Wealth and Welfare States

Wealth and Welfare States

Is America a Laggard or Leader?

Irwin Garfinkel, Lee Rainwater, and Timothy Smeeding

OXFORD
UNIVERSITY PRESS

OXFORD
UNIVERSITY PRESS

Great Clarendon Street, Oxford OX2 6DP

Oxford University Press is a department of the University of Oxford.
It furthers the University's objective of excellence in research, scholarship,
and education by publishing worldwide in

Oxford New York

Auckland Cape Town Dar es Salaam Hong Kong Karachi
Kuala Lumpur Madrid Melbourne Mexico City Nairobi
New Delhi Shanghai Taipei Toronto

With offices in

Argentina Austria Brazil Chile Czech Republic France Greece
Guatemala Hungary Italy Japan Poland Portugal Singapore
South Korea Switzerland Thailand Turkey Ukraine Vietnam

Oxford is a registered trade mark of Oxford University Press
in the UK and in certain other countries

Published in the United States
by Oxford University Press Inc., New York

British Library Cataloguing in Publication Data

Data available

Library of Congress Cataloging in Publication Data

Data available

Typeset by SPI Publisher Services, Pondicherry, India
Printed in Great Britain
on acid-free paper by
Clays Ltd, St Ives plc

ISBN 978–0–19–957930–3 (Hbk)
       978–0–19–957931–0 (Pbk)

1 3 5 7 9 10 8 6 4 2

Preface

As *Wealth and Welfare States* goes to print in late Fall, 2009, the US Congress appears to be on the verge of enacting major health care reform legislation that would achieve nearly universal health insurance coverage. That health care reform is the centerpiece of President Obama's domestic policy agenda and the most important domestic issue in the US today suggests our book is important and timely.

Whatever the outcome of this round of health care reform, however, achieving equal access to health care and restraining the growth of costs will remain a fundamental challenge for the future of the American welfare state. In contrast to those who fear that welfare state programs impoverish nations, we argue that these programs—public education, health care, and social security—in combination with capitalism make nations rich. But poorly designed programs can also impoverish a nation. Americans now spend one of six dollars on health care. If costs grow as rapidly in the next 60 years as they've grown in the past 30 years, we will be spending one of every three dollars on health care. More generally, because welfare state programs already play a huge role in the lives of citizens in all rich nations, a clear understanding of the benefits and costs of these programs is essential. This book aims to enhance understanding of these issues.

In the course of the 9 years we have spent writing this book, we owe thanks to many institutions and people. The Center for Advanced Study in the Social and Behavioral Sciences and the Russell Sage Foundation provided stimulating and congenial environments for thinking and writing to Irv Garfinkel in, respectively, the 2001/2002 academic year and the Fall of 2006. Russell Sage provided the same opportunities for Tim Smeeding in 2007–2008. The MacArthur Foundation provided funding for a Network on Family and the Economy and members of the network—Jeanne Brooks-Gunn, Ceci Conrad, Greg Duncan, Kathy Edin, Paula England, Nancy Folbre, Lindsay Chase Landsdale, Shelley Lundberg,

Sara McLanahan, Ronald Mincy, Robert Pollack, Robert Willis—provided helpful feedback to Irv Garfinkel and Tim Smeeding on many occasions. A large number of other colleagues who responded to presentations of elements of the book at numerous seminars, and several anonymous referees, helped us sharpen the argument and analysis. Amanda Geller, Nathan Hutto, Jumin Kim, Afshin Zilanawala provided research assistance. Brenda Szittya provided editorial support, Helen Gray copy-editing, and Sara Caro critical input to the book title. M.K. Babcock also helped with figures and text. Finally, we thank our wives for patience, understanding, and encouragement.

Contents

Figures and Tables

Figures

Tables

1

Introduction

Many Americans and welfare state scholars believe:

- The welfare state undermines productivity, efficiency, and economic growth.
- The United States has an unusually small welfare state.
- The United States is and always has been a welfare state laggard.

In this book, we argue that in fact:

- Welfare state programs complement capitalism and increase productivity, efficiency, and economic growth.
- Welfare state programs are quite large in the United States.
- The United States was a leader in the most productive part of the welfare state—public education—for most of the nineteenth and twentieth centuries.

In part, these starkly different accounts stem from differences about what should be counted as a welfare state program. Although we are academics, this debate is not just an academic or semantic exercise. If the United States is and always has been a welfare state laggard, but is also, with the exception of Luxembourg, the wealthiest of the world's rich nations, other rich nations might be wise to cut back their welfare states. But if part of the great economic success of the United States is attributable to its leadership in the welfare state program of public education, as we argue in this book, other countries would be wise to imitate the American model—as, indeed, other rich nations have done—and Americans should worry about the fact we are fast losing our educational advantage.

I. The welfare state: a unique blend of capitalism and socialism

All wealthy nations, including the United States, are welfare states—that is, they are primarily capitalist states with large, selective doses of socialism. What have been socialized are institutions that reduce economic insecurity. By its nature, capitalism produces too much economic insecurity. A hallmark objective of welfare state institutions is, therefore, to reduce economic insecurity. Education, health, and some forms of insurance all reduce economic insecurity. Education and health increase human capital, making citizens more capable of dealing with the economic insecurity produced by nature and by the market. Social and health insurance also make citizens more secure by reducing the economic costs of insecurity directly.

Unlike the transfer of resources in the typical capitalist market economy— an explicit trade: "I'll pay you this for that"—social welfare transfers in the form of education, health, and social insurance flow to citizens as a matter of law or entitlement and are paid for by other members of the community by law or requirement.[1] Social welfare transfers are publicly provided or subsidized goods that provide predominantly private benefits. For example, though the public at large benefits from the education of all children, the children who get the schooling and their families reap the largest benefits. Social welfare transfers from one to another part of the population make up the lion's share of the budgets of all rich nations and amount to 30 to 40 percent of the total value of goods and services produced in most of these nations. This book explains why all wealthy nations have such large welfare state programs.

Social welfare transfers are usefully thought of as an extension of family transfers to larger collectives. Within the family, goods are routinely transferred at the beginning of life from parents to children and toward the end of life from children to parents. Furthermore, throughout the life cycle, families transfer resources from the healthy to the sick and from the strong to the weak.[2] Redistribution to the dependent young clearly maximizes a family's chances of survival and long-term success. Likewise, in today's world, where knowledge and education are critical to high productivity, a nation's success hinges on transfers to the young, especially in the form of high-quality public education.

The productivity effects of transfers to the dependent old and more generally from the most to the least productive members of the family are less clear-cut than transfers to the young, but they too are also likely to contribute to the survival and success both of families and of nations.

Health and strength, it bears noting, are not permanent characteristics. Teddy Roosevelt, the rough-rider twenty-sixth president of the United States, was a sickly, asthmatic child who would probably have died had his own parents not been so healthy, wealthy, and wise. "The slow one now," as Bob Dylan put it, "will later be fast." Even when family members' disabilities are permanent, transferring resources to them is likely to contribute to survival in at least two ways. At the most basic biological level, survival depends on reproduction, and the more members of the family who survive to reproduce, the greater the chances of long-term survival. And redistribution from the most to the least productive family members promotes family solidarity and cooperation. The same holds true for nations, especially in the case of redistribution to the aged.

Public education and public pensions redistribute resources from people of working age to the young and old. Health insurance, whether provided publicly in full or subsidized by the state through employer provided insurance, redistributes from the healthy to the sick. All redistribute from the most to the least productive members of society. Economists of all political stripes agree that public education contributes mightily to the long-term survival and success of nations. Many on the right continue to doubt that the benefits of publicly provided health insurance and social security exceed their costs. Many on the left continue to deny that public financing of benefits involves costs. This book explains why those costs exist but also why the benefits of most welfare state programs exceed costs and why, therefore, these programs contribute to the long-term wealth of nations. That benefits exceed costs is the primary reason why all rich nations have large welfare states.

Though this book is about welfare states in all rich nations generally, it focuses disproportionately on the American welfare state for two good reasons. First, almost as many people live in the US welfare state as live in all the other wealthy welfare states in Western Europe, Canada, and Australia combined. The population of Sweden is about the same size as the state of Wisconsin or New York City. Second, because the United States is also the richest, most powerful nation on earth, its institutions merit close examination.

II. Why are welfare states so controversial?

Ideologues of both the right and the left are unhappy about the admixture of capitalism and socialism in the modern welfare state. Socialists are disappointed because the socialist sector is so limited. Karl Marx and his followers identified socialism with public ownership of the means of production. Though some rich nations have socialized a few sectors of production—including coal, trains, and airlines—increasingly, these same nations are re-privatizing even these exceptions. What all wealthy nations have socialized, instead, are three critical aspects of consumption—education, health, and some forms of insurance. On the extreme left, orthodox Marxists continue to regard capitalism as an evil and doomed system and to believe that a decent and humane economy can be achieved only by socializing the means of production. They view social welfare benefits, from public education to pensions to poor relief, as instruments used by the ruling class to keep order and forestall the revolution that will usher in the socialist paradise.[3] But the economic disasters brought on by socializing the means of production in Russia and China have sharply reduced the ranks of orthodox Marxists. Most modern Marxists have become advocates and defenders of social welfare programs, though they remain critics of the limited achievements of welfare states.[4] Socialists of all stripes long for big expansions of the welfare state to eliminate poverty and enhance equality and opportunity.

On the right, free market ideologues—the most influential of which is the late Nobel Prize winning economist Milton Friedman—are appalled by the large size of the socialist sector. In *Capitalism and Freedom*, the popular paean to free markets and minimum government (and the modern Bible of right-wing economists), Friedman argues persuasively that complete socialization is a threat to freedom. He also attributes the phenomenal wealth of the United States solely to the unique freedom of its markets and attacks welfare state programs, including Social Security and public education, but unaccountably overlooks the critical role of free public education in the development of the US economy. As we will see in Chapter 2, economists from right to left agree that education is a fundamental ingredient of human capital and as such a fundamental determinant of long-term economic growth.[5] Friedman's discussion of education may be summarized as a grudging acceptance of the argument for public financing of education and an impassioned argument against public provision of education and for vouchers to pay for private schooling. A more balanced account would have credited some of America's economic success to its leadership in providing free public education and gone on to argue that vouchers might be even better.[6]

What the ideologues of both right and left share is the fervent belief that "if some is good, more is better." They differ only in whether it is socialism or capitalism that is good. The idea that a mixture of capitalism and socialism is superior to the pure version of each is foreign to the ideologue.

The disgruntled extremists on both sides notwithstanding, the vast bulk of the populations in wealthy democratic nations, including the United States, are happy with their country's mix of capitalism and socialism. Most are probably unhappy with at least one or two particulars of their welfare state programs. And many, with good reasons, are particularly unhappy about many of the particulars. But attempts to dismantle the great western welfare states have failed everywhere. And the fast-growing and prosperous nations in Asia have already begun to build welfare states.

Apart from the ideological struggle between capitalism and socialism that animates debates about the welfare state, welfare state programs are also controversial because they involve vast redistributions of resources—mostly, but not exclusively, from the working-age population to the aged and young, from the rich to the poor, and from the healthy to the sick. Even within families, disagreements often arise about how family resources should be shared and redistributed, so it should not be surprising that a nation's citizens, whose bonds to one another are much weaker than a family's ties, disagree vehemently about how the nation's resources should be shared and redistributed.

A final source of controversy springs from the multiple objectives of welfare state programs: reducing economic insecurity; alleviating and preventing poverty; providing equality of opportunity; reducing inequality; promoting solidarity, social inclusion, and social stability; and improving education and health. These objectives, while related, are far from identical. Many analysts of the welfare state tend to focus on one or two objectives, such as reducing poverty or inequality, but all of these goals have played important and varying roles in mobilizing political support for—and disagreement over—welfare state programs.

III. How our perspective on the welfare state differs from others

In this book we build upon a vast scientific literature in economics, sociology, political science, history, and social work. We stand on the shoulders of giants. Our debt is enormous.

Yet our work departs in a few fundamental respects from that of the large majority of welfare state scholars. Most importantly, our account of current and past differences in the welfare states of rich nations encompasses a broader set of social welfare transfers, including education, employer-provided benefits, and all in-kind benefits.

Including public education as a welfare state program, for three reasons, is—or, should be—the least controversial departure from conventional practice. First, the conceptual definitions of welfare states put forth by the leading scholars in the field include education. Second, although education is generally missing from most empirical analyses of the welfare state, an increasingly large minority of welfare state scholars do include education in their inquiries. Third, we have learned a lot from the scholars who do include education in their empirical work.

Our definition of the socialized portion of welfare states—social welfare transfers that provide primarily private benefits that reduce economic insecurity—is consistent with conventional definitions, including those provided by the leading scholars who omit education empirically. In perhaps the most influential book on the welfare state in the sociology and political science literatures, *The Three Worlds of Welfare Capitalism* (1990), Gosta Esping-Anderson begins with a textbook-style definition of the welfare state: "state responsibility for securing some basic modicum of welfare for its citizens." A bit later (pp. 57 and 58) he says:

What then constitutes salient dimensions of welfare state stratification?...The education system is an obvious and much studied instance...At this point, we confine our attention to the welfare state's traditional, and still dominant activity, income maintenance.

In some of his more recent work, Esping-Anderson (2006) focuses on the role of education in welfare states.[7]

In *Fighting Poverty in the US and Europe: A World of Difference* (2004), Alberto Alesina and Edward Glaeser, two of the most influential welfare state scholars in economics, define welfare state programs as "the redistributive side of government policies," but include only cash transfers and health transfers in their analysis. These authors do not explain why they omit education transfers, which clearly involve large redistributions via government budgets.

British scholars of the welfare state have a long tradition of including education in their analyses (Richard Titmus, 1958; John Glennister, 1992; John Hills, 2004). There is also some evidence that welfare state scholars in the economics profession take it for granted that education is part of the welfare state. The authoritative collection of classic readings in the welfare state designed for graduate students in economics, *Economic Theory and the Welfare State* (2001), edited by Nicholas Barr but overseen by the leading economists in the world, has a large section on education, consistent with its operational definition of the welfare state: "For the purposes of these volumes the term 'welfare state' is used for the state's activities in three broad areas: income transfers, health and health care, and education" (p. xiv).

Finally, welfare state scholars who include education have already taught us a great deal. Here we refer only to three scholars upon whose work we build. Our greatest debt is to Professor Robert Lampman, first director of the Institute for Research on Poverty at the University of Wisconsin. In *Social Welfare Spending: Accounting for Changes from 1950 to 1978 (1984)*, Lampman constructed the definition of social welfare transfers that underlies our own definition. He also conducted the first benefit cost analysis of welfare state transfers of which we are aware and found that: (1) benefits are at least as great as costs; and (2) most of the measured benefits come from education. Arnold Heidenheimer (1982) presents convincing evidence that the historical development of the US and German welfare states differed in that Germany led the way in old-age pensions and the US led the way in the development of mass secondary education. Peter Lindert, an economist and historian, in perhaps the finest recent book on welfare state development in rich nations, *Growing Public* (2004), extends the work on the benefits and costs of welfare state institutions, showing that these change over time, and enriches (and in some cases creates) the comparative histories of public assistance, education, and social insurance in rich nations, documenting how welfare state leadership has changed over time.

Including education has huge consequences. Most of the comparative historical accounts of the development of the US welfare state exclude education and conclude that the United States lagged behind other nations in developing welfare state institutions. Most recently, in *Fighting Poverty in the US and Europe: A World of Difference*, economists Alberto Alesina and Edward Glaeser omit education and repeat the assessment that the United States is and always has been a welfare state laggard. But including education completely changes the picture. Although the United States has always been a low spender on poor relief and lagged in the development of social insurance, as documented in *Growing Public* by Peter Lindert and in Chapter 5 of this book, the United States was a world leader in providing mass public elementary education during the nineteenth century and in mass secondary and higher education during the first half of the twentieth century.

The idea that the United States has always been a laggard in welfare state development is not only widespread and misleading, it is also pernicious.

Because education contributes so much to productivity growth, other rich nations have adopted the US model of investing heavily in mass education, and most have caught up, or nearly so. Despite its early lead in mass education, the United States now lags in the development of early education and childcare. Those who mistakenly believe that the United States has always been slow to develop social welfare programs are prone to dismiss the current lag in early education and childcare with the argument that lagging may be a good thing. After all, if, despite always being behind, the United States is the richest nation on earth, why worry about it? But if one of the main reasons why the United States is the world's richest nation is that it has been a world leader in developing mass public education—and if it has now relinquished that lead—this is surely a cause for worry.

Including education in the analysis also shifts the debate about the costs and benefits of welfare state programs. Every welfare state institution, including public education, has been hotly contested from its inception, and the welfare state as a whole continues to come under attack. One charge is constant. Welfare state programs are said to reduce efficiency, productivity, and economic growth. But education is so demonstrably productive that including it completely changes the picture and sets the stage for making the case that, in general, welfare state programs enhance rather than retard productivity, efficiency, and growth in economic well-being.

Besides education, we also include employer-provided health insurance and pensions as part of our welfare state accounts. Employer-provided health insurance involves socialization of the risk of ill health and redistribution from the healthy to the sick, at the firm, rather than the national level. Unlike publicly financed health insurance, employer provided health insurance does not redistribute on the financing side (see Chapter 3, p. 56, for a discussion of the importance of this difference). Given the large role that employer-provided benefits play in the United States, including these benefits is a pre-requisite for identifying similarities and differences between the United States and other countries. Most important, excluding employer-provided benefits leads to a vast understatement of how much the United States as a nation is spending on health insurance and pensions and thereby vastly understates the size and the costs/benefits of the US welfare state. For example, though unlike all the other rich nations, the United States has no national health insurance system that provides universal coverage, once employer-provided insurance is added to the public programs of Medicare for the aged and Medicaid for the poor, the United States has near-universal insurance coverage—nearly 85 percent.

Including the costs of employer-provided health insurance makes clear the fact that the United States pays far more than any other rich countries for less universal health insurance. As the political scientist, Jacob Hacker documents so well in the *Divided Welfare State* (2002), the development of employer-provided benefits is a substitute for and forestalled the development of a National Health Insurance system. Finally, the decentralization of insurance payers that results from employer-provided benefits as opposed to a single national insurer is, as we shall see below in Chapter 8, the most important factor in accounting for the extraordinarily high cost of the US health-care system.

Finally, though spending on in-kind benefits equals or exceeds spending on cash benefits in all countries, most analyses of inequality ignore the effects of in-kind benefits. Most analyses also ignore indirect taxes, which affect the value of cash benefits to recipients. Including health, education, and other in-kind benefits such as health insurance and housing, as well as cash benefits, including employer-provided benefits as well as government-provided benefits, and including the indirect as well as direct taxes that are required to finance benefits, shrinks differences between countries in overall welfare state transfers and in reductions in inequality achieved by welfare state transfers. Once all transfers are counted, the US welfare state is not unusually small. The most important difference between the United States and other rich countries is not how much it transfers, but rather how, through whom, and to whom transfers flow.

IV. Boundaries of the welfare state and aspects not covered

Social welfare transfers, as noted above, are publicly provided or subsidized goods that provide predominantly private benefits. But why do we limit our focus to transfers in the domains of education, health, housing, social insurance, and public assistance? Why not include subsidies for farmers, small business loans, or economic development programs? All of these programs are publicly funded and all provide benefits to particular groups of individuals. One answer to this question is that these other programs are designed to promote objectives other than the traditional welfare state objectives of reducing insecurity, poverty, and inequality. This distinction is slippery, however, because these other programs often serve some social welfare function. Farm subsidies reduce the insecurity of farmers. The Small Business Administration promotes opportunity. A more accurate answer to the question of why some government programs are not included in the welfare state has to do with tradition and convenience. Because academic analysts of the welfare state have focused on education, health, housing, social insurance, and public assistance, government agencies in both the United States and other countries publish data on social welfare expenditures in these domains, and international governmental agencies such as the Organization for Economic Co-operation and Development (OECD) publish cross-national data that use these categories. We follow this tradition.

Some vital parts of modern welfare states, however, do not involve transfers that so clearly provide predominantly private benefits. The most important of these is public health. Public health involves both vast public expenditures on sanitation and clean water that are not counted as part of the welfare state and a vast body of regulations that protect from disease. Sanitation, clean water, inoculations, and other aspects of public health clearly provide large private as well as large public benefits. But whether private benefits are bigger than public benefits is not clear to us and, to our knowledge, has not been seriously studied. What is clear is that expenditures on sanitation and clean water are not counted as social welfare expenditures, while public health doctors and facilities, inoculations, and other aspects of the public health system are counted. We follow this tradition. We discuss the importance of public health to productivity and economic growth in Chapter 2, but otherwise ignore this crucial part of the welfare state.

Other government regulations, such as minimum wages, rent controls, and child support enforcement are also important ingredients of modern welfare states that deserve more analysis. But regulation is beyond the scope of this volume. Many analysts of the welfare state also argue that achieving full employment through the use of Keynesian macro-economic policies is an essential welfare state objective. We do not disagree with this assessment, but an analysis of macro-economic policy is also beyond the scope of this volume. Our book focuses on social welfare transfers and does not deal with either policies to promote full employment or the regulatory aspects of the welfare state.[8]

V. Who should read this book?

Knowledge about the welfare state is important to all citizens. The sheer size of welfare state institutions in all industrialized nations means that they play a huge role in the economic and social life of most people. Welfare state spending substantially exceeds spending on the traditional pure public goods of defense, law and order, and public transportation. Furthermore, because welfare state programs involve socialization, they are inherently a matter of public debate and public policy. To ensure that welfare state institutions meet their objectives, citizens need to understand the accomplishments and shortcomings of their own programs. As a consequence, this book is addressed to the widest possible audience, citizens of all nations. While, as academics, we normally write for a more limited scientific audience, to the maximum extent possible we limit the technical material, jargon, and narrow academic arguments to appendices and footnotes. The most important arguments are addressed in the text in a comprehensible and, we hope, interesting manner.

Professional workers within the welfare state—teachers, doctors, nurses, social workers, and the civil servants who administer programs have a special responsibility to learn about the institutions that employ them. Welfare state workers serve two masters: their employers and their clients. They have a professional responsibility to serve their clients and a professional responsibility to implement the policies of their employers. They therefore have a special obligation to help shape the policies and practices that govern their activities so as to make their dual responsibilities compatible. Similarly self-employed professionals need to balance their client's with their own self-interest. Furthermore, because the welfare state looms gigantic in the lives of the poor, the power of professional employees of the welfare state to affect their lives, for good and ill, is immense.

The book is also addressed to academic social scientists—economists, historians, political scientists, social workers, and sociologists—especially, but not limited to, those who study the welfare state. As noted, we build upon but also depart from the rich existing literature. Thus, this book aims to provide both a useful summary and critique of welfare state literature.

Finally, this book is addressed to advocates for and opponents of welfare state programs. By virtue of its being a socialized sector within a largely capitalist economy, the welfare state is highly contested. Value conflicts exist and cannot be settled by research. Emotions run high. But this does not mean there is no role for science. Even advocates must weigh benefits and costs.

VI. The organization and main findings of the book

In Chapter 2 we show that all rich countries have large welfare states and explain why. The short explanation is that capitalism makes countries rich and welfare state institutions—primarily education, health, and social insurance—make them even richer. Left to itself, the market provides too little of these uniquely valuable goods. Closely related, and equally important, all the rich countries are democratic. Democratic nations are more likely than their non-democratic counterparts to learn from their own and others' experience. That the poor, unhealthy, and ignorant have the right to vote also makes redistributions to them more likely.

Theoretically, democracies may be prone to too much redistribution. Indeed, economic conservatives are obsessed with this theoretical possibility. The decline in economic growth rates during the 1970s and 1980s, following the great expansion of welfare state transfers in the 1960s and 1970s, invigorated and rewarded the obsession—the welfare state was to blame. The socialist welfare state, in their view, was indeed strangling capitalism—the goose that lays the golden eggs. The last part of Chapter 2 explains how, in theory, too much of a good thing (welfare state transfers) can be a bad thing (reduce economic well-being). The last part also explains why, in practice so far in rich nations, welfare state transfers have nourished rather than strangled capitalism.

Chapter 3 describes the current size and structure of the welfare state in 14 rich nations. Similarities and differences are both striking. In all countries, including the United States, welfare state transfers are large—around 30 to 40 percent of each country's total production of goods and services. The domains socialized are also similar and in general similarly sized—old-age pensions, health, education, and cash public assistance for the poor are common to all countries, and, in most, pensions are the most costly, with health insurance second, education third, and public assistance the least expensive. The most striking and important exception to the similarity of domain sizes across nations is the exceptionally large US spending on health care and the exceptionally small US spending on cash benefits and early childhood education.

Welfare states differ in the degree to which benefits are provided universally to all citizens. Universal benefits provide a floor for the entire population. The United States differs dramatically in its heavy reliance on non-universal systems of aid, with the poor receiving benefits from safety-net programs that are limited to the poor, and the middle and upper classes receiving benefits provided by employers or the federal income tax, or both—what we call platforms. This bi-furcated system results in a U-shaped distribution of benefits in which the poorest and richest get the largest benefits and the working poor, near poor, lower middle class, and even the middle class fall between the cracks. The US distribution of public subsidies for housing may be the most egregious example—with the richest fifth of the population receiving subsidies that are nearly four times those of the poorest fifth. In the case of medical care benefits for families with children, the richest fifth gets benefits that are not quite two times larger than that of the poorest fifth. But medical transfers are two and a half times bigger than housing transfers and therefore more important.

In Chapter 4 we describe the effects of welfare state benefits—and the taxes required to finance them—on poverty and inequality. In all the rich nations, net benefits (social welfare benefits minus the taxes that finance them) are progressively distributed. The poorest families gain a substantial proportion of their incomes from welfare state transfers and the richest lose modest proportions of their incomes. Similarly, in all the rich nations, the elderly are big net gainers. Nations also vary substantially in the reliance of the poorest groups and the elderly on welfare state transfers and in the degree to which welfare state transfers reduce the incomes of their top strata. The United States is at the low end of the continuum with respect to the extent to which the poor and elderly rely on welfare state transfers and reduction of upper-income shares. With respect to the low reliance of poor families with children on welfare state transfers, the United States closely resembles Sweden and France: the poorest fifth of these families, largely single-mother families, are less dependent on transfers because they derive a large share of their income from work.

Rich nations also differ substantially in the degree to which cash transfers reduce income poverty and inequality of cash income. The Scandinavian countries are big spenders and reduce inequality the most; the English-speaking countries spend the least and reduce inequality the least; and the continental European countries spend a lot, but achieve less equality than the Scandinavians. Among English-speaking countries, the United States stands out for being the least generous and having the highest income inequality.

Counting in-kind benefits and indirect taxes substantially shrinks cross-national differences in inequality of resources at the bottom of the income distribution. Because the United States spends so much on health, valuing in-kind benefits at government cost shows that it is transferring substantially greater resources to its poorest citizens than previous research has suggested. This raises the question of whether the American poor and the United States as a whole would be better off if it transferred less in health insurance and more in cash benefits and early childhood education.

The last section of chapter 4 describes how rich nations currently compare on three other outcomes of welfare state institutions—the level and

13

distribution of education and health and equality of opportunity. The US is at the high end of educational achievement if attainment is measured by high school and college degrees, but when measured by enrollments in early education or by achievement test scores, the US is at or near bottom. The US also has the most unequal distribution of achievement test scores. The United States gets its money's worth from its health-care system in the sense that the benefits exceed the extraordinarily high costs, but it fails to get its money's worth in the sense that other rich nations achieve the same or greater benefits at lower cost. Moreover, in terms of both infant mortality and life expectancy for the elderly—the single best measures of health status—the US ranks last or near last. While the United States prides itself on being known as the land of opportunity, during the last quarter of the twentieth century, opportunity to move up the economic ladder in the US was lower than opportunity in other rich nations.

Chapters 5, 6, and 7 present a short American-centric history of the development of welfare states in rich nations. Chapter 5 addresses the question of whether the current similarities and differences across nations go back a long way in time or are of relatively recent origin. In particular, we ask in what ways and for how long has the US been exceptional? Has the US always been a low spender in cash and relatively high spender on education, had lower than average health and education outcomes, been more unequal and provided below average chances to move up in the world? We find that, throughout its history, the US has been a consistent laggard in poor relief and social insurance, but also a leader in the provision of mass public education throughout most of the nineteenth and twentieth centuries.

In the last quarter of the twentieth century, however, most other rich nations narrowed the gap and some moved ahead in secondary and higher education, while nearly all surged ahead in early childhood education and care and measures of reading and mathematical achievement at age 15. Until recently, opportunity for upward mobility, for Americans who were not black, was also greater in the US than in most European nations. Blacks in America were held down by law and custom to the bottom rungs of society. Opportunities improved for blacks at the century's end, but discrimination remains, and intergenerational mobility for the population as a whole is lower in the US than elsewhere. Similarly, greater inequality in the US is a recent phenomenon.

Chapter 6 seeks to explain the two key features of US welfare state exceptionalism—the long-term lead in education and lag in poor relief and social insurance. The argument is that US exceptionalism stems from the unique American mix of Protestantism with religiosity, capitalism with no feudal past, early democratization and a revolutionary ethos, being an immigrant and frontier nation, and race, ethnic, and religious diversity. Protestantism privileges education and stigmatizes poor relief. Unlike most adults in other rich nations, Americans are religious. Education, as discussed in Chapter 2, is complementary to capitalism, and most capitalists support education and are wary of poor relief. The landed aristocracy in Europe and the plantation slave-owning elite in the US South generally opposed mass education as a threat to social order. The feudal legacy of class, hierarchy, and social distinctions was also fertile ground for a belief that status is inherited and mobility impossible. Democracy presupposes an educated citizenry and also arms the lower classes with the ballot. Both increased political support for education. Immigrants, almost by definition, believe in mobility and the frontier experience strengthened the value of self-reliance—both of which privilege education and stigmatize cash. Finally, wherever it occurs, diversity depresses poor relief and the US is the most diverse nation. While slavery depressed education in the South, religious, ethnic, and national diversity in the North probably promoted public education. The success of capitalism, democracy, and education in America—high incomes, high mobility, and, for most of its history, high equality—weakened the appeal of socialism for all white Americans and, in combination with the phenomenal diversity of even the white American population, prevented the emergence of strong unionism and a majority socialist party. In all currently rich nations, the threat of socialism spawned social insurance and the electoral success of left-wing, mostly socialist parties hastened its spread. Throughout the twentieth century, the relative weakness of the left in the US accounts for the country's lag in social insurance.

Chapter 7 seeks to explain the dramatic US departures in the last quarter of the twentieth century. Inspired by the American Civil Rights Movement and led by President Lyndon Baines Johnson, between 1963 and 1968, US politics swung substantially left. The United States made gigantic strides toward equality of civil rights and opportunity for its black population, as well as economic security for its aged population. In 1968, however, for a variety of reasons, including most immediately an unpopular war in Vietnam, but most fundamentally fear of social disorder and a backlash against civil rights, the Republican candidate Richard M. Nixon defeated the Democratic candidate Vice President Hubert Humphrey, to win the presidency, and the US began a long, though uneven, political swing to the right, which culminated in 2002 when the Republicans took control of the presidency and both houses of Congress for the first time since 1928. This long swing right is the key to explaining why at century's end the United States fell further behind in social insurance, lost its lead in education, and sank to the bottom in opportunity and equality. This story is told in three parts in Chapter 7.

The last part examines the origins and consequences of the controversial US 1996 welfare reform, which ended the entitlement to cash relief for poor single mothers and their children, required mothers to work for benefits, and strengthened requirements, especially for poor fathers, to pay child support. Soon after the Personal Responsibility and Work Opportunity Reconciliation Act (PRWORA) of 1996 was enacted, welfare caseloads plummeted, labor-force participation rates of single mothers increased dramatically, and poverty rates tumbled. Some other nations, rich and on the way to becoming rich, have already adopted similar laws and many more are considering adopting similar laws. In this recent case, the US is a leader. This leadership justifies a close look at the origins and consequences of PRWORA.

PRWORA followed a huge expansion of the Earned Income Tax Credit (EITC) that Congress enacted in 1993 as part of President Clinton's first-year budget package. Assistance for childcare and other benefits that supported work were also expanded. Thus, although PRWORA cut welfare assistance, total assistance to poor single mothers and their children more than doubled. The reductions in caseloads, increases in labor-force participation, and reductions in poverty that followed the enactment of PRWORA were due not just to PRWORA, but also to the increase in the EITC and other benefits and to the most vibrant economic expansion of the post-World War II era. Furthermore, rigorous experiments with welfare in the US and Canada indicate that toughening welfare by itself reduces caseloads and increases employment, but does not reduce poverty. In short, seen in the broader context of other policies that encouraged work and reduced poverty, PROWRA accomplished much less good than is commonly asserted. US leadership in this area is worth both emulating and avoiding.

Whereas Chapters 2 through 7 examine current and past welfare state programs in rich nations, Chapter 8 is forward-looking, asking how the United States can strengthen its welfare state. In particular, we address three specific challenges and one overarching challenge that confront the American welfare state: making the old-age insurance program fiscally sound; achieving universal health insurance and restraining the growth in health-care costs; and making sufficient education and other investments in children in the face of an aging population. The overarching challenge is to reduce inequality and poverty in ways that promote growth and efficiency. Though the specific proposals examined are limited to the United States, the challenges faced by the US are not unique and analyses have implications for the welfare states of all rich nations.

The projected future shortfall between legislated taxes and promised benefits in the Old Age Insurance (OAI) program in the US is small compared with that in many other rich nations, and compared with the projected shortfall in revenues and promised benefits for old-age health insurance in the US. The OAI shortfall can be relatively easily resolved by a combination of small increases in taxes and small reductions in benefits. Extending the social security tax to cover very high earnings should play a large role in resolving this shortfall because this is an equitable way for the very rich to share their windfall gains that have resulted from the great increase in inequality.

Restraining the growth in health-care spending will be more difficult. The most certain way to restrain spending growth would be to adopt a federal, tax-financed, National Health Insurance system—commonly called the single-payer system. Financing National Health Insurance via an explicit tax will restrain costs because politicians will be reluctant to increase a dedicated tax of 15 percent or 16 percent. Financing National Health Insurance through taxation would also substantially reduce inequality and free up state revenues that have been devoted to Medicaid to shift into education. Though desirable in our view, in the short term, a single-payer system is probably not politically feasible. Adoption of a universal health insurance program for children, and achieving universality of coverage for adults via building on the current employer-based system, would be desirable steps, but by themselves would involve only a small increase in equity on the financing side and would increase rather than restrain costs.

Investing now in the future productivity of American children will reduce the burden on them of supporting an aging population. Investing in children will also increase equality and opportunity in the current and succeeding generations. Good investments in children abound. The overall objective should be to restore American pre-eminence in education. Universal pre-school education for three and four year olds will more than pay for itself. Increasing teacher quality is the key to improving K-12 education and requires increasing teachers' salaries and improving their work environment—both of which will require increases in taxes. There is no shortage of other productive investments in families with children that will complement investments in education. We describe four such investments: paid parental leave, a post-birth universal nurse home-visiting service, a child allowance, and a government guaranteed minimum benefit for children legally entitled to receive private child support. All of these programs will require some increase in taxes or some reduction in other government programs, which is always a challenge in the US and is especially challenging in the face of an aging population.

Whether any, some, most, or all of the reforms discussed are adopted will depend upon the political power and ability of the advocates of reform, upon whether and how far the country swings back to the left, and ultimately upon the knowledge, beliefs, and actions of millions of American citizens and their political leaders.

Notes

1. Employer-provided benefits are both market trade and socialization. All economists agree that health insurance and pensions are part of the total compensation package for workers. On the other hand, health insurance is different from wages and by its nature transfers resources from the healthy to the sick.
2. The evidence with respect to transferring to more and less able children is more mixed. Becker (1991) predicts that parents will invest more in the human capital of abler children, but use non-human capital transfers to compensate less able children. Behrman, Pollak, and Taubman (1982), Ashenfelter and Rouse (1998), and Ermish and Francesconi (2000), McGarry and Schoeni (1995 and 1997), Dunn and Phillips (1997), McGarry (1999 and 2000), and Hochguerel and Ohlsson (2000) report compensatory human investment transfers to less well-endowed children. By way of contrast, Behrman, Rosenzweig, and Taubman (1994), and Miller Mulvey and Martin (1995), find that parents invest more educationally in abler children, and Kim (2005) finds that parents favor abler children in both human capital investments and non-human capital transfers.
3. See O'Connor (1973); Gough (1979); and Offe (1972).
4. Wright (1996–2006); and Bowles, Roosevelt, and Edwards (2005).
5. Indeed, the theoretical contributions to the importance of human capital came from Milton Friedman's colleagues at the Chicago and Columbia departments of economics. See Schulz (1971 and 1973); Becker (1986 and 1993); and Mincer (1993).
6. Friedman was awarded the Nobel Prize for his more careful and balanced scientific work, especially in monetary theory. Such is the difference between paeans and science and between ideologues, or true believers, and practical people looking for practical solutions. Friedman himself took a certain amount of pride in his extreme position, saying in response to an accusation of going

overboard in his anti-statism, "In every generation, there's got to be somebody who goes the whole way, and that's why I believe as I do" (Noble, 2006).

7. In another example in the sociology literature, Wilensky (2002) explicitly includes education in his definition as the following quote illustrates: "The essence of the welfare state is government-protected minimum standards of income, nutrition, health and safety, education, and housing assured to every citizen as a social right, not as charity." He also explicitly excludes higher education on the following grounds: "While pensions, health and disability insurance, family allowances and related family policies, job-injury insurance programs, and housing programs hang together as a welfare-state package, higher education, because of its stronger meritocratic component, is different; it is generally negatively correlated with spending as a percentage of GNP for pensions, health care, work injuries, war victims, and family allowances (216)." But, inexplicably, he leaves out elementary and secondary education from his empirical analyses.

8. Aside from employer-provided health insurance, pensions, and other benefits, we also do not deal directly with the "third sector"—voluntary non-profit institutions and charities. One common perception is that state provision of the social welfare transfers in the US is less than in Europe because there is greater voluntary provision funded by a higher level of charitable giving. There is some truth to this because much of the third sector consists of employer-provided benefits and voluntary organizations, such as hospitals, that are funded by government or employer-provided benefits. (See Amy Blackman, Kenndard T. Wing, and Thomas Pollack. 2008, *The Non-Profit Sector in Brief*, National Center for Charitable Statistics, Urban Institute). As we show in Chapter 3, counting employer-provided health insurance and pensions does narrow the gap between the US and other rich nations in welfare state transfers as a percent of national income. But, employer-provided benefits hardly constitute "charitable giving." Charitable contributions to churches and other non-profit institutions, such as the United Way, appear to play a much larger role in the US than in other rich nations, but the amounts transferred are quite small compared to the rest of the welfare state. While a comparative/historical study of the third sector would be useful, it is beyond the scope of this volume.

2

Why All Rich Nations Have Large Welfare States

Most analyses of welfare states focus exclusively on rich nations. This book follows this tradition for the most part. Limiting the analysis of welfare states to rich countries, however, obscures a fundamental similarity among them: all these rich countries have large welfare states.

Figure 2.1 displays the relationship between a country's income and the size of its welfare state.[1] The size of welfare state, as measured by the share of the country's total income devoted to welfare state transfers, is displayed from the bottom to top of the diagram; income per person is displayed from left to right. (Both variables are logged so that the chart displays the relationship of percentage increases.) Each of the 162 dots in the figure represents a country and describes both the size of its welfare state and its average income per person. The poorest countries cluster in the bottom left-hand corner of the diagram, while the richest countries cluster in the top right-hand corner. Clearly, the richer the country, the greater the share of their income that citizens devote to welfare state transfers. The same pattern holds within the United States and within Europe. The higher the income of states or countries, the greater the share of income that they devote to welfare state transfers.[2]

The black dots represent the 14 rich countries we describe in more detail in the following chapters. The US is represented by a white square, as well as the black dot with the highest LN GDP. The black dot includes only explicit government expenditures, while the white square also includes government subsidized, employer-provided benefits. In the big international picture, the difference is small, converting the large US welfare state from slightly below to more noticeably below the rich average. In either case, all of these rich nations have large welfare states.[3]

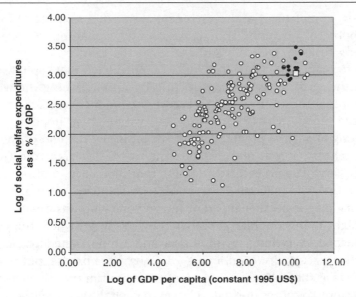

Figure 2.1: Log social welfare expenditures as a percent of GDP by log GDP per capita in 162 nations (1998)

If the welfare state is a drag on nations, as the critics would have us believe, how could it be that all these rich nations have large welfare states? The first section of this chapter explains how the critics have it backwards, or upside down. Like capitalism itself, the socialized portion of welfare states enriches, not impoverishes, nations. The second section argues that democracy promotes welfare state development. The third section examines and mostly debunks the claim that excessive social insurance has generated a crisis in the welfare state. The final section examines and mostly debunks the longstanding claim that welfare state programs can attain greater equality only at the expense of efficiency.

I. How capitalism accompanied by critical doses of socialism enriches nations

All rich nations have large welfare states because capitalism makes countries rich and welfare state programs make them even richer. To understand how welfare state institutions, or the socialized sector of a mixed economy, complement and enrich capitalism, it is necessary to understand both the strengths and weaknesses of capitalism. "Capitalism," according to its arch-enemy Karl Marx, "is the most productive system known to mankind." Of course, Marx also predicted that capitalism was sowing the seeds of its own destruction by impoverishing the working class and that socialism would be even more productive. Marx was right about the productivity of capitalism, but wrong about impoverishment and wrong about the productivity of socialism. By the end of the nineteenth century, it was already apparent to the leader of the German Socialist Party, Eduard Bernstein (1899), that capitalism, far from impoverishing the working class, was raising its standard of living. Nearly 100 years later, it became apparent to everyone who was capable of seeing straight that economies dominated by socialism, where the government owned everything, as in Russia and China, were not nearly as productive as capitalist economies—or, to be more precise, not nearly as productive as the welfare state versions of capitalism that characterize all rich Western countries. Indeed, relative to capitalism, socialism had impoverished the masses. Both China and Russia have already abandoned a great deal of this form of socialism and are encouraging the development of capitalism in their countries along with Western-style welfare state institutions.

Whole books, including Adam Smith's classic, *The Wealth of Nations* (1776), have been written on the topic of why capitalism makes countries rich. All American undergraduate economics textbooks build on Smith's seminal work and emphasize the importance of self-interest, economic incentives, and, most important, competition in propelling economies forward. Though human beings frequently act in an altruistic manner, especially toward family members, and occasionally perform selfless heroic acts, most human beings often do what is in their own best interest. This is particularly true when it comes to surviving and thriving—that is, to economic life. Economies that build on the powerful motive of self-interest through competition, which creates the incentives, are more likely to thrive.

Joseph Schumpeter, in *Capitalism, Socialism and Democracy* (1942), emphasized one aspect of competition that is particularly important to understanding both the strength and weakness of capitalism. He called it "creative destruction." By that he meant that competition weeds out inefficient producers. In a capitalist system, mass production of automobiles puts horse buggy-makers out of business. Good restaurants drive out the bad. Business failures, bankruptcies, and unemployment are not just an accidental by-product of capitalism, but are an essential feature of its productivity. The upside of competition and creative destruction is prodigious riches. The downside is economic insecurity.

Economic insecurity is much broader than poverty. It arises not just from low income, but also from irregular or uncertain income, as well as from high, irregular, and uncertain expenses. All welfare state institutions reduce economic insecurity. A whole body of economic theory and a more limited but growing body of empirical research attests to the economic value to individuals of reducing uncertainty and risk. By reducing the insecurity of capitalism, welfare state institutions further enrich capitalist nations.[4]

Private markets, left to themselves, will produce too little of the critical goods that reduce economic insecurity—education, health, and insurance.[5] It is no accident that education, health, and insurance are the goods that welfare states provide. By providing more of these goods than the market, welfare states enrich nations.

Education

Interestingly enough, most of the literature on economic insecurity, like the broader welfare state literature, has focused on social insurance and ignored education. Yet knowledge and, therefore, education may be the single most important ingredient in reducing uncertainty and risk. Knowledge cannot by itself eliminate uncertainty or risk because some things are inherently uncertain. But ignorance is certainly one large source of uncertainty. Knowledge—being able to read and write, add, subtract, multiply, and divide—reduces the range of uncertainty. Knowledge of science and history further narrows the range. What better way to equip citizens to cope with the economic insecurity produced by a vibrant capitalist economy than to educate them?

Another, older, body of economic theory explains why markets produce too little education and provides a strong rationale for public financing of elementary and secondary education. That rationale is that the benefits of education spill over beyond the individual child and the child's family to other members of society. Economists refer to this spillover as an externality. Each of us has an interest not only in our own children's education, but also in the education of other children as well. Poorly educated children are more likely to be unhealthy, dependent on public assistance, and criminal when they become adults. Education reduces these social costs of ignorance. More educated children are also more likely as adults to be more informed citizens and more generally capable of a higher level of social and economic interaction. Finally, particularly important for nations like the United States, whose population includes such a diversity of nationalities, religions, and races, public education transmits a common set of social values to children—helping to make them American children. Sociologists call this "increasing social cohesion." In making decisions about how much to invest in their own child's education, parents acting individually do not take account of these public benefits. Thus, reliance on the market leads to underinvestment in education. Collective action is required to reach the optimum level of education. Of course, government financing or provision of education, or both, does not guarantee the optimal level of education. Governments are no more perfect than markets are. With respect to education, however, we know that the market fails to invest enough. Government at least has a fighting chance to get it right.[6]

The empirical evidence is overwhelming that public education promotes productivity and growth. Economists agree that improvements in education account for a good deal of economic growth (Denison, 1962; Mankiw et al., 1992; Barro, 2001; Lucas, 1988). Indeed, today, the controversy in economics is over whether education is a great public investment or an unbelievably great public investment. And although education's acknowledged role in economic growth has pretty much eliminated controversy over public financing of elementary and secondary education, economists and other social scientists do still disagree about whether education should be publicly provided as well as publicly financed (in Chapter 8, we return briefly to this issue).

Public health

The theoretical case for public health measures such as sanitation, inoculation, even isolation, and, most generally, the prevention of infectious disease is identical in principle to the externality, or spillover, argument for education. As with education, the benefits of public health programs are not limited to the individual but extend society-wide. And, as with ignorance, the disadvantages of poor sanitation extend far beyond the individual. Our neighbors' failure to be sanitary imposes costs not just on them but also on us. If each of us were to pay only for our own sanitation, we would have too little. If each of us were to weigh the individual benefits and costs of purchasing an inoculation, we would get too few inoculations and too much disease.

Scientific evidence also indicates that the public health measures described above have large social benefits and, like public education, promote productivity and growth. Though some disagreement exists about the relative importance of nutrition and public health in accounting for declines in mortality between the seventeenth and nineteenth centuries, scholars agree that the huge gains in life expectancy during the twentieth century are due primarily to public health. (Samuel Preston, 1975, 1980, 1996; Robert W. Fogel, 2004; and Cutler, Deaton, and Lleras-Muney, 2006). Indeed, Robert Fogel, who stresses the role of nutrition in *The Escape From Hunger and Premature Death*, attributes the remarkable increase in life expectancy between 1890 and 1930—a gain of 14 years in the United Kingdom and 16 years in the United States—to public health investments in the late nineteenth and early twentieth centuries. The gains in health and life expectancy attributable to public health have led in turn to large gains in productivity and economic growth, though, unlike the case for education, economists have not estimated economic rates of return for massive public health investments.

Social insurance

The scientific evidence for the argument that social insurance, health insurance, and other cash transfers promote economic productivity and growth is not so clear—although the evidence for the argument that social insurance retards economic productivity and growth is equally unclear. We review the empirical evidence on the opposing hypotheses in the next section and show that the best estimate of the effect of the current high levels of social insurance on growth is zero. Combining a null effect with the positive effects of education and public health on productivity and growth indicates that the welfare state as a whole increases productivity and growth.

In this section, we explain how social insurance enriches us even if it has no effect on economic productivity and growth. Unfortunately, quantitative research on the economic worth of reducing insecurity is in its infancy.[7] Still, again, economists across the political spectrum agree that social insurance reduces economic uncertainty, thereby improving individual utility and economic well-being.

Work by three Nobel Prize-winning economists, Kenneth Arrow (1963), George Akerlof (1970), and Joseph Stiglitz, together with Michael Rothschild

(1976), explains why government-provided health insurance is likely to lead to an increase in economic well-being. Given the irregularity and uncertainty of health-care costs and most people's aversion to risk, health insurance improves well-being by reducing risk. Private health insurance markets cannot succeed because of what economists call asymmetric information and adverse selection. Individuals know more about their own health than insurers do. Those who are healthy are more likely to risk being uninsured. To the extent that only the sick enroll, the price of insurance goes up, reinforcing the proclivity of the healthy to avoid insurance—further increasing costs and making insurance unaffordable. On the provider side, insurers have a stake in insuring only the healthy and weeding out the unhealthy. The private market, left to itself, produces too little health insurance. The only way to make health insurance affordable is to eliminate the element of choice, make insurance mandatory, and spread the risk across a broad population. Employer-provided health insurance performs this function at the firm level and, more generally, government does it at the city, state, or federal level. Today, virtually all economists accept the argument that some form of government-financed or -provided health insurance would be efficient. Conservative economists favor limiting the insurance to "catastrophic" coverage—that is, to very expensive health-care costs. While, as we explain in Chapter 8, we do not share this view, these differences should not obscure the fundamental agreement that some government role in financing and providing health insurance is efficient and makes sense. Finally, it is worth noting that the gains in economic well-being from the reduction in risk that comes from social insurance are likely to be quite large.

Just as the private market will provide too little education and too little health insurance, so it will provide too little insurance against the risk of becoming unemployed, or disabled, or dying prematurely, or even against the happy risk of living too long. Once again, those who are most likely to need the insurance will buy it, while those least likely to need it will not, thus driving up the price. Old-age insurance, for example, addresses the risk of living too long in retirement. One such form of insurance provided by the private market is an annuity, which pays a fixed sum periodically as long as a person lives. Those people who anticipate living long into retirement (perhaps because of family history, their insight into their own health, and other personal characteristics) will be more likely to purchase an annuity as they will expect to enjoy more years of payouts than those who expect to live only a few years in retirement. As the annuity market comes to be overpopulated by purchasers who are relatively expensive to insurers, insurers will raise the price of annuities. As annuities get more expensive, they will become attractive only to those with the longest expected lifespans, and retirees with relatively few years of expected retirement will be priced out of the market. By pooling risk across the population and using a centralized administrative system, social insurance avoids the adverse selection issues that arise with voluntary coverage and provides insurance against this risk more efficiently than the private market can.

American economists now agree that there is a role for government in assuring that the aged have sufficient income in retirement. Most also agree that government can achieve this end more efficiently than private markets and the family alone (Becker and Murphy, 1988; Buchanan, 1968; Aaron, 1982; Musgrave and Musgrave, 1984; Blinder, 1988; Steuerle and Bakija, 1994; Feldstein, 1987 and 2005). Only a few ideologues reject any government role. Conservatives such as James Buchanan and Martin Feldstein want the government to require people to save for their retirement. We address the issue of private accounts in Chapter 8.

II. How democracy encourages the growth of welfare states

That capitalism makes nations rich and that welfare state institutions make them even richer is no guarantee that nations will adopt either capitalism or welfare state institutions. Certainly, history offers plenty of counter-examples. Among the minority of nations that have become rich welfare states, as we shall see below in Chapters 6 and 7, democracy appears to have been a driving force. It is no accident that all of today's rich nations have democratic institutions. Democracy is associated with good governance—at least in the relative sense. Compared with their non-democratic counterparts, democratic nations find more effective solutions to common problems. They are also more likely to learn from the experience of other nations. Why this is so is a matter of debate. One explanation is that abilities and knowledge are widely dispersed among the population and that allowing all adults to vote—universal suffrage—maximizes the expression of this diversity. Another explanation is that power corrupts and that universal suffrage restrains the power of elites.[8] Whatever the explanation, few would contest that democracy does produce relatively good government. Perhaps the most important element of "good government" is the encouragement of capitalism accompanied by large doses of socialization of investment in human capital and insurance. All the democratic states have chosen this mixture because experience indicates that capitalism makes countries rich and welfare state institutions make capitalist nations even richer.

It is also true that allowing all adults to vote makes democracies more prone to support public programs that redistribute from the rich to the rest of the population. Both simple and very sophisticated economic models of political behavior predict that extending the right to vote should increase redistribution. The median voter model, the most popular of these models, is easy to understand in terms of the redistributive effects by income class described in Chapter 4 below. The net fiscal benefits of the US welfare state are very large for the poor; quite substantial for the near-poor and lower middle class; positive but quite small for the middle class; negative, but not very large for the upper middle class; and negative and noticeable, though not huge, for the richest fifth. If everyone has the vote and each group knows and votes their own self-interest, the middle group or median voter group is the swing group. So long as they get net benefits, they should support redistribution. If, however, only the top fifth can vote, they would likely decide to provide little to no welfare state programs. Consider, for example, education. Although it is true that the rich benefit from the education of the poor, it is also true that if self-interest alone guided the rich man's voting, the benefit to him from educating the poor would have to exceed the cost to him of paying for poor children's education. Enlightened self-interest might conceivably cause voters at the top of the distribution to provide some limited public financing of education for the very poorest citizens. But, as the franchise is extended downward, public funding for education would likely increase until it became universal provision—which is part of Peter Lindert's explanation of why the United States was a leader in providing education (2004). More generally, Lindert argues persuasively that as voting rights are extended increasingly down the income scale, theory predicts and empirical evidence confirms that extending the vote increases welfare state spending and redistribution.

Indeed, conservative theorists have for centuries feared that democracies might redistribute and redistribute until incentives are killed and the economy degenerates.[9] More recently, the remarkable post-World War II prosperity in the United States and Europe spurred major welfare state expansions during the 1960s and 1970s. The 1972 OPEC oil crisis marked the end of this golden era and set the stage for stagflation and substantial declines in growth in both productivity and income. The slowdown, however, was not well understood. By the end of the 1970s, conservative economists were blaming the social insurance portion of the welfare state for declining economic growth. Martin Feldstein, in a series of papers, argued that health insurance was inefficient, old-age insurance discouraged saving and thereby led to a fall in investment and long-term wealth, and unemployment insurance increased unemployment (Feldstein, 1973, 1974, and 1976). As citizens in the rich nations continued to live longer and healthier lives and to have fewer babies, economists began to talk about an impending crisis in the welfare state (OECD, 1980). More recently, Assar Lindbeck, a well-respected Swedish economist, argued that the Swedish welfare state had gone too far and was responsible for a decline in the Swedish economic growth rate (1997). All these charges, it should be noted, were directed social insurance rather than education or public health.

III. Is there a crisis in the welfare state? Or do we have too much social insurance?

While social insurance may increase economic well-being by reducing risk, at first blush it would appear hard to make the case that cash transfers from the working population to the retired, disabled, and non-working populations also increase productivity and growth. This section first explains how theory predicts that social insurance programs both reduce and increase productivity and growth, and then reviews the empirical evidence, which suggests small to no net effects.

How social insurance programs reduce productivity and growth

Why might welfare state programs reduce the productivity of capitalism? Standard economic analysis suggests three reasons. The first and most important source of inefficiency is the taxation required to finance welfare state services. Taxes distort and blunt incentives. A tax on earnings reduces the reward for work, which, other things being equal, reduces work. At the individual level, taxes on earnings also reduce income, which leads to more work. In general, it is not clear which effect dominates. But at the societal level, while taxes reduce incomes, social welfare benefits increase incomes. Thus, to a first approximation, there is no income effect at the social level and the net social effect is to reduce work. Similarly, taxes on capital decrease incentives to save and invest.

The inefficiency costs of taxes, it should be said, apply to all government services—including education, public health, defense, roads, and other infrastructure. One implication is that even if the benefits of every program taken individually exceed the costs, if the public sector is very large, the costs of the aggregate tax burden for all the programs added together could exceed the total benefits. If taxes are already 60 percent, the costs of adding another program that would raise the tax burden 10 percentage points are higher than if taxes were only 30 percent.

The second source of inefficiency is the distortion costs of provision. For example, because public assistance benefits are sharply reduced as earnings increase, they reduce the incentive to work. Because health-care benefits are provided free of cost at the margin (or nearly so) consumers are apt to use more health care than if they had to pay for the service. Government-guaranteed retirement pensions may decrease private saving for retirement.

The third source of inefficiency involves the administrative costs of collecting taxes and distributing benefits. That welfare state programs have costs that could in principle be very large would not be denied by anyone who is economically literate. Imagine an economy in which all goods were provided by the government and all incomes were fully taxed. There would be no economic incentive to earn legitimate income. The underground economy would grow, but the above-ground economy would begin to grow more slowly and perhaps even to shrink. If only 90 percent of goods were publicly provided, some economic incentives would remain, but fewer than if 50 percent of goods were publicly provided. Similarly, economic incentives would be greater if only 20 percent rather than 50 percent of goods were publicly provided. But, while theory tells us that 20 percent dulls incentives less than 50 percent, it says nothing about the magnitude of the difference.[10]

Moreover, all goods have costs. As economists are fond of saying, there is no free lunch. To say that there are costs, however, is not the same as saying that the costs exceed the benefits. As we have seen, economic theory and empirical research confirm that public education and public health increase efficiency, productivity, and growth. Social insurance reduces uncertainty more and more efficiently than private insurance does, thereby increasing efficiency and economic well-being. But does insurance promote productivity and growth?

How social insurance programs increase productivity and growth

Pensions for the aged, the disabled, and survivors promote social stability, and social stability promotes productivity and growth. As described in Chapter 6, the Conservative German Chancellor Otto von Bismarck pioneered social insurance to undercut the rapidly increasing appeal of the German Socialist Party and thereby promote social stability. The young know that they will one day be old. Ensuring that citizens get adequate pensions and health care in their old age gives the working-age population something to look forward to, rather than something to dread. Similarly, ensuring that workers get adequate compensation for injuries on the job makes workers from poor backgrounds who wind up working at the most dangerous jobs feel that there is some fairness in the system. Thus, old-age and work-injury insurance not only increase the economic security of the aged and disabled, but also increase solidarity among the working-age population by giving them a common stake in the system. Even public relief programs, by creating a safety net to aid the poorest victims of the system, increase the fairness of the system and quell discontent, thereby increasing political stability (Piven and Cloward, 1972), productivity, and growth.[11] Furthermore, by reducing economic insecurity, social insurance and safety nets make people more willing to take economic risks. Although critics like Feldstein attack unemployment insurance for prolonging unemployment, it may be that an unemployed worker who can take the risk of remaining jobless a little longer will in the end find a job that is a better match for his or her skills, thus increasing productivity. Thus, economic theory does not offer a firm prediction of the effects on productivity and growth of increasing or decreasing social insurance or, more generally, of the size of the welfare state. The loss of efficiency that arises from increases in tax rates may be larger than, equal to, or smaller than the gains in efficiency that arise from the benefits. The net effect of social insurance programs on productivity and economic growth is therefore an empirical question. What is the evidence?

So what is the empirical evidence?

The empirical literature that addresses the question of the effects of the welfare state includes only social insurance in its measure of welfare state spending. It ignores education and public health. Thus, it addresses more precisely the question of how spending on social insurance affects economic growth.

The country most often discussed in both the economics and wider welfare state literature is Sweden. Just as many advocates of welfare state expansion in the 1970s and 1980s pointed to Sweden's extraordinary success in reducing poverty and inequality, many critics have since called attention to Sweden's relatively low growth rate after its massive expansion of the social welfare system during the 1970s.[12] It is possible that the Swedish tax burden, the highest among all rich nations, and some overly generous benefits were discouraging growth. But if one listens to what the critics are saying it is equally possible that certain Swedish regulations of labor and capital markets discouraged growth. On the other hand, that Norway, whose social welfare spending is only slightly less than Sweden's, had growth rates between 1970 and 2004 slightly larger than that of the United States suggests that the focus on Sweden may be a bit narrow. Even more important, though Sweden had low growth rates during the 1980s and early 1990s, from 1995 to 2006, among our 14 rich nations, only Finland and Ireland had a higher growth rate in per capita GDP than Sweden.

Anthony Atkinson (1999), after reviewing nine studies that examine the effects of the welfare state on growth rates in 13 to 19 OECD countries[13] in different periods between 1950 and 1987, concludes:

The results of econometric studies of the relationship between social transfer spending and growth rates are mixed: some find that high spending on social transfers leads to lower growth, others find the reverse. The largest of the estimated effects—in either direction—do not, however, seem believable.

In the most recent study, Lindert (2004) examines three periods of growth in the OECD welfare states—1880–1930, 1962–81, and 1978–95—and finds a statistically significant positive effect of cash transfers on economic growth during the first two but none during the third. These findings suggest that early expansions in social insurance increased growth and that the most recent expansions have not harmed it. The findings also suggest that at some point further expansions of social insurance will hamper growth. If increases in spending have positive effects at low levels and null effects at high levels, the negative effects are growing faster than the positive effects as spending grows. At some point, if the least productive transfers continue to grow as a percentage of GDP, the negative effects will outweigh the positive effects. That makes sense. But we haven't reached that point yet.

A longer historical perspective reinforces our conclusion that the effects of the welfare state on economic growth have been positive. Table 2.1 presents growth rates in per capital GDP for the 14 rich nations examined in this book for two recent time periods—1960 to 1975 and 1975 to 2006—and for one long period before the growth of the welfare state, 1870 to 1913. Except for Ireland and the UK, growth

Table 2.1: Growth rates in per capita GDP: 14 currently rich nations in three time periods

	1960–1975	1975–2006	1870–1913
Australia	2.36	1.83	1.07
Canada	2.89	1.76	2.14
Ireland	3.41	4.09	no data
United Kingdom	1.97	2.08	0.65
United States	2.15	2.04	2.63
Belgium	3.72	1.89	no data
France	3.77	1.74	1.32
Italy	3.90	1.91	0.86
Germany	no data	1.95	1.57
Netherlands	3.25	1.80	no data
Spain	5.25	2.03	no data
Finland	3.97	2.24	1.50
Norway	3.39	2.60	1.43
Sweden	3.11	1.67	1.97

Source: Data for 1870–1913 is from Mitchell, B.R. (1998). *International Historical Statistics: 1750–1993*. London: Macmillan Reference. Other periods are from World Bank World Development Indicators.

rates are higher in all countries, and much higher in most from 1960 to 1975 than they are from 1975 to 2006. The Swedish growth rate drops from 3.11 to 1.67, or by nearly a half! This sharp drop in growth rates helped fuel the belief that the welfare state was strangling capitalism. That Sweden's growth rate from 1994 to 2006 was back up to 2.5 percent, as we have already noted, provides some evidence to the contrary.

The longer historical perspective shown by the data in column three provides evidence that the growth rates in the 1960 to 1975 period were unusually high. This earlier period comes after the American Civil War and the Franco-Prussian War, and before World War I. Although not shown in the table, economic growth before this period and afterwards—during World War I, the Great Depression, and World War II—was dramatically lower. A country-by-country comparison of columns one, two, and three indicates that economic growth rates in the 1960–75 period were un-usually high. While growth was substantially higher in most countries between 1960 and 1975, as compared to the post-1975 period, in all countries except the US growth rates were dramatically higher in the 1960–75 period than they were between 1870 and 1913. Even more im-portant, most of the currently rich nations have higher growth rates in the large welfare state 1975–2006 era than they did in the pre-large welfare state 1870–1913 era. Look first at the United Kingdom, the first nation to industrialize. It is useful to begin with the industrial leader because countries that industrialized later were able to grow faster, as they caught up by copying the successful technologies of the leader(s). The annual growth rate of the UK during the Victorian era was a paltry 0.65 percent, compared to a robust 2 percent per year in the large welfare state era. In Germany, the second leading European nation, growth is also higher in the large welfare state era, though the difference is not nearly as great. In only three countries—Canada, the US, and Sweden—are annual growth rates higher in the earlier than the later period. The largest difference is for the US—nearly one half-percentage point. But the initial US figure is unusually high for two reasons: catching up from incorporating foreign technology and recovering from the Civil War. If we divide the period into two sub-periods, growth is 2.95 percent from 1870 to 1890 and only 2.25 percent from 1890 to 1913, or only slightly higher than the 2.04 growth rate from 1975 to 2006.[14] Thus, results are sensitive to the particular years chosen for comparison. But the big picture is clear. Incomes in most of the currently rich nations are now growing faster, not slower than they have in the past. Of course, many other things besides social welfare spending have changed during the past 150 years. But, as we have seen, welfare state spending is now very large relative to the total production of goods and services in all advanced industrialized nations. If such spending had large adverse effects, it is doubtful that growth rates would have been so large in the last quarter of the twentieth century. The crude historical relationship suggests, at a minimum, no great ill effects and, more likely, a positive effect.

The burden of proof clearly lies on the side of those who claim that welfare state programs are strangling productivity and growth. If they are right, they need to explain why all rich nations have large welfare states and they need to explain why growth rates have grown in most rich nations as their welfare states have grown larger. The fact is there is no satisfactory explanation that omits the positive effects of welfare state programs.

As the populations of welfare states age, transfers to the aged will increase, as will the tax burden on the working-age population. It is possible that these future increases will slow economic growth. But, even if they do, the slowdown will be taking place from remarkably high rates of economic growth. To use the term "crisis" to describe the current and future of the welfare state is simply alarmist.

It is also true that some rich nations, including the United States, face a future shortfall between legislated taxes and promised benefits in their old-age insurance programs. But, as discussed in Chapter 8, the US short-fall can be relatively easily resolved by a combination of small increases in taxes and small reductions in benefits.

IV. What about the trade-off between equality and efficiency?

In this chapter, we have shown that welfare state programs increase efficiency, productivity, and economic growth. Achieving greater equality is both an objective and, as we shall see in Chapter 5, an accomplishment of welfare state programs. Yet, in 1975, in *Equality and Efficiency: The Big Trade-off*, Arthur Okun argued that equality could usually be increased only through a loss in economic efficiency. Okun was not a conservative. He served on President John Kennedy's council of economic advisors. And his book is the all-time best-seller at the Brookings Institution, the oldest and probably most respected Washington think tank. Was Okun wrong about the necessity of a big trade-off? Much as we have learned from his book and respect Okun's work, the answer is yes.

Okun makes an exception for public education, which he sees as promoting equality of opportunity as well as equality and therefore also efficiency. He also treats old-age insurance as an exception on the grounds that work disincentives for the aged are of little concern. These are pretty big exceptions. More fundamentally, Okun does not refer to efficiency gains from insurance, perhaps because the economics literature was just beginning to address this issue.

In the most quoted passage of the book, Okun asks his readers to think about what he calls the "leaky bucket experiment." The bucket, explains Okun, is the means by which transfers are made from one part of the population to another, so leaks—the costs necessarily attending on the transfers—are inevitable. The leaks from the bucket include the disincentive effects of taxation, the incentive effects of provision, and administrative costs. But these various costs, as we have already discussed, do not necessarily make transfers inefficient. The costs must be weighed against the benefits. Okun's leaky bucket experiment implicitly assumes that transfers have no individual or social benefits beyond the amount being transferred. That assumption is clearly wrong for both public education and public health, where external and social benefits are high. It is also clearly wrong for social insurance, where all of the insured, not just those who collect the insurance, benefit from the reduction in risk. The transfer described in Okun's leaky bucket experiment was a pure cash transfer. Of all possible kinds of transfers, those in pure cash are least likely to have benefits that extend beyond the value of the transfer itself (Currie, 2006). But, as we have seen, even poor-relief cash benefits are worth something to the rest of the population and therefore are probably efficient and contribute to productivity and growth. As a whole, therefore, as Walter Korpi says, the welfare state is more akin to an irrigation ditch than to a leaky bucket.[15]

Though it is possible to imagine a set of circumstances in which greater equality can be achieved only at the expense of efficiency, for those circumstances to pertain, the world would have to be both much more equal and much more efficient than the imperfect world we inhabit. In practice, by enhancing the human capital and economic security of the entire population, welfare state programs in rich nations have achieved greater equality and greater efficiency, productivity, and economic growth.[16]

Notes

1. Social welfare expenditures are the sum of social security, health, and education spending. Expenditure data is taken from IMF Government Finance Statistics Yearbooks (1998–2006). The IMF provides social security, health, and education expenditures in local currency. Each expenditure is then divided by that country's GDP for the year of expenditure and the quotients are summed. This is the total social welfare expenditures as a percent of GDP for each country. GDP and per-capita GDP are taken from the World Bank World Development Indictors. All data are presented as natural logarithms.

2. Internationally, spending increases a little less than 1 percent for each 1 percent increase in income. Amongst the 50 American states, for every 1 percent increase in state income, welfare state spending increases by at least 1 percent, with some studies suggesting that state spending goes up by more than 1 percent. In general, public spending on health care seems more responsive to increases in income than other types of social welfare spending, particularly cash assistance (Chernick, 1998).

3. The alert and questioning reader will note that there are three countries that are very rich but have decidedly smaller welfare states than all the other rich nations. The exceptional nations—Hong Kong, Singapore, and the United Arab Emirates—have not been included in previous research on welfare states in rich nations and we make no attempt to analyze or explain their exceptionalism. Not because doing so is unimportant, but because completing a book requires not exploring every issue. We trust that future scholars will deal with this one.

4. The theory and evidence are collected and summarized best in the three-volume set on *Economic Theory and the Welfare State* (2001), edited by Nicholas Barr. For a shorter summary see Barr (1992).

5. Most economists would agree in practice if not in principle to the argument that macro-economic stability is another good under-produced by the market. Milton Friedman, of course, has argued the opposite. But Alan Greenspan, fan of Ayn Rand, did not adopt Friedman's recommendations to adopt an automatic rule rather than rely on the discretion of the Federal Reserve in changing interest rates.

6. Gary Becker and Kevin Murphy (1988) have a new and different explanation for public financing of education. If parents could adjust the inheritance they leave their children, they would, as selfish human beings, invest optimally in their children's education because they, as well as their children, have an interest in their children being well educated. But, many parents, especially those in poor economic circumstances, cannot save enough money both to live well in retirement and to give inheritances to their children. Thus, there is a need for public financing.

7. Amy Finkelstein and colleagues have done the pioneering research in this area. Finkelstein and McKnight (2005) find that the economic gains are quite large for health insurance for the aged, but Brown and Finkelstein (2007) find they are quite small for old-age insurance.

8. The federalist essays by Alexander Hamilton, John Jay, and James Madison (1787) are the best expression of the classical arguments.

9. Josephine Shaw Lowell (1890), the head of the Charity Organization Society and one of the founding mothers of the social work profession in the US, gives a beautifully crafted literary expression of this fear. Tanzi and Schuknecht (2000) is a modern-day, numerically filled expression of this fear.

10. Theory does predict that the inefficiency costs increase with the square of the tax rate.

11. In "Transfers, the Social Safety Net, and Economic Growth," Xavier Sala-I-Martin (1997) develops a theoretical economic model in which transfers quell social and political discontent and thereby increase growth. He also reports that in most empirical studies of economic growth, transfers have a positive effect. Alesina, Ozler, Roubini, and Swagel (1996) find that political instability substantially retards economic growth. The empirical evidence on the effects of transfers on growth is discussed in the next subsection.

12. Lindbeck (1994, 1996, and 1997); Freeman et al. (1997). For alternative views see Korpi (1996) and Agell (1996). For the latest exchange, see Lindert (2006) and comment by Bergh (2006) and response by Lindert (2006).

13. A few of the studies also include Japan. A tenth study uses a worldwide sample of 74 countries.

14. In Canada, which industrialized more slowly than the US and had no civil war, the growth in the second sub-period was higher than the first—2.4 compared to 1.75.

15. See Korpi (1985). Unfortunately, this otherwise very fine paper is marred by Korpi's denial of any ill effects of the leaks.
16. See also Pontussan (2005) who gives four reasons why increasing equality might facilitate economic growth: (1) a more equal distribution of wages facilitates wage restraint & thereby a better balance between inflation & un-employment; (2) increasing the minimum wage forces companies to be more productive; (3) some of big government, such as education and training, is productive; and (4) providing generous social insurance benefits facilitates political acceptance of trade. The first two relate to labor market regulations, which are not considered in this book. The third and fourth relate to transfers and are similar to arguments made in the text.

3

The Size, Nature, and Universality
of Welfare State Transfers

All rich nations are mixed economies, with very large private, capitalist sectors accompanied by large public sectors that go well beyond the classic public goods of defense, law and order, and public transport. Education, public health, health insurance, social insurance, public assistance, and housing are all publicly provided, subsidized, and/or regulated.

These welfare state institutions play a large role in the everyday lives of citizens. Most children attend public schools. Old-age insurance benefits are the main source of income for most of the elderly. When citizens are sick, nearly all count on health insurance that is partially or fully publicly funded to pay the bills. Citizens in every rich nation also take for granted clean water, well functioning sewerage, inoculations against infectious diseases, and other public health functions.[1] Welfare state services are expensive and citizens of rich countries devote a large share of their incomes via taxes and payroll deductions to paying for these services.

In this chapter we describe the size and structure of the welfare states in rich nations using data on social welfare expenditures. The data, which come from official government publications in each country, have been made consistent and compiled by the Organization for Economic Co-operation and Development (OECD).[2] The first section disputes the claim that the American welfare state is unusually small. The second and third sections substantiate the claim that the structure of the American welfare state differs in fundamental ways from the welfare state structures of other rich nations. The US differs from other rich nations in its extraordinarily high expenditures on health care and low expenditures on cash and early childhood education and its heavy reliance on safety nets and platforms as opposed to floors.

I. The size of welfare states

The most common measure of the size of a welfare state is a country's total social welfare transfers as a share of its total annual income, or its gross domestic product (GDP). Roughly speaking, this share measures both the share of the total income of the average citizen that comes from welfare state transfers[3] and the average tax rate required to finance all welfare state benefits.[4] This is the measure we use in Chapter 2. Another measure of the size of a welfare state is the total amount of social welfare transfers per person. As we shall see, these measures do not always coincide, but taken together they yield the unambiguous conclusion that the US welfare state is not—as it is often described—unusually small but, in reality, quite large.

As noted in Chapter 1, our analysis of welfare state spending departs from most previous analyses by including education, employer-provided health insurance and pension benefits, and tax expenditures. We also include social welfare spending by all levels of government. Tax expenditures (savings in income tax payments) and tax-subsidized employer-provided expenditures are alternative (and, as we shall see, less progressive) ways to achieve some of the social goals of direct government spending—among them, providing health insurance, housing, or income security in old age. As such, including them gives a more accurate description of the size of welfare states.

Most economists treat tax expenditures as economically equivalent to explicit budget expenditures and would therefore agree that, at a minimum, the tax-subsidized portion of employer-provided health insurance (between one fifth and one quarter of the total) should be included as welfare state expenditures (Adema and Ladaique, 2005). Although a case can be made for counting only the tax-subsidized portion on the grounds that state funding differs from funding stimulated and regulated by the state, some economists and political scientists—whose practice and rationale we follow—argue for including the entire amount of employer expenditures on the grounds that these benefits are publicly subsidized and regulated; that employer-provided health insurance involves social-ization of the risk of ill health and redistribution from the healthy to the sick, at the firm rather than the national level; and, finally, that failing to include these benefits underestimates the share of the population with insurance and mis-characterizes the US welfare state by obscuring and minimizing how much it spends on subsidized health insurance.[5]

By the same logic, at a minimum, the tax-subsidized portion of employer-provided pensions should also be included as a welfare state transfer.

The case for including all of employers' spending for pensions, however, is weaker than the case for including all of their spending for health insurance. Health insurance, by its nature, redistributes from the healthy to the sick. Employer-provided pensions may involve no interpersonal redistribution (other than the tax subsidy) if, for example, the pension is a defined-contribution plan that involves private accounts and no spousal or survivor benefits. Unfortunately, we cannot distinguish between pensions that do and do not involve interpersonal transfers. For simplicity, we calculate the size of welfare states in two ways—by counting both all and no employer-provided benefits as social welfare transfers.

Figure 3.1 depicts the overall size of welfare states as measured by social welfare transfers as a share of GDP in 14 rich nations. For each nation, the first bar excludes and the second includes employer-provided benefits and tax expenditures. The share of income that is devoted to social welfare transfers increases from the bottom to the top of the diagram. The higher the bar, the larger is the welfare state. (The figure also depicts the size of each of the five major domains, which we discuss in the next section.).

The 14 nations are grouped into five predominantly English-speaking nations (Australia, Canada, Ireland, the United Kingdom, and the United States), six continental European nations (Belgium, France, Germany, the Netherlands, Italy, and Spain), and three Scandinavian or Nordic nations (Finland, Norway, and Sweden). In adopting this grouping, we follow a tradition, most closely associated with Gosta Esping-Anderson's superbly titled "Three Worlds of Welfare Capitalism." The same distinctions were also made in earlier works by Kahn and Kamerman (1978) and even earlier by Wilensky and Lebeaux's (1965) groundbreaking study, *Industrial Society and Social Welfare*. The classification is based entirely on cash benefits, predominantly pensions. According to Esping-Anderson, social welfare policy in the English-speaking countries is dominated by the nineteenth-century *liberal* belief in limited government, which results in heavy reliance on income testing and private benefits or what we call platforms. Policy in the *social democratic* regimes of the Nordic countries is dominated by the social democratic commitment to greater equality, which results in universal benefits with high floors. Policy in the *corporatist* regimes of continental Europe is dominated by the conservative belief in preserving both status differentials and social peace, which results in universal benefits closely tied to previous earnings. The Southern European countries, such as Italy and Spain, were for the most part not included in these analyses and most analysts agree that they don't fit neatly into any of the three regimes. More important, education, health insurance, and

Figure 3.1: Social welfare transfers as a percent of GDP in 14 rich nations: with and without employer-provided benefits (2001)

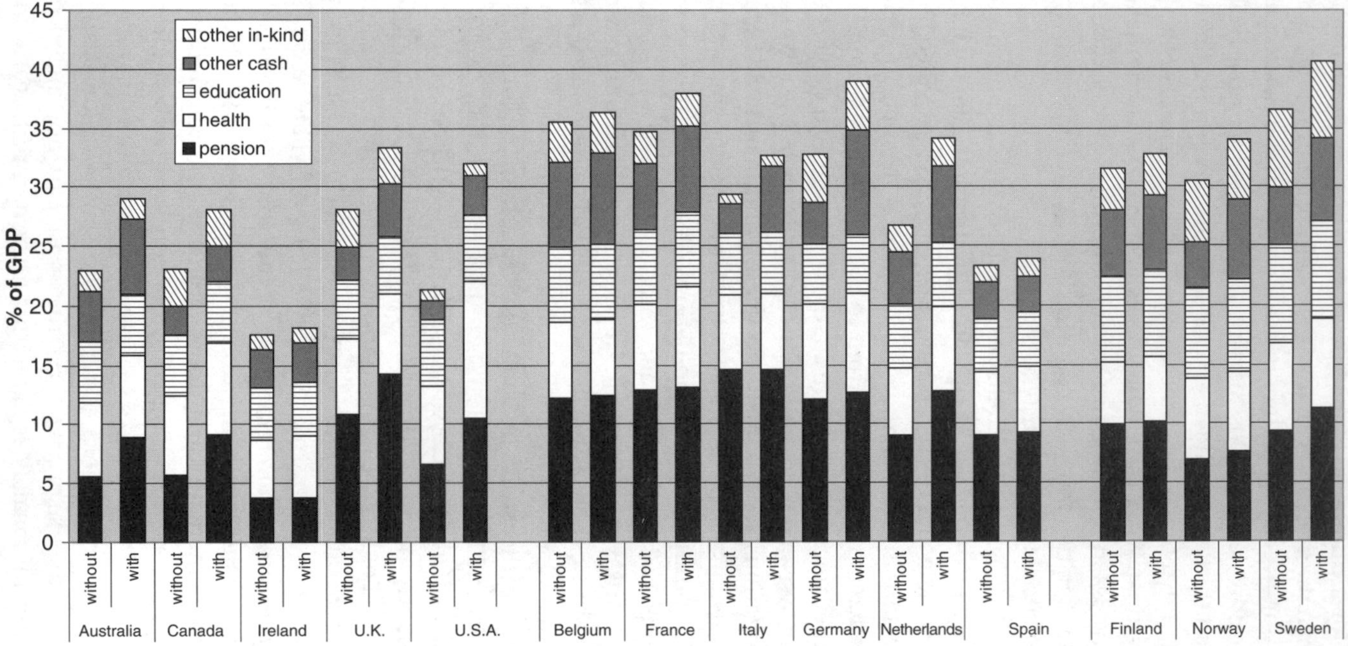

Sources: For data sources, see note 2 of this chapter.

other in-kind transfers were not included. In fact, as we shall see, while several very important aspects of the welfare states of rich nations do conform to "the three worlds of welfare capitalism," several others do not. As we discuss the size and structure of welfare states, we will comment on the conformities and non-conformities.

We begin the discussion by examining social welfare expenditures the old-fashioned way, in part, by not counting employer-provided benefits and tax expenditures. Recall, however, that the first bars do include education. (Later on, we will discuss the pure old-fashioned way, omitting education and employer-provided benefits, and tax benefits.) The first bars indicate each of the countries spends a substantial fraction of its GDP on social welfare—from 17 to 38 percent. As a share of total government spending, social benefits are at the very least 55 percent of government outlays (in the United States) and at the most 90 percent (in Sweden) (Osberg, Smeeding, and Schwabish, 2004). Most of what governments spend money on involves taxing one set of persons and providing benefits to another, and is therefore represented in Figure 3.1.

Not counting employer-provided benefits, the English-speaking nations spend the least—Ireland and the United States, the very least. The European nations spend substantially more, and the Scandinavian nations spend the most. These patterns are consistent with findings of other comparative studies (Kamerman and Kahn, 1978; Smeeding, O'Higgins, and Rainwater, 1990; Esping-Andersen, 1990; Smeeding, 2004).[6]

Unlike previous studies, however, the second bar, which includes employer-provided benefits, indicates that, within the English-speaking group, the United States spends nearly as much as the United Kingdom does and more than Canada and Australia do. Including employer-provided health insurance and pensions and tax expenditures increases the estimated size of the US welfare state by nearly 50 percent! More generally, including employer-provided benefits and tax expenditures substantially narrows cross-national differences in the size of welfare states because the English-speaking nations rely more on them than do most of the continental West European and Scandinavian countries. But note that Germany, the Netherlands, and Sweden also rely moderately on employer-provided benefits and tax subsidies.

Finally, note that if you want to make the case that the US welfare state is small, it helps to omit education, as well as employer-provided benefits and tax benefits. Counting spending on education increases the size of the old-fashioned or "traditionally measured" American welfare state by 38 percent!

Figure 3.2: Social welfare transfers in US $ per person in 14 rich nations: with and without employer-provided benefits (2001)

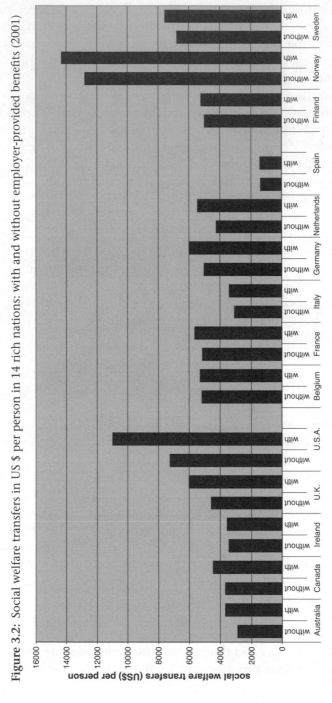

Sources: For data sources, see note 2 of this chapter.

Although welfare state spending relative to GDP is a good indicator of the degree to which countries differ in the share of their incomes devoted to the welfare state, such differences are not a good indication of the absolute amounts of social welfare transfers per person in each country. For example, though Sweden devotes more than 41 percent of GDP to welfare state expenditures, compared with the US share of 32 percent, Sweden's GDP per capita is only 79 percent of the US GDP per capita. Consequently, in absolute terms, the United States spends a lot more than 32/41 of what Sweden spends on a per capita basis. Therefore, to compare absolute levels of spending across countries, we multiply the share of GDP devoted to social welfare spending in each nation (Figure 3.1) by the ratio of its per capita GDP to the US per capita GDP. The results are presented in Figure 3.2. For those who believe that the absolute size of the US welfare state is small, the data in Figure 3.2 are shocking and constitute a wake-up call. Once health and education benefits are counted, real per capita social welfare spending in the United States is larger than that in almost all other countries! Even if employer-provided benefits and tax expenditures are excluded, the United States is still the third biggest spender on a per capita basis.[7]

II. The structure of welfare states

Describing the structure of a welfare state is more difficult than describing its overall size because every country has dozens of different welfare state programs. Each program has many provisions that determine who is eligible to receive benefits and what benefits each receives. Because a detailed description of all these programs would be overwhelming, we simplify and describe broad patterns.[8] We focus in this section on the kinds of benefits received and in the next section on how widely and fairly they are distributed—both of which can be measured by the same internationally available data on social welfare spending we use to describe the size of welfare states. (In the next chapter, we use survey data to describe two other aspects of the structure of welfare states: the concentration of benefits on the elderly and children and the effects of welfare state benefits and taxes on poverty and inequality.) Focusing on the kinds of benefits received helps describe what welfare states do. We categorize all spending into five broad domains: pensions (old-age, survivors', and disability insurance), health care, education, cash benefits other than pensions, and services and in-kind benefits other than health and education. Pensions are the largest source of spending for all countries except the United States, where health care is the largest.

Domains of welfare state benefits

In addition to depicting the overall size of welfare states, Figure 3.1 also conveys important information about the relative sizes of different domains of the welfare state within and across the 14 rich nations. In Figure 3.1, the five domains are ordered from the bottom to the top of the bars by largest to smallest for most countries—pensions, health care, education, other cash benefits, and other services or in-kind benefits.

Pensions include benefits from disability and survivors' insurance as well as benefits from old-age insurance, and, as noted, employer-provided pension benefits. Together, these benefits are designed to deal with the risk of becoming economically dependent because of either ill health (due to either old age or disability) or death. All citizens who have an established work history or are spouses or children of those with an established work history are eligible for old-age, survivors', and disability insurance. In nearly all rich countries, many employers also provide private pension benefits. On average, old-age pensions account for about 80 percent of total pensions. In all countries, social insurance cash benefits are a mixture of a minimum benefit paid to all who are eligible and a benefit that is related to previous earnings.

Health-care benefits include publicly financed health insurance (Medicare and Medicaid in the United States), publicly provided health care (as in the United Kingdom and as in the United States for military and military veterans), and, in the United States, tax-subsidized employer-provided health insurance.

Education includes primary, secondary, and post-secondary education, as well as early childhood education and childcare (ECEC).

Other cash transfers include unemployment compensation, occupational injury and disease (workman's compensation in the United States), child welfare, tax breaks for social purposes that are similar to cash, such as the Earned Income Tax Credit in the United States, public assistance for the poor, and several other benefits that are available in the United States on a very limited basis, but common in other countries, such as sickness insurance, family allowance, and paid parental leave.

Finally, other services or in-kind benefits include services for the elderly and physically and mentally disabled, housing subsidies for low-income families, job-training programs (or, to use the European term, active labor-market programs), and miscellaneous programs such as food stamps, nutrition programs for women and children, low-income home energy assistance, and other family services.

Figure 3.1 highlights several similarities across countries. With a few exceptions, the biggest single expenditure is for pensions, health is second, and education is third. The few country exceptions to this ordering are all quite interesting and are discussed below. In all countries, these three transfers also account for the bulk of social welfare transfers. This striking similarity in structure reinforces our finding that welfare states in rich countries are more similar in size than previous analyses indicate.

In discussing differences, we begin with pensions, the biggest single source of welfare state spending in all rich countries except for the United States. The United Kingdom is the biggest spender—about 15 percent of GDP and about half of its total welfare state transfers. (If we count only public pensions, however, the United Kingdom drops below all continental West European countries.) The smallest spenders, at approximately 10 percent, are the other English-speaking nations. Part of the difference in spending is attributable to differences in the share of the population that is older than age 65; part, to differences in generosity toward the aged. The share of GDP devoted to pensions per 10,000 persons aged 65 or older (a simple measure of generosity) ranges from .03 percent in the United States to 0.13 percent in Finland. There is also wide variation across countries (not shown in Figure 3.1) in transfers to the disabled—ranging from 0.44 in Canada to 2.7 in the Netherlands, which is more reflective of differences in policy. The Netherlands is widely known for treating the physically and mentally disabled most generously.

The mix of pension benefits that are flat and those that are earnings-related differs across nations and is a distinguishing feature of the different worlds of welfare capitalism. Throughout most of the twentieth century, social insurance benefits in Germany were strictly related to previous earnings; there was no minimum benefit. Danish and Swedish benefits, by contrast, were the same for everyone. During the early post-World War II period, the United Kingdom had, like the Scandinavian countries, flat benefits.

Initially, the United States followed most closely the German model, with benefits related to previous earnings, but the US benefit formula has always been progressive—the lower the earnings, the higher the share of earnings that is replaced by old-age, survivors', and disability insurance. Over time, the United States adopted a minimum benefit, and the United

Kingdom and the Scandinavian countries adopted earnings-related benefits.

Probably the single most important distinction in pensions today is how the minimum benefit relates to average earnings in the country. The minimums tend to be very high in Scandinavia, a bit lower in the continental European countries, and much lower in the English-speaking countries. As we shall see in Chapter 4, this pattern leads to the so-called three worlds of welfare capitalism. But pensions, though the largest single item in all welfare state spending, are at most half of total spending in a few countries and in most countries less than a third of the total.

In health, the second biggest domain, the United States, at nearly 12 percent of GDP, is the biggest spender. Indeed, more than a third of US social welfare transfers are spent on health. Furthermore, Figure 3.1 understates how much more Americans spend on health than do citizens of other countries because it does not reflect privately purchased insurance and out-of-pocket health expenditures, which are trivial in other countries, but quite substantial in the United States—another 3.2 percent of GDP. The lowest spender is Finland at about 5.5 percent of GDP. As with pensions, part of the differences in health expenditures is related to the share of the population that is aged. But the high-spending United States has a younger population than most European countries, including France and Germany, the next biggest spenders. So the United States, with a smaller share of aged citizens and with about 15 percent of its residents lacking health insurance, still spends much more on health transfers than any other country. That anomaly raises the question of whether the United States is overspending on health care or getting superior quality care. We take up this question in Chapters 4, 6, and 8. Except for the United States, nations provide health insurance that guarantees equal access to basic health care for all citizens. In the United States, benefits are provided on an equal access basis to a large share of the population, including the elderly, disabled, and survivors and their dependents, and veterans and their dependents. The United States also provides a less costly form of health insurance to low-income families and individuals through Medicaid. Benefits from employer-provided health insurance are distributed quite unequally among the working population—with the highest-paid workers having the best insurance coverage and the lowest-paid workers having no coverage.

Education is the third largest domain. Spending ranges from a low of 4.5 percent of GDP in Ireland to a high of 8.25 percent in Sweden. At 5.6 percent, US spending is in the middle of the pack, toward the high end.

The United States does spend more than all the other English-speaking nations and more than Germany, Italy, the Netherlands, and Spain, but it spends less than Belgium, France, Finland, Norway, and Sweden.

As with health-care spending, Figure 3.1 understates total US spending on education because more of US spending comes directly out of the pocket of the recipient of the service. Private payments for college and other forms of post-secondary education are particularly important in the United States. When private spending on education is added to transfers on education, the US share of total spending increases to 7.6 percent of GDP, which puts it at the higher end of the rich countries. US institutions of higher education are acknowledged to be among the best in the world. Higher shares of US citizens still get college degrees than citizens in most, but no longer all, other rich countries. But in terms of mass early child-hood education and care, the United States lags in transfer spending and total enrollments.

Spending on cash transfers other than pensions is the fourth largest domain, slightly smaller than spending on education. The United States stands out, along with Canada, as a small spender in this area. These two nations devote 3 percent or less to all other cash transfers besides pensions. Australia spends nearly twice as much, putting it close to the average. Germany and Belgium, at 8.5 percent and 7.75 percent respectively, are the leading spenders.[9]

The pattern of spending on other in-kind benefits is similar to that of cash benefits, with the United States and Canada at the bottom, but, in this case, the Scandinavian countries at the top. The most generous country in this category is Sweden, with 6 percent of GDP devoted to these social service expenditures. A large part of Swedish spending in this category is for elder care. Note that while Finland, at 3.5 percent, is also near the top, Belgium spends as much as Finland, and Germany, at 4 percent, spends more.

The balance between cash and in-kind benefits and the effects of taxes

Figure 3.3 sharpens our analysis of similarities and differences across welfare states by collapsing the five domains into only two kinds of benefits: those paid in cash and those received as services or in-kind benefits. The bottom black part of each bar represents cash benefits. The top white part represents in-kind benefits.

Figure 3.3 also takes account of how taxes affect the value of cash benefits. Scandinavian and continental European countries, for example, are more

Figure 3.3: The shares of cash (gross and net) and in-kind transfers (2001)

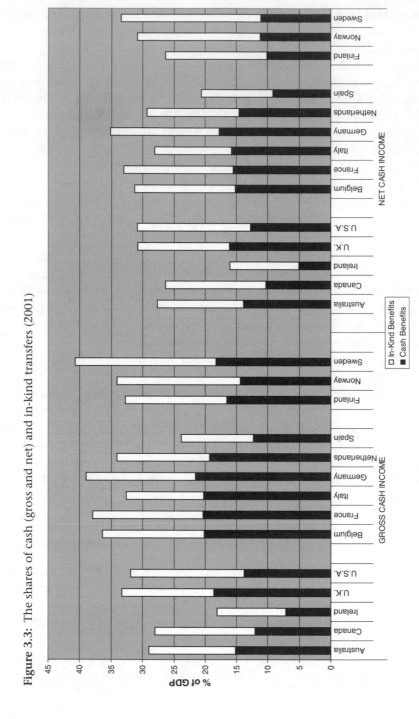

Sources: For data sources, see note 2 of this chapter.

likely to tax cash transfers and to finance social welfare spending and other government services through indirect taxes than the English-speaking countries, so it is important to capture the effects of these taxes as well as those of direct (payroll and income) taxes. The value-added tax, which may be thought of most simply as a variant of a sales tax, is close to 20 percent in most Scandinavian and continental countries, as compared with sales tax rates of about 6 percent or 7 percent in the United States. A cash transfer of $1,000 that will in the United States buy $930 to $940 worth of goods will buy only about $800 worth of goods and services in Europe. Among the English-speaking countries, the United States relies least on indirect taxes and also ranks last in taxing cash transfers under its income tax.

In the first set of bars for each country, cash benefits are measured on a gross basis; in the second, they are measured according to their after-tax value. The measurement of non-cash benefits is identical in both bars.

In the gross expenditures bars in Figure 3.3, two points stand out. First, except for the continental European nations, where the shares are about 40 percent, non-cash spending amounts to half or more of total welfare state spending. Studies that take account of only cash transfers are thus omitting about half of the total redistribution accomplished by welfare states. Second, the Anglo-Saxon nations, and particularly the United States, spend a greater share on non-cash benefits than do the other nations. Americans are small spenders on cash support but big spenders on education and especially health care.

Differences across countries in the net expenditures bars are much smaller than differences in the gross expenditure bars. The net expenditure bars provide no hint of the three worlds of welfare capitalism. The value of total benefits is highest in Germany and Sweden, followed by France and Belgium. The United States, the United Kingdom, and Norway are just below France and Belgium. The dramatic ways in which differences among countries shrink and rankings shift suggest that earlier estimates of cross-national differences in economic well-being may also be quite misleading. We confirm this in Chapter 4.

Universality of benefits

FLOORS, SAFETY NETS, AND PLATFORMS: CROSS-COUNTRY COMPARISONS

Benefits are categorized as floors, safety nets, and platforms in order to compare countries in terms of the universality and fairness of benefit provision. Floors serve all regardless of income. The most universal of benefits are based on citizenship and are available to all members of a nation, including in some cases even non-citizen residents. These benefits include public elementary and secondary education; public health and national health service and health insurance systems; family allowances; and, in Denmark, Finland, Sweden, and France, early childhood education and care. The next most universal are the social insurance systems, which cover all who work in the legitimate labor market and have social security taxes withheld from their wages. In these programs, funding is provided almost entirely by those who will eventually or could potentially benefit from them. These benefits include pensions—old-age, disability, and sur-vivors'—and occupational compensation for unemployment, injury, and parental leave. To simplify somewhat we lump these two sets of programs together and label both as floors.

Safety nets serve a more limited range of people—specifically, the poor or near-poor, who cannot function economically at adequate levels with-out special assistance. Safety nets in the United States include public assistance (cash and services), child welfare, Head Start, Medicaid, housing subsidies for the poor, food and nutrition programs, and labor market programs.

The term "floor" has long been used to describe universal programs, just as "safety net" has long been used to describe programs for the poor. Yet another set of public programs, which we call platforms, includes employer-provided health insurance and pensions and tax benefits. Plat-forms are characterized by widespread eligibility, but are more restrictive than floors; their benefits generally targeted more to the rich. Are rich nations relatively similar in their reliance on floors, platforms, and safety nets? Or are there stark differences?

Figure 3.4 provides evidence of strong similarity in the universality of benefits across countries, with one notable and another extreme excep-tion. All the rich countries have floors, safety nets, and platforms. In all except the United States, welfare state transfers consist predominantly—in most cases 70 percent or more—of floors. In general, the English-speaking nations tend to rely more heavily on safety nets and platforms—bifurcated aid systems as compared to universal aid systems—than either the contin-ental West European or Scandinavian nations. But, even within the English-speaking nations, the United States stands out. Over half of total US welfare state transfers come through platforms and safety nets. Further, recall that tax expenditures for housing in the United States are not counted in Figure 3.4.

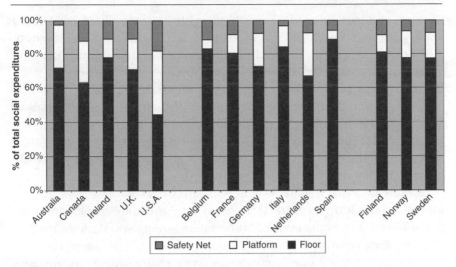

Figure 3.4: Universality of social welfare transfers in 14 rich nations (2001)

Sources: For data sources, see note 2 of this chapter.

Note: Most of Australia's expenditures are income-tested. However, a number of its expenditures are categorized as universal because of their broad eligibility, which qualify up to 85% of the state's population.

No other country transfers as large a share of GDP using either safety nets or platforms.[10] The US safety-net transfers amount to 5.7 percent of GDP, as compared with 4 percent in Belgium and only 3 percent in the Scandinavian countries. US platform transfers amount to 12 percent of GDP, as compared with a bit under 9 percent and 8 percent, respectively, in the Netherlands and Germany, and around 7 percent in Australia and Canada. These discrepancies arise because American social expenditures on health are so large and for the non-aged population consist of income-tested and employer-based benefits.

SO WHAT: DO FLOORS, SAFETY NETS AND PLATFORMS DIFFER?

Our three categories—floors, safety nets, and platforms—oversimplify, but some categorization is far superior to no categorization. Old-age insurance in the United States and other nations combines a floor with a platform. Coverage is (near) universal. Benefits create a floor under the income of all the aged, while providing greater benefits (platforms) to those who have earned more in the market. Free public education might also be thought of as platforms combined with floors or, better yet, as an uneven or tilted

53

floor: all children are entitled to attend public schools, but in the United States and, we suspect, other nations as well, the quality of their school depends on where they live and ultimately on their family income. We categorize these programs as floors, because we believe that their universality of provision is more important than the degree to which they contain platforms or are uneven. But uneven floor or combination floor-and-platform universal public education is clearly not a safety net. Nor is Social Security a safety net. The United States, does, however, have a safety net for the elderly and disabled poor. Called Supplementary Security Income, it provides benefits only to the poor.

Labeling all social welfare programs as safety nets as many have done— including both former President Bush, on the right, and Paul Krugman, on the left—obfuscates the essential differences among social programs and devalues floors and platforms.[11]

Safety nets relieve abject poverty, prevent malnourishment, increase fairness, quell discontent, and thereby also increase productivity. This is no small achievement. But safety nets increase productivity minimally because they invest in only the poorest citizens. Because they aid only the poor, safety nets do nothing to prevent poverty.

As the circus imagery implies, safety nets are also for the fallen, the economic losers. As a consequence, safety nets stigmatize their beneficiaries. Non-beneficiaries dislike beneficiaries, who also dislike themselves (Rainwater, 1982). Safety nets are also uncomfortable and, for those who are weak economically, difficult to escape. Heavy reliance on safety-net programs produces what British economists have referred to as poverty traps (Atkinson, 1999). If you cannot earn much, it is hard to escape the safety net and to improve your condition because safety-net programs take away benefits as income increases. Reducing benefits as income increases is equivalent to taxing earnings. The tax rates on working that confront the welfare poor are much higher than the tax rates confronted by everyone else in society.[12]

Heavy reliance on safety nets also creates greater incentives for the poor to work at intermittent, informal, and even illegal jobs where the earnings go unreported. Similarly, in the United States safety-net programs for single mothers—TANF and, before it, AFDC—create incentives for couples to avoid marriage and live together informally so that the earnings of fathers will not be reported. These adverse incentives may be thought of as an immorality trap, which further stigmatizes the poor.

Safety-net programs, by their nature, also create special bureaucracies that serve the poor alone and thereby isolate and segregate them.

Safety-net programs also undermine social cohesion by creating a sharp distinction between the poor, who are eligible for the safety net, and the lower-middle class, who are not. Finally, safety-net programs also breed mutual distrust between beneficiaries and program administrators. Because these programs must "test each case individually, they are to a greater extent subject to suspicions of cheating, arbitrariness, and discrimination compared with universal public agencies" (Kumlin and Rothstein, 2005). For all these reasons, safety-net programs are viewed negatively by both their beneficiaries and the populace as a whole.[13]

In contrast, floors, like universal elementary and secondary public education, Social Security, Medicare, and, in all other rich countries, National Health Insurance, provide benefits to all citizens. As a consequence, floors prevent poverty, reduce dependence on safety nets, integrate the poor into mainstream society, and increase the productivity and economic security of all citizens. Existing floors in rich nations are universally popular.

Platforms are like floors in that they provide a solid foundation on which to build. But they differ from floors because they cover only portions of the population. Like floors, platforms also reduce poverty and dependence on safety nets. But, unlike floors, platforms do not integrate the poor into mainstream society. Nor do they eliminate poverty and immorality traps. Equally important, benefits in platforms generally increase with income—they are worth nearly nothing to the poor and near-poor and are worth a great deal more to the most well-off members of society. In the United States, the biggest tax expenditures, in order of dollars expended, are for health insurance, pensions, housing, and the EITC. Only the last benefits those in the lower-income brackets. (Subsidies to higher education, which we are not counting in our analysis, like most tax expenditures, disproportionately go to upper-middle and upper-income families.)

Health insurance (HI), whether publicly financed or provided by employers, redistributes on the benefit side from the well to the sick. But, unlike publicly financed HI, employer-provided HI does not redistribute on the financing side. Economists agree that fringe benefits such as HI are paid for in the form of reduced earnings by employees. If HI costs $5,000 per person, under employer-provided HI, each employee pays $5,000. If HI were publicly financed by a proportional tax, the richest fifth of the population which earns about 60 percent of total income would pay for 60 percent of the cost or about $15,000 per person, while the poorest fifth which earns only about 5 percent of total income would pay only about $1,500 per person.

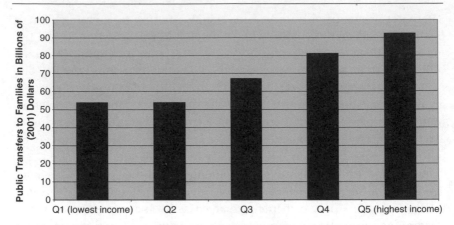

Figure 3.5: Distribution of healthcare transfers to families with children, by income quintile (2001)

Source: Based on authors' calculations.

Floors also distribute benefits more fairly than safety nets, or, to be more precise, than the combination of floors and safety nets. Figure 3.5 shows the distribution of Medicaid and CHIP plus employer-provided health insurance benefits by income class for US families with children. We follow common practice by economists and other social scientists and divide the families with children, from poorest to richest, into five equal-sized groups, or quintiles. To simplify, we will refer to those in the bottom fifth as the poor and near-poor, those in the next fifth up as the lower-middle class, those in the middle fifth as the middle class, those in the fifth next to the top as the upper-middle class, and those in the top fifth as the rich. The picture of the distribution of benefits (taxes are considered later) by income class is not pretty. Despite the fact that their children are healthier, the benefits to the wealthiest fifth of American families with children are almost twice as large as the benefits to the poorest fifth. In view of the fact that the poor are less healthy and more in need of health care than the rich, from an equity point of view, the figure is upside down. The most should be spent at the bottom and the least at the top.

US housing benefits, shown in Figure 3.6, are distributed even more perversely—in a very pronounced U-shape. The richest and poorest quintiles get the greatest benefits, though as in the case of health insurance the richest receive the largest share—$77 billion as against $21 billion for the poorest. The upper-middle-income group gets the next most, $19 billion. The lower-middle-income class is at the very bottom, with $8 billion; the

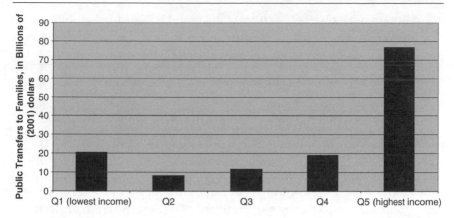

Figure 3.6: Distribution of housing transfers to families with children, by income quintile (2001)

Source: Based on authors' calculations. See note 14 of this chapter for a description.

middle class, very near the bottom, with $12 billion.[14] The drop-off from the richest to all the other groups is dramatic. It is hard to think of a normative justification for this distribution of benefits.

Sometimes, safety nets vis-à-vis floors are justified on the basis of being cheaper. This is an example of a half-truth and nonsense. It is true that safety nets entail lower taxes. But for most of the population the benefits received from floors exceed the taxes they pay to finance the program. In fact, safety nets are cheaper only to the top income group. The arithmetic is easy to grasp. In safety-net programs, only the poor get benefits and everyone else helps pay for the benefits. The top-income group loses the most from universal programs because they gain only the benefit of the floor, while having to pay the largest share not only for the poor but also for everyone else, including themselves. The near-poor and lower-middle class gain the most from a universal floor because they get the full benefit of the floor but have the least ability to pay taxes to finance the benefit.[15] In view of the large inequality in the US today, not only the near-poor and lower-middle class, but also the middle class and even the upper-middle class would all derive greater net benefits from floors than safety nets.

So, why, if floors are superior to safety nets, do all rich nations have both floors and safety nets? Part of the answer has already been given: complete socialization—floors so high that to finance them would require tax rates of 100 percent—is economically inefficient and would smother productivity and economic growth. Even near-complete socialization will have strong adverse effects. Thus, the height of the floor is limited by the need to maintain a balance between capitalism and socialism. Another part of the answer has to do with the nature of a floor and the nature of poverty. Because floors are common to all, they are taken for granted by the population. Everyone is expected to do better than the floor, and when inevitably some individuals fail to do so, citizens of democratic rich nations believe their standard of living is too low by contemporary standards in rich nations, label them as poor, and aid them using safety nets.

But the foregoing cannot explain why the US, alone among rich nations, relies so heavily on safety nets and platforms in the provision of health insurance. The combination of safety nets and platforms results in substantial socialization of medical care costs for 85 percent of citizens, but compared to countries with universal coverage there is little to no efficiency gain to our model. Indeed, as we have seen in this chapter, we spend a great deal more on health insurance than other rich nations. In the next chapter, we show that health outcomes are lower in the US. In Chapters 5, 6, and especially 7, we offer an explanation for this aspect of American exceptionalism.

In short, the US welfare state differs from those in other rich countries not so much in its size as in its extraordinarily high spending on health insurance and its disproportionate reliance on safety nets and platforms rather than floors.

Notes

1. Clean water and sewerage services, however, are not counted as part of welfare state services.
2. We use several data sources to construct our measures of welfare state program transfers. The aggregate public expenditure data is derived from the *OECD 1980–2001: 20 Years of Social Expenditure—the OECD Database* (2004d), with the exception of education data, which is derived from *OECD Education at a Glance* (2002c), and early childhood education (ECE), which is taken from Gornick and Meyers (2003). The *Social Expenditure Database* includes the following categories of benefits: old-age cash benefits; disability cash benefits; occupational injury and disease; sickness benefits; services for the elderly and disabled; survivors; family cash benefits; family services; active labor market policies; unemployment compensation; housing benefits; public health expenditure; and other contingencies (e.g., cash benefits to those with low income). Such benefits may be cash transfers or direct in-kind provision of goods and services. While data on public benefits encompasses expenditures paid and controlled by all levels of government (federal, state, and local), the quality of the data varies

across countries, particularly with respect to expenditures by lower tiers of government (OECD, 2002c). The OECD housing data includes only cash expenditures tied to housing; in-kind and tax expenditures for housing are omitted. Finally, aggregate employer-provided benefits are derived from Adema and Ladaique's OECD report (2005). The OECD data on ECE is unreliable. In the US, for example, expenditures on Head Start, a national program for poor children between the ages of three to five, are easy to count, but state and local expenditures on pre-school education and childcare are more recent and not counted systematically in government publications. In the other rich countries, ECEC is reported sometimes as part of education expenditures, sometimes as part of other social welfare expenditures, and sometimes as both.

3. With respect to income, we are referring to what in the next chapter we label as full income, which includes in-kind transfers such as education and health care valued at government cost. With respect to taxes, although employer-provided benefits are paid for by employers, economists agree that ultimately it is workers who pay for these benefits in the form of lower wages. Thus, these benefits are financed by reductions in wages that are akin to a tax.

4. The percent of GDP spent on social welfare transfers is also a very good and simple measure of the extent to which welfare states de-commodify. A ratio of 30 percent, for example, indicates that, in the overall economy, 30 percent of the income of the country's populace comes from transfers rather than earnings and other market sources of income. Though Esping-Anderson goes to great lengths to construct an alternative measure of de-commodification, his criticisms of the percent GDP measure are either corrected by our comprehensive measure or are conceptually incorrect. An example of the latter is critiquing the conventional measure because it includes pensions to civil servants—a favorably treated non-poor group. This criticism is conceptually correct—though empirically minor—if one is using percent of GDP devoted to social welfare transfers to measure the equality-producing effects of the welfare state. (In general, the percent of GDP devoted to social welfare transfers is a good crude indicator of the equalizing effect of the welfare state.) But the distribution of de-commodification is a separate issue from its average presence in the economy—which is why Esping-Anderson treats equalization and de-commodification as distinct outcomes.

5. Lampman (1984) makes this argument. See also Hacker (2002) for a political science perspective on the issue of employer-provided health benefits. Only the United States heavily subsidizes private health insurance via employers (see Adema and Ladaique, 2005).

6. The other studies referred to in the text omit Ireland and do not count education. Note that if Ireland were omitted, the US would be the lowest spender and that if education were also omitted US expenditures would fall below 20 percent and the difference between the US and other countries would be even greater.

7. We use per capita here, not per recipient. We believe that the latter, though much harder to measure, would show the same pattern.

8. Schematic descriptions of the cash and health insurance programs of more than 170 countries are available in *Social Security Programs Throughout the World* (2005).

9. In Germany, employer-provided benefits and tax expenditures are quite large, amounting to 4.2 percent of GDP, or about half of total cash benefits other than pensions. Tax expenditures, mostly for child tax credit, account for 1.2 percent of GDP. The rest is accounted for by mandatory employer-provided social expenditures, including paid sick leave and maternity and parental leave and continued payment of wages.

10. Australia is an ambiguous case. A large proportion of Australia's social welfare system is income tested, but the income test is designed to eliminate benefits for the rich rather than limit benefits to the poor. Given that Australian programs cover the vast majority of the population we categorized them as universal.

11. Following his proposal to privatize social security accounts in his 2005 State of the Union address, President Bush referred to social security programs as "safety nets" in several speeches. Examples include speeches in Pensacola, FL (3/18/05), Tucson, AZ (3/21/05), and Albuquerque, NM (3/22/05). *New York Times* columnist and economist Paul Krugman has referred to social security programs as "safety nets" in numerous editorials, including "Always Low Wages. Always" (5/13/05), "Americans Want Security" (5/23/05), and "Played for a Sucker" (11/16/07).

12. The tax rates (benefit reduction rates) that safety-net programs impose on the poor are higher than the tax rates imposed on the non-poor to finance the programs (Garfinkel, 1982). Whereas the rich lose part of what they earn through taxes, the poor lose an even bigger part of what they earn through benefit reductions. Eugene Steurle and Adam Carasso (2005) estimate that in the United States today, the marginal tax rates on earnings of the poor range from 36 to 89 percent.

13. Rainwater (1982) discusses how beneficiaries of income-tested programs internalize their stigmatized position. One of the most interesting and consistent findings in US public opinion data is the strong support for increased funding to help the poor and the equally strong opposition to increased funding for welfare programs. Shaw and Shapiro (2002) report that 62 percent of Americans believe we are spending too little to help the poor and another 24 percent think we are spending about the right amount. But only 17 percent believe federal spending on welfare should increase, while 38 percent favored decreases in welfare spending.

14. The estimate is an update of Garfinkel (1996), and is based on 2000 Green Book projections of HUD outlays for housing assistance (Table 15.32, year 2000, inflated to 2001$) and homeownership tax exemptions (Table 13.2, year

2001). Of total outlays for housing assistance, an estimated 47 percent go to families with children (Burke, 1998). This figure is likely an underestimate because, while 47 percent of housing-aid recipients are households with children, these families likely have larger apartments than households without children, and thus receive a disproportionate amount of aid. Garfinkel (1996) estimates that 80 percent of housing aid goes to the lowest quintile, while 20 percent is allocated to the near-poor.

Of outlays for homeowners' tax benefits, an estimated 33 percent go to families with children (Census, 2000, stating that 33 percent of households include their "own children"). To allocate this amount, approximately $111B, we follow the benefit distribution of Follain and Ling (1991), and project that in the 1991 distribution, the lowest quintile had incomes up to $15,000, the second quintile had incomes between $15,001 and $30,000, the third had incomes between $30,001 and $45,000, the fourth had incomes between $45,001 and $60,000, and the top quintile had incomes over $60,000. Following Follain and Ling, we project the lowest quintile to receive almost nothing in tax benefits (0.2 percent of the total benefit), the second quintile to receive 2.3 percent of the total benefit, the third quintile to receive 8.5 percent, the fourth to 13.8 percent, and the top quintile to receive the vast majority of benefits, 55.9 percent.

Combining the housing-aid benefits, which accrue to the lowest two quintiles, with the homeowners' tax benefits, which accrue primarily to the top quintiles, yields an overall U-shaped distribution.

15. For a discussion of the income distribution effects of floors versus safety nets, see, Tullock (1982); Downs (1982); and Orr (1982). All agree that the top-income group loses the most and the near-poor gain the most from floors as compared to safety nets. Tullock argues that the poor also lose from safety nets, but Downs questions this conclusion and shows that it depends upon the nature of the safety net and the taxes used to fund the alternatives.

4

How Welfare State Programs Redistribute Income, Reduce Poverty and Inequality, Build and Sustain Human Capital, and Promote Opportunity

All rich nations redistribute large shares of national income through welfare state programs. Who gains and who loses from this vast redistribution of resources—and by how much? What are the effects on poverty and inequality and on education and health? In this chapter we address these questions, focusing again on how the rich nations resemble each other and how they differ.

We begin with the strategy that led Robert Woodward and Carl Bernstein (1974) to unravel the Watergate scandal by "following the money" in one nation, the United States. We show how welfare state benefits and taxes are distributed by income class and over the life cycle—from childhood through retirement. We walk the reader through the nuts and bolts of the process of redistribution in one country because, even amongst sophisticated researchers, there is some confusion about the redistributive effects of social welfare transfers. For example, some have claimed that welfare state benefits only appear to reduce poverty and inequality because they transfer resources to the old and young who have low incomes during that life stage, but higher incomes in between childhood and old age. Similarly, others claim that because most welfare state benefits go to everyone in society they are "middle-class entitlements" which do not reduce inequality.[1] Both of these assertions, as we shall see, are false. Though much of the redistribution accomplished by the American welfare state is across the life cycle to the young and the old, the American welfare state also substantially reduces economic inequality and substantially increases the incomes of the poorest fifth of the population at very modest costs to the richest fifth. Benefits provided on a universal basis to everyone in society reduce poverty and inequality.

In the second, third, fourth, and fifth sections, we examine how rich nations differ in the net redistribution of resources across income class and over the life cycle, the degree to which cash transfers reduce poverty and inequality, and how the picture changes by taking account of in-kind benefits and indirect taxes. When differences in "relative poverty" and inequality across nations are measured by cash incomes and transfers, the rich nations do break roughly into three distinct worlds. Within the low-spending, high-poverty and inequality-liberal, English-speaking world, the United States spends the least on cash transfers and has the highest "relative" poverty rates and greatest inequality. This provides evidence for the argument that the US welfare state is a world apart. But either measuring poverty in real purchasing power terms, rather than relative to the country's average standard of living, or counting in-kind benefits and indirect taxes substantially shrinks these cross-national differences in poverty, lifts the US from the very bottom, and further blurs, but does not make unrecognizable, the picture of three distinct worlds.

The sixth and final section examines national differences in education, health, and equality of opportunity. In health and opportunity, there are hints of the three worlds and clear evidence that the United States is near or at the bottom of the rich nations. The evidence in education is more mixed.

I. Welfare state redistribution, by life cycle and income group, in the United States

Table 4.1 describes in some detail how the US welfare state redistributes resources by income class. The figures on redistributive effects presented below are only first approximations of the net redistributive effects of the welfare state because they reflect changes in work, savings, marriage, and private family transfers that are induced by welfare state benefits and taxes. In the absence of welfare state transfers, market incomes of the poorest groups would be somewhat higher and thus the amount of redistribution is overestimated. They are very useful first approximations, however, because taking account of these changes in behaviors does not alter any of the broad conclusions discussed in the text.[2]

The data come from the Current Population Survey (CPS), conducted by the US Census Bureau, and are used by the government and academics for

Table 4.1: Redistribution of welfare state benefits in the US by households (2000)

A. All Households		QUINTILES				AVERAGE
	Poor	Lower middle	Middle	Upper middle	Upper	
Market Income (Mean)	8900	28200	48800	73400	145300	60900
Cash Transfers (Mean)	10800	6400	3500	2400	2300	5100
In-Kind Transfers (Mean)	13600	14600	13300	12000	10000	12700
Welfare State Benefits (Mean)	24400	21000	16800	14400	12400	17800
Taxes (Mean)	6200	9400	14100	20300	38900	17800
Net Benefits (Mean)	18200	11600	2700	−5900	−26500	0
Full Income (Mean)	27100	39800	51500	67500	118800	60900
Net Benefits as % of	67%	29%	5%	−9%	−22%	0

B. Households with Children		QUINTILES				AVERAGE
	Poor	Lower middle	Middle	Upper middle	Upper	
Market Income (Mean)	17000	39000	58900	84100	169600	73700
Cash Transfers (Mean)	7620	3570	2297	1880	1492	3400
In-Kind Transfers (Mean)	23800	21500	20700	20200	19600	21200
Welfare State Benefits (Mean)	31500	25100	# 23000	22100	21100	24600
Taxes (Mean)	7800	11700	16200	22600	44100	20500
Net Benefits (Mean)	23700	13400	6800	−500	−23000	4100
Full Income (Mean)	40700	52400	65700	83600	146600	77800
Net Benefits as % of	58%	26%	10%	−1%	−16%	5%

C. Elder Households		QUINTILES				AVERAGE
	Poor	Lower middle	Middle	Upper middle	Upper	
Market Income (Mean)	5200	7300	14600	27600	83700	27700
Cash Transfers (Mean)	12600	12400	13800	13200	13600	13100
In-Kind Transfers (Mean)	11900	10900	12000	12000	12200	11800
Welfare State Benefits (Mean)	24500	23300	25800	25400	25700	24900
Taxes (Mean)	5700	5800	6400	8300	21500	9500
Net Benefits (Mean)	18800	17500	19400	17100	4200	15400
Full Income (Mean)	24000	24800	34000	44700	87900	43100
Net Benefits as % of	78%	71%	57%	38%	5%	36%

Source: Based on authors' calculations. See Appendix for further information.

reporting income and poverty rates. Panel A describes the effects for the whole population (panels B and C are described below). As in the previous chapter, income is measured at the household level and the population is divided into five equal-sized groups, or income classes.[3] Thus, the table has six columns, one for each income class and one for the population as a whole.

The first row in the table gives the average income before welfare state transfers and taxes, or what economists refer to as "market income" (earnings, interest, dividends, and rents) for each of the five income classes.[4] The average income for the country as a whole in 2000 was nearly $61,000.

Market incomes are distributed very unequally. For the poorest fifth of the population, mean market income was only $8,900; for the richest fifth, it was more than $145,000, or about sixteen times higher.[5]

The second row of the table gives the mean value of cash and near *cash transfers* received by each income group. These data also come directly from the CPS. Employer-provided pensions are not included because, as discussed above, part of such pensions are akin to a private savings account and therefore involve no transfer. Otherwise, the cash transfers are the same as those described in Chapter 3. Average cash and near-cash benefits in 2000 were $5,100, with the poorest fifth of the population receiving $10,800, the richest fifth receiving $2,300.

In-kind transfers are reported in the third row. The in-kind transfers consist primarily of health and education. Because of the difficulties of assigning higher-education transfers to particular families, they are not included in the distributional analyses in this chapter. The in-kind transfers average $12,700 per household (the data and methods for estimating the distribution of in-kind transfers are described in detail in the Appendix). Note that in-kind transfers are distributed more equally than cash transfers: the poorest fifth receive $13,600; the richest fifth, $10,000.

The fourth row of the table gives the mean value of all (cash plus in-kind) *welfare state transfers*. The last column indicates that the average value of transfers in 2000 was $17,800. Note that, as a whole, social welfare transfers are distributed very progressively, with the poorest fifth getting an average of $24,400 and the richest fifth getting only about half that. As explained below, most of this progressivity is due to the concentration of the aged at the bottom of the income distribution.

The fifth row gives the mean value of *taxes* required to finance all the transfers. Although governments can and do run deficits, in the long run, transfers cannot be financed by deficits, but must be paid for. In practice, in the rich welfare states, deficits play little to no role in financing welfare state benefits.[6] Thus, taxes must equal welfare state transfers (We describe in the appendix how we estimate the distribution of taxes). The upper-income groups pay much more in taxes than the lower-income groups. The rich pay much more in taxes, not because the tax system is progressive (taxes increase more than in proportion to income) but because their incomes are so much higher. Indeed, though not shown in the table, taxes are roughly proportional to gross cash income (market income plus cash transfers). Taxes (row 5) divided by gross cash income (row 1 plus row 2) equal about 26 or 27 percent of income for all income groups, except for the lowest, where taxes equal about 33 percent.

The sixth row subtracts taxes paid from benefits received to calculate each income group's *net benefit*. For the country as a whole, because taxes must equal benefits, net benefits are zero. But the net benefits vary widely by income group, from minus $26,500 for the highest to plus $18,200 for the poorest.

The seventh row presents estimates of *full income*, which equals market income plus all welfare state benefits valued at government cost minus taxes. Full income varies much less widely, by income group, than market income. Although the average market income of the top fifth of the population is 16 times that of the bottom fifth (approximately $145,000 divided by $9,000), the full income of the top fifth is only 4.4 times that of the bottom fifth ($118,800 divided by $27,100.) The American welfare state, therefore, appears to substantially reduce inequality.

In the eighth and bottom row of the table, we show how important welfare state redistribution is to each income class by dividing the mean net benefit by the mean full income of each. This measure of *net benefits as a percent of full income* is a useful summary measure of the redistributive effect of welfare state programs. Because the gap between the rich and poor in the United States is so large, the redistribution adds substantially to the total resources of the poor and lower-middle class at a relatively small cost in percentage terms to the upper-middle and upper income groups. The poorest fifth gets nearly 70 percent of their full income from their net benefits from welfare state transfers minus taxes. The lower-middle-income group gets 29 percent. The middle-income group also derives net benefits from the welfare state, but they are small—only 5 percent of full income. The upper-middle income group loses 9 percent of full income, and the top group loses 22 percent, because the taxes they pay for welfare state benefits exceed the benefits they receive.[7]

Panels B and C of Table 4.1 show how resources are redistributed across income class within the population of households with children age 18 or less and within the population of households with at least one person over age 65.[8] There are two reasons for looking separately at these two sub-groups of the population. First, they get the bulk of all welfare state benefits. Second, by analyzing the two groups separately, we can roughly distinguish between redistribution by income class and redistribution across the life cycle.[9] Childrearing families represent the first stage and the elderly the last stage of the life cycle.

The last column and last row in panels B and C indicate that the American welfare state redistributes across the life cycle to both families with children and the elderly, both of whom derive net benefits from the American welfare state. (Not shown in the tables are the negative net transfers from households who neither have children nor are aged. Since most individuals have children at some point in their lifetime, most members of this population are in one of two very different stages of their life cycle—either before they have children or after their children have left home, but below age 65.) Note that the redistribution to families with children is quite small. Only 5 percent of their full income is attributable to net welfare state transfers, as against 36 percent of the full income of the elderly. But the average gross benefit for the two groups is nearly identical—approximately $24,000. The differences arise because the market incomes, and therefore the taxes, of the elderly are much smaller than those of families with children.

The distribution of gross benefits across income class for both families with children and the elderly differ considerably from the pattern for the overall population. Indeed, benefits for the elderly are actually slightly higher at the top than the bottom of the income distribution. For families with children, the poor get the most—$31,500. Benefits decline going up the income scale, but much less than they do for the population as a whole.[10] Because the pattern for the population as a whole mixes life cycle with across-class redistribution, it overstates the progressivity of the distribution of welfare state benefits across income class.

Contrary to the claims of some that the welfare state only redistributes across the life cycle and has no effect on economic inequality over the life cycle, there is still substantial redistribution by income class. The pattern across income class of the bottom line (net benefits as a share of full income) for households with children is remarkably similar to the pattern for the whole population. In families with children, the poor get somewhat less of their incomes from welfare state transfers and the rich lose a bit less because gross benefits are less pro-poor and more equally distributed than for the population as a whole. Most important, the ratio of incomes in the top as compared to the bottom fifth drops from 10.0 for market income to only 3.6 for full income. For the aged, reductions in inequality achieved by welfare state transfers are even greater despite the fact that the benefits are slightly pro-rich. The market incomes of the richest elderly are 16 times the market incomes of the poorest elderly, while the ratio of full incomes is only 3.6.

How can benefits that are equally distributed across income class, let alone those that are pro-rich, reduce inequality? Don't benefits have to be greater for the poor to reduce poverty and inequality? The answer is no because equal benefits, or, as we have seen, even slightly pro-rich benefits, are far more equal than the very unequal market distribution of income. There are two sources of income—the market and social welfare transfers. The market distributes income very unequally and the social welfare transfer system distributes benefits equally. If two thirds of income come from the market and one-third from transfers, two thirds of income will be very unequal and one third will be equal. If the share of income coming from transfers increases, equality will increase.

II. Welfare state redistribution by life cycle and income class in rich nations

In this section we compare redistribution in the American welfare state with that in nine other rich nations. We focus on the bottom line identified in the previous section—net benefits as a share of full income—and examine similarities and differences in rich nations' patterns of redistribution by age and income class. We use data from the Luxembourg Income Study (LIS), the most widely used data set for cross-national studies of rich nations. The LIS takes independent national surveys like the CPS in the United States and makes them comparable by defining variables like income similarly. The data and methods are described in detail in the Appendix. Though four of the 14 nations that we examined in the previous chapter are omitted because of data limitations, the 10 nations examined still represent each of the three worlds of welfare capitalism.[11]

Redistribution across the life cycle

Table 4.2 presents the data showing redistribution across the life cycle. The table displays in four columns the mean net benefits as a share of full income for three groups in each nation—the elderly, childrearing families, and the non-elderly childless—and for the country as a whole. Each row describes a country. The last column for each country is zero because for the entire population, taxes levied must equal total benefits.

Table 4.2: Net benefits as a percent of full income across the life cycle[1]

Country	Year	Elder Households	Households with Children	Childless Households	Full Population
Australia	1994	62%	0%	−22%	0
Canada	1997	50%	1%	−18%	0
United Kingdom	1999	54%	6%	−24%	0
United States	2000	36%	5%	−19%	0
Belgium	1997	71%	−11%	−22%	0
France	1994	80%	−9%	−30%	0
Germany	2000	72%	−7%	−38%	0
Netherlands	1999	53%	2%	−21%	0
Finland	2000	29%	5%	−14%	0
Sweden	2000	76%	−8%	−36%	0
Average[2]		58%	−2%	−25%	0%

Source: Authors' calculations from the Luxembourg Income Study.
Notes: [1]This table uses the difference between taxes paid and total benefits received as a percent of "final" or "full" income.
[2]Simple average, not weighted by population size.

The first column in Table 4.2 indicates that all countries provide net social welfare transfers to the aged. On average, as the bottom row indicates, transfers provide 58 percent of the total after-tax full income of the aged. Across nations, if we ignore Finland and the Netherlands, we observe a part of the familiar three-world pattern: the English-speaking nations provide the lowest net transfers to the aged and the US is the lowest of the low. But Sweden is not distinctly different from the remaining continental European nations.

The second column of the table indicates that in other rich nations, as in the United States, families with children receive in benefits about what they pay in taxes. Though families with children benefit disproportionately from welfare state benefits, unlike the elderly, they pay a lot in taxes. Thus, it is not surprising that the net benefits to families with children are close to zero.

The third column shows that the childless are net taxpayers in all 10 countries, averaging 25 percent in net taxes. Because the overwhelming majority of people in all the countries have children at some point in their life, the transfers away from the childless to the elderly should be viewed as reflecting primarily redistribution across the life cycle.[12]

Redistribution across income classes

Tables 4.3(A) and 4.3(B) show redistribution by income class among families with children and among the aged. As for the United States, we divide

Table 4.3: Net benefits as a percent of full income by quintiles[1]

A. Households with Children

Country	Year	LOW	2	3	4	HIGH
Australia	1994	89%	30%	3%	−13%	−38%
Canada	1997	68%	24%	4%	−8%	−24%
United Kingdom	1999	99%	47%	5%	−11%	−29%
United States	2000	58%	25%	10%	−1%	−16%
Belgium	1997	70%	9%	−10%	−24%	−44%
France	1994	40%	5%	−8%	−16%	−36%
Germany	2000	67%	14%	−7%	−21%	−42%
Netherlands	1999	57%	14%	1%	−8%	−20%
Finland	2000	65%	23%	7%	−9%	−22%
Sweden	2000	66%	15%	−9%	−24%	−42%
Average[2]		68%	21%	0%	−14%	−31%

B. Elder Households

Country	Year	LOW	2	3	4	HIGH
Australia	1994	100%	99%	95%	66%	4%
Canada	1997	100%	92%	70%	46%	11%
United Kingdom	1999	100%	97%	82%	53%	9%
United States	2000	78%	71%	57%	38%	5%
Belgium	1997	100%	98%	93%	87%	30%
France	1994	100%	99%	98%	93%	41%
Germany	2000	97%	95%	93%	79%	25%
Netherlands	1999	97%	86%	70%	48%	14%
Finland	2000	83%	57%	37%	20%	−2%
Sweden	2000	100%	95%	90%	82%	39%
Average[2]		95%	89%	78%	61%	18%

Source: Authors' calcuations from the Luxembourg Income Study.
Notes: (1) This table uses the difference between taxes paid and total benefits received as a percent of "final" or
"full" income.
(2) Simple average, not weighted by population size.

these two groups in each country into five equal-sized income groups. The five columns of the tables present the mean net transfer as a share of full income for each of the five groups.

Three striking similarities across countries stand out in Table 4.3(A). First, in every country, welfare state benefits, net of taxes, substantially and systematically redistribute resources away from the top toward the bottom of the income distribution. Poor families and those in the lower-middle class gain the most in all countries. Those in the middle class neither gain nor lose much—10 percent either way. Families in the upper-middle class pay net taxes that average 14 percent of full incomes. Only the richest fifth of families with children in each nation pay substantially more in taxes than they receive in benefits (31 percent).

Second, the increase in resources available to the poorest quintile of families in every nation is very large. On average, net transfers make up 68 percent of full income, indicating that welfare states more than double the market incomes of the poor. The increases are so large because the poorest quintile in all these countries consists primarily of single-mother families and families in which fathers are disabled or unemployed. These families have no or very low market earnings and high social welfare benefits.

Third, in all countries the taxes required to finance welfare state benefits take away a non-trivial share of resources from families in the top quintile—on average 31 percent of full income.

Two differences across countries are also quite interesting. First, countries differ substantially in the degree to which the poorest fifth get resources from welfare state transfers or the market, but the differences are not consistent with the three worlds of welfare capitalism. The United States is below average, with 58 percent of total resources coming from net transfers, but so are the two Scandinavian nations, at 65 percent and 66 percent. At 40 percent, France has the smallest share of all countries. Two English-speaking countries, the United Kingdom and Australia, provide the greatest share of resources to the poorest groups. Finland, France, Sweden, and the United States are below average because they encourage poor single mothers to work.

Second, countries differ substantially in the degree to which the welfare state reduces the incomes of those at the top of the income distribution. Here the pattern conforms a little more closely to the three worlds, but exceptions abound. In general, the English-speaking nations take the least from the richest fifth, with the US taking least of all.[13] But Australia is closer to the continental European nations and Sweden than to the other English-speaking nations, while Finland and Holland are closer to the US.

Table 4.3 presents data on net benefits as a share of full income by income class for the elderly. Five commonalities, accompanied by exceptions for the US, stand out. While the latter seems to provide evidence for the US being a world apart, Finland is as exceptional as the US and both stand apart for the same reason: not counting employer-provided pensions. First, except for the top income class in Finland, the net transfers to all aged income groups in every country are positive. Second, in all countries, except for the United States and Finland, nearly all of the full income—between 97 percent and 100 percent—of the poorest fifth of the elderly population comes from social welfare transfers. The US and Finland, at 78 percent and 83 percent, would be much closer to 100 percent if employer-provided transfers were counted as transfers. Third, on average, the elderly in the lower-middle class and middle class get more than three-fourths of their full incomes from net welfare state transfers. Fourth, outside of the United States and Finland, even the upper-middle class gets from near half to more than three-quarters of their full income from transfers. If employer-provided pensions were counted, both the US and Finland would be above 50 percent. Fifth, in all countries, less than half of the incomes of the top fifth of the elderly come from transfers. The differences among rich nations are greatest in the top fifth of the income distribution. The proportions of income from transfers in France and Sweden at 41 and 39 are four to eight times higher than the proportions in the English-speaking nations' 4–11 percent.

III. Cash transfers, relative and absolute poverty, and social exclusion

A large body of research finds that rich nations differ in both poverty rates and the generosity of cash transfers.[14] Though there are many exceptions, which we shall note, in general, the "social democratic" Scandinavian countries are big spenders and reduce poverty the most; the "liberal" English-speaking countries spend the least and reduce poverty the least; and the "corporatist" continental European countries fall in between. Among the English-speaking countries, the United States stands out as being the least generous and having the greatest income inequality. These cross-national differences are consistent with Esping-Andersen's view of the three worlds of welfare capitalism. Whether the differences are large or small, however, depends upon the way poverty is measured.

Figure 4.1 displays this research visually. The figures present two measures of poverty for each of our 10 countries. The first set of black bars depicts the most commonly used measure in cross-national research, relative poverty rates. The second set of white bars depicts absolute poverty rates. The absolute poverty rate used is the US poverty line. Incomes in other countries are converted to US dollars.[15] (Data on absolute poverty rates for Australia and France were not calculated because the surveys that provided the data for these countries are much older than surveys for the other countries.) Clearly, the pictures conveyed by the two measures are strikingly different. Thus we need to know the difference between these two measures of poverty.

The relative measure of poverty is the proportion of households in each country with incomes below one half of the income of the household in each country at the exact center of the income distribution. This household is referred to as the median-income household because one half of

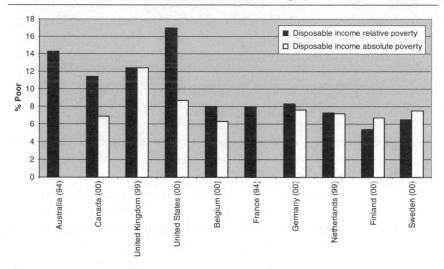

Figure 4.1: Effects of cash transfers on relative and absolute poverty rates in 10 rich nations: all households
Source: Smeeding, T. (2006b).

the population has more income and one half of the population has less income. Households who have less than half the income of the median-income households are "relatively" poor in that their incomes are below a standard set by the average income in the country. By way of contrast, the absolute measure of poverty is the proportion of households in each country with incomes below an amount needed to purchase a minimum standard of living. The minimum standard is related to the costs of buying food, clothing, shelter, and other necessities.

Relative poverty rates are a measure of inequality at the bottom of the income distribution. The larger the gap between the income of the poorest citizens and that of the median, the larger will be the share of the population with less than half of median income. Relative poverty rates can increase, as they did in Ireland and China in the last two decades of the twentieth century, even when the incomes of the poor are increasing and absolute poverty rates are declining. All that is required is that median income grows faster than low incomes. Rapid economic growth in the early stages of industrialization of currently rich nations was accompanied by increasing inequality. When both incomes of the poor are rising and absolute poverty rates are declining rapidly, even if relative poverty rates are going up, most people would agree that poverty is declining.

One might ask, therefore, why most academic students of the welfare state, including all three of this book's authors, have utilized the relative measure of poverty. A relative poverty rate is useful because although the standard of living of the poor in any rich country today is dramatically higher than that of the overwhelming majority of people in the rest of the world today and of the overwhelming majority of people of their own country 100 years ago, the poor in any rich country today do not live in the rest of the world or in their own country of 100 years ago. Within their own world, they are poor because their incomes are so much below average that they cannot participate in and take advantage of mainstream opportunities. They think of themselves as poor and so do their fellow citizens. This was true in Great Britain in 1776 when Adam Smith wrote the *Wealth of Nations* and is equally true today in the United States of America. Smith explained clearly why poverty was a relative as well as an absolute phenomenon. Necessities, including, most obviously, the quality of shelter, are socially defined. Indoor plumbing was considered a luxury in the United States 70 years ago and today 40 percent of the world's population does not use a toilet, but, in the US, indoor plumbing is now considered a necessity. No one in the US had phones 100 years, but most Americans would agree that to be unable to afford to pay for a phone today would be a good designation of poverty. Amartya Sen (1982) has suggested that while "relative" poverty is measuring something important it should be called something else other than poverty. Perhaps, in rich nations, a better term for relative poverty would be "socially excluded." The term "social exclusion" has been used increasingly in Europe to describe relative poverty as well as other forms of social exclusion. On the other hand, in the long run, social and official definitions of poverty go up in tandem with average incomes.[16] As a measurement tool, therefore, a relative definition of poverty may, in the long run, be a better reflection than an absolute measure of citizen's perceptions of what it means to be poor. Thus, we present both absolute and relative poverty rates.

The picture conveyed by relative poverty rates is consistent with both the notion of three worlds of welfare capitalism and the notion that the US and Europe are worlds apart. The Scandinavian nations have the lowest poverty rates, the English-speaking nations the highest poverty rates, and the continental European nations are in between. The US poverty rate at 17 percent is much higher than European poverty rates, which with the exception of the UK are well below 10 percent, and more than three times the Swedish poverty rate of 5.4 percent.

The picture conveyed by absolute poverty rates is dramatically different in most but not all respects. First, differences between the US and other nations are much smaller. The ratio of the US to Swedish poverty rate shrinks from over 3 to 1 to only 1.16 to 1. The US doesn't even have the highest poverty rate, that distinction belonging to the UK. This picture does not suggest the US is a world apart. This point echoes the finding in Chapter 2 that when an absolute measure of welfare state transfers per person is used, rather than transfers relative to national income, US spending is much closer to (indeed, higher than that of) most other rich nations. Second, the three-world classification breaks down completely. Canada, Belgium, and the Netherlands all have lower rates than Sweden. Still, even when poverty is measured in terms of real purchasing power, the US poverty rate is among the highest in the richest nations.

In short, when absolute standards of living are compared, US poverty rates are only a bit higher than European poverty rates, but relative poverty rates or rates of social exclusion are much higher in the US.

IV. The effects of cash and in-kind transfers on inequality

Just as differences across nations in poverty depend upon how poverty is measured, so too do differences in inequality depend upon how income is measured. In the last section, income was measured as cash disposable income. As described in the previous section, a large body of research finds large differences among rich nations in relative poverty rates that are closely associated with the generosity of cash welfare state transfers. But the research on relative poverty is limited in that it restricts analysis of transfers and their effects on inequality to cash or near-cash transfers. (Atkinson, Rainwater, and Smeeding, 1995; Hacker, Mettler, and Pinder-hughes, 2005; Kenworthy, 2004; Smeeding, 2005, Smeeding, 2006a). Similarly, cross-national analyses of inequality are based on cash disposable incomes (Gustafsson and Johansson, 1999; Alderson and Nielsen, 2002; Moller, Bradley, Huber, Nielsen, and Stephens, 2003; Kenworthy, 2004). Yet, as we have seen in Chapter 3, in all of these rich countries, about half of welfare state transfers consist of in-kind benefits such as health insurance, education, childcare, elder care, and other services. And, like cash transfers, in-kind transfers reduce inequalities in standards of living, as documented in research within selected countries (Lampman, 1984, for the United States; McLennan, 1996, for Australia; and Harris, 1999, and Sefton, 2002, for the United Kingdom).

A second major limit of existing cross-national studies is that they take into account only direct (income and payroll) taxes and fail to incorporate differences across nations in indirect (sales, value-added, and property) taxes. Unlike the United States, which relies modestly on sales taxes, most rich countries rely heavily on value-added taxes (Adema and Ladaique, 2005), which can be relatively burdensome. The value-added tax is close to 20 percent in most Scandinavian and continental countries, for example, whereas state sales taxes in the United States are roughly 6 to 7 percent. A cash transfer of $1,000 therefore buys $930 to $940 worth of goods in the United States but only about $800 in Europe. Within the English-speaking countries, the United States relies least on indirect taxes and also taxes cash transfers least under its income tax. To the extent that the mix of cash and in-kind benefits and tax structures differ across rich nations, ignoring in-kind benefits and indirect taxes gives an incomplete and perhaps misleading picture of the generosity of welfare states and the effects of welfare state programs on cross-national differences in inequality. It may also contribute to a misunderstanding of the distinctiveness and nature of welfare state regimes.

In this section we extend previous analyses of how welfare state programs affect inequality in rich countries by taking into account both in-kind benefits and all the taxes required to finance these benefits. As described above, we call this new measure of income "full income." Economists who study income distribution are agreed that, as compared to disposable income, full income is a conceptually superior measure of a household's command over economic resources.[17] We use the new measure of full income to examine whether taking account of in-kind benefits and indirect taxes substantially changes cross-national differences in inequality and alters country rankings.[18]

Once again, we depict the effects of differences in measurement visually. In this case, we use economic distance bars. For each measure of income, households are arrayed from poorest to richest. Within each country, households at three points of the income distribution are compared: the middle, the bottom, and the top. The middle-income household is at the median income—half the households in the country are poorer and half richer. The low-income household is the one with 10 percent poorer and 90 percent richer, and the high-income household is the one with 90 percent poorer and 10 percent richer. The economic distance bars are centered on the median income (denoted by the vertical line at 100 percent of the median) and measure the ratio of incomes of the poor and rich to the middle-income household. The further to the left the distance bars go, the greater the economic distance between the poor and median-income family, and the further to the right the bars go, the greater the distance between the rich and the median-income family. Overall inequality is measured by the entire length of the bar. The longer the bar, the greater is inequality. For example, in Figure 4.2, panel A, the far left of the economic distance bar for Australia is just to the left of the 50 percent line, indicating that the disposable income of the low-income household is equal to 49 percent of that of the middle-income household. The income of the rich household (the far right of the bar) is equal to 175 percent of the median-income household and 360 percent of that of the poor household. The numerical values of these three ratios are also presented respectively in the one column to the left and two columns to the right of the distance bars. The economic distance bars depict the big picture, and the numerical values give the specific details.

As before, we analyze families with children and the elderly separately, in Figures 4.2 and 4.3. Panels A and B present economic distance bars for

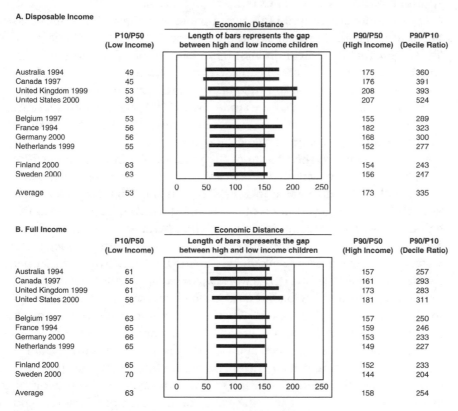

Figure 4.2: Two measures of relative economic well-being: children
Source: Authors' calculations from the Luxembourg Income Study.

the two different measures of income—cash disposable incomes and full income. We begin with the children.

The picture for disposable income in panel A of Figure 4.2 corresponds exactly to existing research and to both descriptions of three distinct worlds of welfare capitalism and the US as a world apart. It depicts substantial differences in inequality across nations in the overall distribution of income and at both the bottom and the top of the income distribution. The English-speaking countries have the longest bars and are the most unequal and the United States is the most unequal of all. The continental European nations are less unequal than the English-speaking nations, and the Scandinavian nations are the most equal. Note, in particular, the differences at the low end, where nations fight poverty. Visually, here, as elsewhere, the United States appears to be a world apart. It has the lowest ratio of low to middle disposable incomes—39—compared to the other European nations, whose ratios range from 53 to 63.[19]

The overall picture for full income in panel B of Figure 4.2 is similar to the picture in panel A insofar as the English-speaking nations still have the greatest inequality, the continental European nations fall in the middle, and the Scandinavians are the most equal. But the differences across countries in inequality of full income are much smaller than the differences in disposable income. For example, the US 90/10 ratio for disposable income (5.24) is more than twice the Swedish ratio (2.47). For full income, the US ratio is only 1.5 times higher than Sweden's.[20]

More important, at the bottom of the income distribution, the picture for full income is a very muted, and in a way quite different one, compared to the picture for disposable income. Though the English-speaking nations still have the lowest ratios of low to middle income, and Sweden the highest, those ratios are now in a much tighter band, varying only from 55 percent to 70 percent. Within the English-speaking countries, the United States is no longer the lowest country. Canada has that distinction. Visual evidence of either the US being a world apart or of three distinct worlds of welfare capitalism is weak because differences across nations are so small.[21] The US ratio, 0.58, is only 7 percentage points below the European level of 0.65. The US level is thus nearly 90 percent of the European level. The difference between Sweden and Germany is only 4 percentage points. Finland is not distinguishable from the other continental European nations. Why do the differences shrink so dramatically at the bottom of the distribution when we include the value of the in-kind education and health benefits and take account of the taxes required to finance these benefits? There are two reasons, both of which have already been discussed in conjunction with Figure 3.3 in the previous chapter. First, compared with other advanced industrialized nations, the United States and the other English-speaking countries are short on cash and long on in-kind benefits. Second, the big-spending welfare states rely more heavily on indirect taxes and taxation of cash benefits than does the United States.

Figures 4.3(A) and 4.3(B) display economic distance bars for disposable income and full income measures for elderly population. As was the case for children, full income mutes the differences between nations in disposable income and the muting is greater at the bottom of the income distribution. Even after muting, differences in inequality at the bottom of the distribution remain large enough to provide crude visual evidence of the three worlds. In general, the English-speaking countries are the most unequal, the continental European nations are more equal, and the

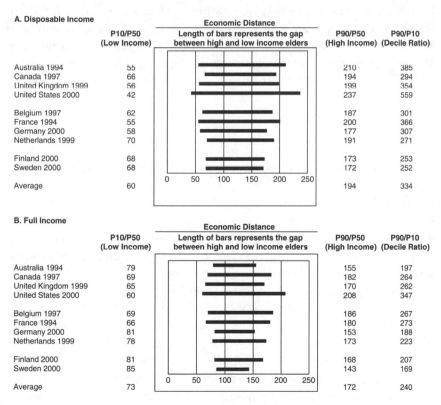

Figure 4.3: Two measures of relative economic well-being: elders
Source: Authors' calculations from the Luxembourg Income Study.

Scandinavians the most equal. But exceptions abound. Australia is closer to Finland and Sweden than to the other English-speaking nations. Similarly, Germany and the Netherlands are closer to Finland and Sweden than to France and Belgium. And France and Belgium are closer to Canada and the United Kingdom than they are to Germany and the Netherlands. Evidence that the US and Europe are a world apart is similarly mixed. On the one hand, the US ratio is only 5 and 6 percentage points, or 10 percent, lower than the UK and French ratios. Compared to Finland, Germany, the Netherlands, and Sweden, however, the US is 20 percentage points, or about 25 percent lower.

V. Human capital and opportunity

In this section, we assess how rich nations compare on three other desirable outcomes of welfare state institutions—achieving high and equitable levels of education and health and promoting equality of opportunity. Though welfare state institutions are not the only determinants of the education, health, and opportunity of a nation's population, they bear the principal responsibility.[22]

Education

In Chapter 3, we saw that spending on education transfers is now the third largest domain of social welfare transfers in most rich nations. US spending as a proportion of GDP on education transfers at all levels of education is somewhat above average. Spending on post-secondary education is quite a bit above average, while spending on early education and childcare is below average.[23] In this section we provide some indication of how the spending translates into educational attainment.

Educational attainment is measured both by the percent of the country's population that attains degrees or is enrolled in school and by test scores. Figure 4.4 shows the proportion of adults age 25–34 in each country who have completed the equivalent of US high school and college degrees (in panels A and B) and the proportions of children age four who are enrolled in early education and childcare.[24] In most rich nations, the overwhelming majority of the population attains at least the equivalent of a US high school degree. In the US, Canada, and the Scandinavian countries, the proportion is just above or below 90 percent. Australia,

Figure 4.4: Educational attainment as a percentage of the population (2001 and 2002)

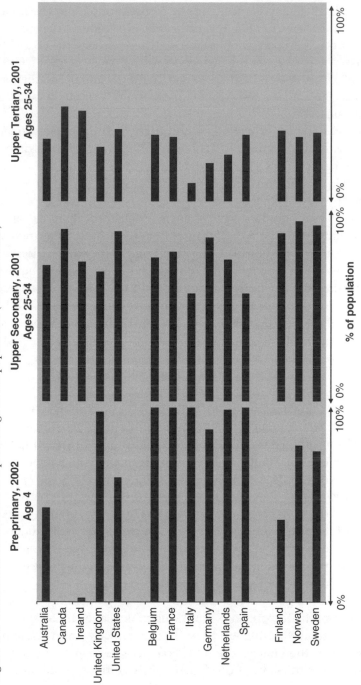

Source: OECD Education at a Glance (2002), Tables A1.2 and A2.3. OECD Education Database (2005).
Note: The pre-primary education data is limited to organized center-based programs designed to foster learning and emotional and social development in children age three to compulsory school age. Day care, play groups, and developmental activities may not be included in these data.

Ireland, the UK, Belgium, France, and the Netherlands are in the middle between 70 and 75 percent, while Spain and Italy are the lowest at 57 percent. The pattern for college completion is quite different. Though the US and the Scandinavian countries are at the high end—with 33 to 39 percent with the equivalent of college degrees, they are joined there by Belgium, France, Spain, and Australia. But Canada and Ireland, at 50 and 48 percent respectively, stand out as the leaders.

In short, with respect to secondary and higher education attainment, there is no evidence in Figure 4.4 of three worlds of welfare capitalism and no evidence that the US is a world apart from or even lags behind Europe. Indeed, the US appears to be ahead of most European nations in college completion. By way of contrast, the early education and care enrollment figures for four year olds do suggest that the English-speaking nations in general, including the US, are substantially behind most other rich nations. Note that the UK is ahead of the other English-speaking nations and looks more like the other continental European nations.

Another indicator of educational attainment is obtained from scores on achievement tests. The OECD's Program for International Student Achievement (PISA) in 2000, 2003c, and 2006 conducted tests of educational achievement of 15 year olds in most rich nations. PISA measures how well these students, who are approaching the end of compulsory education, have acquired the knowledge and skills essential for full participation in society. Identical (or nearly identical) tests in all nations provide a comparable measure of the output of the education system.

In Figure 4.5, we reproduce the raw scores in math and reading for 9 of the 10 nations examined in this chapter (excluding the United Kingdom) for 2003. We plot each country's scores at the 10th and 90th percentiles of their country's distribution and each country's mean score.

In math, the United States has the lowest score at the 10th percentile, the mean, and the 90th percentile. Finland has by far the highest score at the bottom of the distribution. Indeed the 10th percentile math student in Finland scores above the 25th percentile math student in the United States (the latter is not displayed in the graph). Finland also has the highest mean score and the third highest score at the 90th percentile.

In reading, the top US students—those at the 90th percentile—are in the middle of the pack. Top students from Australia, Canada, Finland, and Belgium score somewhat higher; those from Germany and the Netherlands score about the same; those from France score a bit lower. But the mean US score and the score of US students at the 10th percentile are at or

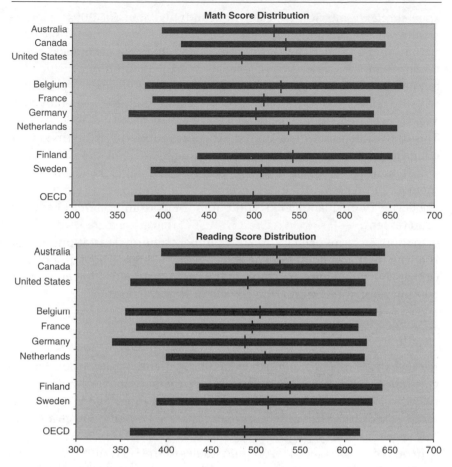

Figure 4.5: PISA 2003 raw scores at 10th and 90th percentiles and the mean in 9 rich nations

near the bottom. Only Belgium and Germany do worse at the bottom and only Germany at the mean.

The distance between the 10th and 90th percentile PISA scores, like the economic distance bars in the previous section, provides information about inequalities in educational achievement. These distances indicate that the US not only does poorly on average, but also has one of the most unequal distributions. Finland and Canada have the least unequal outcomes. Other achievement tests administered to children of different ages show similar results. John Micklewright and Sylke Schnepf (2004) examine results of other achievement tests administered in six English-speaking nations and 12 other European nations, and find that differences across countries in both average achievement and inequalities of achievement are notable, but differences in inequality are even greater. As compared with other OECD countries, the English-speaking countries generally have average achievement levels, but above-average inequality of achievement. The United States and the United Kingdom stand out as high variance countries and are a third to a half more unequal than the continental OECD countries. Canada is an exception—with higher average achievement and lower variance in achievement. The United States ranks first in the degree of inequality and second from the bottom in terms of average achievement.

In short, in terms of educational attainment among rich nations, the US is at the high end if attainment is measured by high school and college degrees, but when measured by enrollments in early education and care or by achievement test scores, the US is at or near the bottom.

Health

Because the US spends so much more than other rich nations on health-care transfers, we frame our discussion of cross-national health outcomes in terms of the broader question of: "Is the United States getting its money's worth for its vastly disproportionate spending on health care?" The answer is both yes and no.

In one of the best recent economic studies of the US health-care system, *Your Money or Your Life,* David Cutler (2004) provides strong evidence that overall benefits exceed costs. Though US life expectancy improved throughout the twentieth century, before 1940 most of the decline in mortality was attributable to public health measures. During the second half of the century, most of the decline was attributable to medical care. Total health-care spending per person in the United States rose from $500 in 1950 to $5,000 in 2000. During roughly this same period (1960–2000), life expectancy increased by 6.6 years; 4.2 of which went to people age 65 or older. Cutler conducts a benefit-cost analysis of three specific medical interventions: beginning-of-life care of low-birthweight babies, new drugs for mental illness, and new procedures and drugs for dealing with heart attacks. The estimated benefits of these interventions, measured by increases in years and quality of life, is large. Increased longevity from infant care and heart interventions alone yield about $50,000 in benefits per person, which is about equal to the total increase in cost in all of medical care spending between 1950 and 2000. Thus, although spending on health care in the United States is huge and still growing rapidly, the benefits are much larger than costs.

Cutler also shows that the US system is plagued by serious waste and inefficiencies, including both over- and under-use, and that the current method of reimbursing hospitals' and doctors' costs is at the root of the problem because it rewards intensive, technological, surgical intervention rather than making sure everyone gets what is known to be best practice—which entails more clerk-like work. Lack of insurance is one serious problem that leads to under-use. Cutler cites an Institute of Medicine estimate that 20,000 non-elderly adults die each year because they lack insurance coverage, a loss valued at $33 billion annually. Despite the waste and inefficiency, the benefits of the US health-care system still far exceed costs and Cutler is reluctant to advocate a universal government-run health insurance system because as an economist he prefers competition to monopoly.

Cutler's study is confined to the United States and does not include a comparative analysis. Two pieces of evidence, however, suggest that other rich nations gain the same large health benefits but at lower costs than the United States, suggesting that the United States is not getting its money's worth. First, in a 2003 article, "It's the Prices, Stupid: Why the United States Is So Different from Other Countries," using OECD data, Gerald Anderson and several colleagues compare US health-care services and spending with those of other rich nations. The US supply of physicians and nurses, the number of doctor visits, hospital stays, and utilization of most services are all about or slightly below average as compared with other OECD nations. Just as an example, although Henry Aaron and William Schwartz in *The Painful Prescription* (1984) report that hip replacements were severely limited in the United Kingdom, replacement rates in the United Kingdom are now similar to those in the United States, and both are about average as compared with other rich nations.[25] Given the comparability of this and other aspects of medical care, why are US costs so high? Among the most important explanations are higher administrative costs, a greater likelihood that doctors are specialists and thus more highly paid, and the greater amenities provided by hospitals.

The second piece of evidence that other rich nations reap the same large benefits as the United States but at lower cost comes from data on mortality, which is recognized as the single best indicator of health. Table 4.4

Table 4.4: Healthcare outcomes in 10 rich nations: 2002

	Outcomes		
Country	Infant Mortality Rate Per 1000 Births (Index)	Life Expectancy as of Age 60: Females	Life Expectancy as of Age 60: Males
		Years	Years
Australia	4.6	85.2	81.4
Canada	5.0	84.8	81.1
United Kingdom	5.2	83.2	79.9
United States	7.0	83.5	80.2
Belgium	4.4	83.9	79.6
France	4.4	85.7	80.8
Germany	4.2	83.9*	79.9*
Netherlands	4.5	83.5	79.5
Finland	3.0	84.0	79.5
Sweden	3.3	84.3	80.9

*data from 2003.
Source: OECD (2002d).

shows that of the 10 rich nations under study, the United States has both the highest infant mortality rate, with conditional upon living to age 60, average life-expectancy rates for men and one of the lowest life-expectancy rates for women.

In sum, the United States gets its money's worth from its health-care system in the sense that the benefits exceed the extraordinarily high costs, but it fails to get its money's worth in the sense that other rich nations achieve the same or greater benefits at lower cost.

The US distribution of health-care spending and consumption is also more unequal than that of other nations. The United States is the only rich nation in which a significant share of its population dies, as in the extreme case noted above, because of a lack of health insurance. Finally, the link between individual out-of-pocket health-care spending and income is unique to the United States. Jessica Banthin and Didem Bernard (2006) find that, in 2003, 19 percent of US citizens lived in families that spent more than 10 percent of family income on health care. Of these people, about 18.7 million (7.3 percent) were spending more than 20 percent of family income. Among the Americans with a higher-than-average risk of incurring high total burdens are poor and low-income citizens, those in fair or poor health, and those with any type of limitation or a chronic medical condition. Although cross-national evidence on differences in health-care spending by income level is sketchy at best, a recent study of the United Kingdom, New Zealand, the United States, Australia, and

Canada by the Commonwealth Fund (Hussey et al, 2004) finds that in each of these five countries, adults with below-average incomes are more likely to forgo needed health care because of cost considerations than are other adults. The study also finds that the highest share of adults who forgo care live in the United States, a figure that includes not only those with below-average incomes but at all income levels.

Equality of opportunity and intergenerational mobility

Throughout most of the nineteenth and twentieth centuries, Americans (and the rest of the world as well) viewed the United States as the land of opportunity. In the next chapter we examine whether or not this perception was true in the past. Here, we are concerned with current differences in opportunities across rich nations.

Although measuring cross-national equality of opportunity directly is difficult, sociologists and economists can and have measured a closely related, but not identical, phenomenon known as social mobility—the extent to which people's occupations or incomes as adults depend on their parents' occupations or incomes.[26] If every adult wound up in the same relative socioeconomic position as his or her parents, there would be no mobility and no equality of opportunity.[27] Perfect equality of opportunity, however, would not necessarily imply complete social mobility because mobility depends not only on parental socioeconomic status but on abilities, some of which are inherited. Because it seems highly unlikely that countries themselves differ in the degree to which people's abilities are transmitted genetically, in principle cross-national differences in mobility are likely to reflect cross-national differences in equality of opportunity.

But comparing differences across nations is still complicated. To begin with, virtually all studies have been carried out within, not across, nations. Studies of mobility are based on unique sample surveys that include data on both fathers and sons and, more recently, also on both fathers and daughters. These studies differ in many ways both within and across nations. One difference is that sociologists tend to measure the average correlation between the occupations of fathers and sons, while economists typically measure the share of the difference in incomes between families in the parents' generation that shows up in differences in incomes in the sons' generation—the so-called elasticity between fathers' and sons' earnings.[28] Despite these challenges, there is now a considerable and growing literature on intergenerational mobility in comparative perspective.[29] We summarize three of the most recent and informative studies.

Emily Beller and Michael Hout (2006) review research by sociologists on mobility and find that the correlation between fathers' and sons' occupations in the United States is between 0.3 and 0.4, indicating that between 60 and 70 percent of the variation in sons' occupations is due to something other than their fathers' occupations (a low correlation indicates high mobility). These mobility rates place the United States in the middle of occupational mobility rates—rates in Canada, Norway, and Sweden are higher, while those in Ireland, the United Kingdom, Germany, Italy, and France are lower.

Two 2006 studies, one by Miles Corak and the other by Marcus Jantti and several colleagues, review and extend research by economists. The Jantti study is notable as being the first cross-national analysis explicitly designed and based on comparable data, with all sons born in 1958 and all fathers' and sons' earnings observed at age 40. The results of both studies are reproduced in Table 4.5, which compares intergenerational income elasticities in the 10 rich nations (a high elasticity indicates low mobility). Corak finds that the United States ranks next to the bottom in mobility, just above the United Kingdom, while Jantti finds that order reversed, with the United States at the bottom and the United Kingdom next to last.

In sum, sociological research suggests that mobility in the United States is no longer exceptionally high, and economics research suggests that it is exceptionally low.

Table 4.5: Immobility rates (inter-generational income elasticities) in rich nations

Country	Preferred	Corak Estimate Lower Bound	Upper Bound	Jantii, et al. Estimates With Harmonized Data
Canada	0.19	0.16	0.21	–
United Kingdom	0.5	0.43	0.55	0.31
United States	0.47	0.4	0.52	0.52
France	0.41	0.35	0.45	–
Germany	0.32	0.27	0.35	–
Denmark	0.15	0.13	0.16	0.07
Finland	0.18	0.16	0.21	0.17
Norway	0.17	0.15	0.19	–
Sweden	0.27	0.23	0.3	0.26

Source: Compiled and calculated by Corak (2006) and Jantii et al. (2005).
Note: Intergenerational elasticities are derived by regressing the natural logarithm of son's earnings (or incomes) on the log of father's earnings (or incomes).

Summary

Welfare state programs redistribute large shares of national income in all rich nations. Net benefits are progressively distributed. On average, the poorest families with children gain 68 percent of their incomes from welfare state transfers, while the richest families lose 31 percent of their incomes. The elderly are also big net gainers. Welfare state transfers make up more than half the income of the elderly as a whole and almost all the income (95 percent) of the poorest elderly. Nations vary widely, however, in the degree to which their poor and elderly citizens rely on welfare state transfers and the degree to which such transfers reduce the income of the wealthy.

In the United States, the poor and elderly tend to rely less on social welfare transfers than they do in other countries, and the wealthy tend to lose less of their income. The United States spends the least on cash transfers and has the highest poverty rates and greatest inequality. Counting in-kind benefits and indirect taxes substantially shrinks these cross-national differences. Amongst rich nations, the United States currently ranks last or near last in promoting education, health, and equality of opportunity.

The welfare states of other rich nations reduce inequality, increase the incomes of the poorest fifth, and reduce the incomes of the top fifth somewhat more than the US. Many other rich welfare states also do more to redistribute resources to the aged, but the US is in the middle in terms of redistributing resources to the families with children. In one important respect, the US welfare state more closely resembles the Swedish and French welfare states than the welfare states in other English-speaking nations or other continental European nations. In these three nations, the poorest fifth of families with children, largely single-mother families, derive a large share of their income from work.

Appendix 4.A: Data and Methods

The micro data are from the Luxembourg Income Study (LIS) database, which now contains over 140 household income data files for 30 nations, covering the period 1967 to 2002 (<www.lisproject.org>). The data and methods are identical to those described in our paper (Garfinkel, Rainwater, and Smeeding, 2006), with one exception. In the paper, we did not include in-kind benefits other than health and education. These benefits, as described in Figure 3.1, are large in Scandinavian and low in English-speaking nations. Omitting these benefits tilted the scales against the three distinct worlds or worlds-apart hypotheses. Thus, for the book, we added the other in-kind benefits.

How we distributed in-kind benefits other than health and education is described below in the context of a full description of the data and methods. The new section is shown in bold typeface.

We limit our LIS analysis to 10 nations, and their most recent data sets. Within each country, we develop three measures of the economic resources of households. The first measure is market income, which is the sum of earnings, interest, dividends, and rents. The second measure is "disposable income," which is the standard measure utilized in cross-national research on inequality and its determinants. Disposable income is equal to income earned in the market (earnings, interest, dividends, and rents), minus direct (income and payroll) taxes, plus cash and near cash transfers, such as food stamps and housing allowances (all of these items are reported by respondents in the LIS data base). The third measure, which we call "full income," differs from disposable income because it adds the value of health, education, and other in-kind benefits, and subtracts the direct and indirect taxes required to finance cash, near cash, health, and education benefits (all of the additional items are imputed). The disposable income and full income measures also differ in that income taxes which finance other, non-transfer government services are not subtracted from full income.

Because it is a new measure and represents the heart of our empirical contribution, we describe in more detail the construction of the full income measure. We begin with the LIS measure of disposable income and add third-party health-care subsidies (public spending in all nations, plus employer subsidies in the US), education subsidies (public-sector support for early childhood education) and elementary and secondary schooling, and all other in-kind benefits, such as elder care and family services. From disposable income, we subtract indirect taxes, including value added taxes (VAT) (sales, excise), corporate taxes, and real property taxes. We exclude all taxes paid for government final goods and services, and only subtract taxes to the extent that they equal overall social welfare benefits paid in each country. If we included the value of other taxes, we should also include the value of the benefits they finance. But we are describing the redistributive effect of only social welfare transfers. Defense, law and order, roads, bridges, and other government activities all have distributional effects. But these are beyond the scope of this book. Though ignored in practice in most studies of the effects of welfare state benefits on incomes, public finance economists agree that such a balanced budget analysis is the theoretically appropriate procedure for estimating the distributional impacts of public programs (Musgrave, 1959; Fullerton and Rogers, 1993).

We ignore post-secondary (tertiary) education benefits and childcare subsidies for children under age three. Omitting these benefits is a limitation, but the LIS provides insufficient data to allow us to impute the value of higher education benefits to households. OECD data on early childhood education are by their own admission incomplete and inaccurate.

With the exception of health in the United States, we assume an equal distribution of health and education expenditures across the income distribution within all nations. This is a strong assumption, which, based upon scattered evidence for particular countries (LeGrand, 1978; Card and Payne, 1998; Wilson, 2000) is almost certainly false. Other in-kind benefits are distributed equally across the entire distribution if they are provided to the entire population without income or assets tests and only to the lowest income quintile if they are provided only to the low-income population.

Education benefits

We used OECD (2002b) data to obtain average primary and secondary public expenditure per pupil in each country per year (columns 2 and 3 of Table 4.A.1). These were assigned to students according to starting and ending ages of primary and secondary school in each nation up to age 18. No account was taken of dropouts or attendees of non-public schools. Each person received the same national average benefit according to OECD estimates.

OECD (2002c) outlays for early childhood education (ECE) in some countries are at odds with other available data sources because countries classify childcare expenditures differently—some put them in education, in social welfare, or in both budgets. Marcia Meyers (2003) was kind enough to share the data used in her recent book with Janet Gornick (Gornick and Meyers, 2003) and to help us update these data. We also used several sources including the Clearinghouse on International Developments in Child, Youth, and Family Policy at Columbia University (<http://www.childpolicyintl.org>) and the European Union "Eurydice" website (<http://www.eurydice.org>) to determine the distribution of these benefits. These sources gave us five parameters: (1) number of children using ECE benefits in each nation; (2) number receiving full-day v. half-day benefits; (3) average amount spent per child per day; (4) average number of days attended; and (5) total spending in each country. The resulting mean benefits per child enrolled in ECE by country are given in the fourth column in Table 4.A.1 (full details are available from authors). We limited benefits to children aged three or over in the survey year; randomly assigned children each benefit amount; and integrated benefits in each nation with the year they began elementary schooling.

Health-care benefits

The average public-health-care expenditure per person by country, taken from OECD (2002a), is given in Table 4.A.1 in 2000 US dollars. We used OECD (2003) purchasing power parities to put all countries' non-cash benefits into 2000 United States PPP adjusted dollars, nationally price indexed to the correct nation year (1997 to 2000 for all but France and Australia, both 1994). The US amount is not just public subsidy, but includes two additional amounts: employer subsidies, taken from the Employment Benefit Research Institute (2004), and an amount for the uninsured (about 15 percent of the population) who are receiving charity or other public care with a value of half of the amount provided by the public sector, taken from Wolfe (2002). For 2000, these per capita amounts are: $2,005 (public subsidy); $2,535 (employer subsidy); $1,002 (uninsured subsidy). From the Current Population Survey (CPS) data which underlie LIS we can separate the US population into those with public subsidy (Medicare, Medicaid, other), those with employer-provided insurance, and the uninsured, and assign each person an average subsidy.

Two points should be stressed about the simulation of health insurance benefits in the US. First, the simulation reflects the unequal distribution of health insurance in the US. Second, the inclusion of employer-provided benefits increases rather than reduces inequality at the bottom of the income distribution because the very poor—those at the 10th percentile—receive virtually no employer-provided health insurance, whereas those at the median receive quite a bit. Omitting the value of employer-provided insurance reduces the well-being of the family at the median and thereby reduces measured inequality.

We impute the "insurance value" of coverage to each person based on their age. That is, we take each national average per capita amount, assign that to 19 to 34 year olds, and from there adjust the insurance subsidy according to a person's age. The insurance value is the amount that an insured person would have to pay in each age category so that the third-party provider (government, employer, other insurer) would just have enough revenue to cover all claims for such persons (Smeeding, 1982). We also implicitly include the insurance value of publicly provided nursing home services for the non-institutionalized population. Each person of a given age receives this benefit regardless of actual health-care usage. The multipliers we used for all countries—taken from Freund and Smeeding (2006)—are 0.75 for persons under age 18; 1.0 for persons age 19 to 34; 1.25 for 35 to 54; 1.75 for 55 to 64; 3.0 for 65 to 74; and 4.0 for those 75 and over. Though the insurance approach has been used by economists for over 30 years, to estimate the benefits of subsidized health care, it has also been questioned by Le Grande (1978) and Atkinson (1983) and therefore alternatives to such valuation should be incorporated in future research.

Other in-kind benefits

The main source for the benefits data is OECD's Social Welfare Expenditure (SOCX) database (2004). The online version provides information from 1980 to 2001. Most of the benefits data are from 2000, but some countries' data are from years 1994, 1997, or 1999. The other in-kind benefits that are calculated and distributed for this particular micro-simulation include the following: active labor market programs (ALMP), family services, Low Income Housing Energy Assistance Program (LIHEAP), services for the elderly and the disabled, Social Services Block Grant, and other in-kind benefits (old age, survivors, and disabled). LIHEAP and the Social Services Block Grant are benefits specific to the United States.

The benefits are distributed by three household and two benefit types. The household types include households with children, elder households, and non-elder childless households. The proportion of each group for each country is calculated in the Luxembourg Income Study (LIS) data, and the distribution of benefits is done proportionately to population groups. The population groups are also divided by income quintiles. Benefits are categorized as universal or means-tested. Within the three demographic population groups, the means-tested benefits are distributed equally to all households in the bottom quintile, and the universal benefits equally to all households in all quintiles.

There are three universal other in-kind benefits considered for this micro-simulation. Family services benefits are distributed to all households with children; similarly, services for the elderly to all elder households. Services for the disabled are divided between households with children and non-elder childless households, according to the population proportion of each country.

The remaining other in-kind benefits are means-tested. LIHEAP is distributed to all three households in the bottom 5th income quintile.[30] Both ALMP[31] and other in-kind benefits for the disabled are distributed to households with children and non-elder childless households in the bottom 5th income quintile. All of the Social Services Block Grant is distributed to households with children.[32] Other in-kind benefits for old age are distributed to elder households in the bottom income quintile, and other in-kind benefits for the survivors to non-elder childless households in the bottom quintile.

The benefits are then summed for each country by type of benefit and household, resulting with six aggregate numbers (per country). The benefits are provided in current prices in local national currency, in millions. These benefits are then converted to US dollars by multiplying them with the purchasing power parity (PPP) from year 2000. For countries whose data are from years other than 2000, the final aggregate amounts are calculated by multiplying the benefits by the PPP of the year and inflating them by the ratio of the Consumer Price Index of that year and of 2000.

Taxes

For each country, we first calculate an aggregate amount of taxes needed to finance cash, near cash, health, education, and other in-kind benefits. All payroll taxes are assumed to be devoted to benefits and the rest of the taxes to be divided according to the country's mix of taxes (not including payroll taxes.) We use OECD data on the relative distribution of taxes by source for each nation, covering five taxes: personal income, payroll, corporate income, property, and "goods and services" (value added, sales, or excise) taxes, as described in Table 4.A.2.

To distribute the taxes by income class, we use actual LIS reports of income and payroll taxes (though the amount of employer payroll tax had to be imputed based on LIS earnings reports and the country's payroll tax structure and then counted in the tax-balancing equations). Following standard practice, we assume that employer payroll taxes and employer-provided health insurance in the US are taken

Table 4.A.1: Health benefits per person and education benefits per beneficiary by country

Country	Year	Health-care[1] (OECD &/person)	Education Elementary	Secondary	ECE
Australia	1994	$1,063	$2,810	$4,530	na
Belgium	1997	1,420	3,633	5,570	3,135
Canada	1997	1,532	5,000	5,900	2,089
Finland	2000	1,276	4,136	6,079	2,666
France	1994	1,398	3,222	5,761	4,030
Germany	2000	2,086	3,929	6,672	2,010
Netherlands	1999	1,461	4,162	5,670	2,537
Sweden	2000	1,866	5,879	5,973	2,291
United Kingdom	1999	1,371	3,627	5,608	2,353
United States	2000	3,175	6,912	8,537	1,113
Overall All Nation Average Benefit Across all types of Beneficiaries		$1,719	$4,331	$6,030	$2,469

Source: OECD.
Note: [1]Includes OECD public subsidies, plus, for US, employer and other third party subsidies.

Table 4.A.2: Tax structures as percentage of total tax receipts, 1999

	Personal Income tax	Corporate Income tax	Social security contributions Employees	Employers	Taxes on goods and services	Other taxes
Australia	43.3	15.9	0.0	0.0	25.0	15.8
Belgium	30.6	7.9	9.7	19.3	25.4	7.1
Canada	38.1	9.8	5.3	8.0	24.7	14.1
Finland	31.9	9.1	4.3	20.1	31.0	3.6
France	17.6	6.4	8.8	25.0	26.8	15.4
Germany	25.1	4.8	17.3	19.3	28.0	5.5
Netherlands	15.2	10.1	27.6*	11.6	28.0	7.5
Sweden	35.6	6.0	5.8	19.1	21.4	12.1
UK	28.8	10.4	7.3	9.7	32.3	11.5
US	40.7	8.3	10.5	12.2	16.4	11.9

Sources: OECD in Figures 2002: Statistics on the Member Countries, Paris: OECD, 2002; Revenue Statistics, 1965–2000, PARIS: OECD, Paris, 2001; Taxing Wages Statistics, 2000–2001, Paris: OECD, 2002; OECD Tax Database; Centre for Tax Policy and Administration, at: <http://www.oecd.org/department/0,3355,en_2649_34897_1_1_1_1_1,00.html>.
Note: * Including self-employment or non-employed.

from wages that employers would otherwise pay (Lampman, 1984; McLennan, 1996; Harris, 1999; Sefton, 2002). Thus, the "incidence" is on labor and, to calculate income gross of benefits, we add these to market income (Brittain, 1971).

With respect to other taxes, we assume the incidence of the corporate tax and of the goods and services tax is on the consumer, and thus distribute according to overall consumption; the incidence of the property tax is similarly assumed to fall on housing consumption. We assign corporate, goods and services, and property taxes according to LIS-calculated ratios of overall expenditure (including housing expenditure) to income ratios by LIS disposable income decile, provided by Eva Sierminska and Thesia Garner from their LIS-based consumption work (Sierminska and Garner, 2002). Decile specific consumption to income ratios are taken from micro-data surveys for four nations (Canada, France, the United Kingdom, and the United States), and an average of the four is applied to other nations. In these four countries, consumption exceeds income in the bottom quintile, which means that consumption and value-added taxes are regressive, not just at the top, but also at the bottom of the income distribution.

Equivalence scales

For cross-national comparisons of inequality, the household is the only comparable income-sharing unit available for most nations. While the household is the unit used for aggregating income, the person is the unit of analysis. Household income is assumed to be equally shared among all individuals within a household. A variety of equivalence scales has been used in cross-national comparisons in order to compare well-being between households with differing compositions. We adjust household incomes (both disposable and full incomes) to reflect differences in household size by dividing income by the square root of household size.

This equivalence scale allows for economies of scale, but does not unduly bias measures toward larger units (with children) or smaller units (with elders) (Atkinson, Rainwater, and Smeeding, 1995). For example, in contrast to using per capita income, which divides by household size, using the square root of household-size equivalence scale, a household of four needs twice as much income rather than four times as much income as a household of one to be equally well off.

Arguments can be made for utilizing a different equivalence scale for cash and in-kind benefits. On the one hand, in-kind benefits do not exhibit economies of scale, which implies they should be divided by household size rather than the square of household size. On the other hand, in-kind benefits are not shared equally by all family members, which suggests that they should be added to equivalized cash income on an individual basis. Education, for example, is targeted to children and, from the child's point of view, their full income equals the equivalized cash value plus the full value of the cost of their schooling. Thus, our use of the same equivalence scale for both cash and in-kind expenditures is a reasonable middle-of-the-road solution, but future research should address the sensitivity of our results to this assumption.

Measures of inequality

Our measure of inequality is the economic distance between households at three points in the income distribution in each country—the 10th, 50th, and 90th deciles. Though proportions of the population below a relative poverty line and Gini coefficients are more commonly used, the economic distance measure has been used in previous studies of income distribution (most recently in Smeeding, 2005) because it allows for comparisons at both the bottom and the top of the income distribution and is more readily interpretable. Utilizing relative poverty rates to focus on the bottom of the income distribution also has the disadvantage that if one includes more resources in the measure of income in a poverty measure, one should also raise the poverty needs level. When we use full income rather than disposable income, we find no families with children or elders in any country that lie below 50 percent of the median-adjusted full income. While this is the most common measure of relative poverty in cross-national research in rich nations (Rainwater and Smeeding, 2004), future research should examine the effects on relative poverty rates with varying definitions of the poverty line that take account of needs for health and education. Also, it is possible to compute Gini coefficients for the bottom and top halves of the income distribution. Future research should also examine whether our findings would hold if the Gini coefficient, rather than economic distance, was the dependent variable.

Finally, though examining how families at the 10th percentile are faring is justified by a Rawlsian (Rawls, 1972) focus on maximizing minimum incomes, other points in the lower half of the income distribution may also be of interest. In particular, future research might focus on the 20th to 35th percentiles, the near-poor and lower-middle class that fare the worst under welfare states, such as the United States, which rely heavily upon income testing (Tullock, 1982; Garfinkel, 1996).

Notes

1. For the argument that all of welfare state redistribution in the US is cross-life cycle, see Morton Paglin (1975). Danziger et al. (1977) effectively rebut the claim for the US. Falkingham and Hills (1995) present the most careful estimates and, using UK data, conclude that half the redistribution of old-age pensions is attributable to life cycle and about half to cross-class redistribution.
2. For evidence that taking account of changes in behavior would not change any of the broad conclusions discussed in the text, see Danziger, Haveman, and Plotnick (1981), "How Income Transfer Programs Affect Work, Savings, and the Income Distribution: A Critical Review." See Garfinkel and McLanahan (1986) and Moffitt (1992, 1996) for reviews of the effects of safety-net benefits on marriage. There is also evidence that public income transfers reduce private family transfers (Smeeding and Lampman, 1983; Jensen, 2003). The reductions are not very great—from under 10 percent to perhaps as much as 25 percent,

but, more important, because the giving and receiving families in private family transfers are in the same part of the income distribution, the reduction in private transfers that occurs in response to public transfers has little effect on the inequality-reducing feature of public transfers.

3. In addition, income is measured at the household level and equivalized.

4. Households are ranked by market income adjusted to account for differences in household size. See the Appendix for a discussion of the equivalence scale.

5. The CPS data understates the share of the top fifth because, in order to protect anonymity, the Census Bureau codes all incomes above $100,000 as if the income was only $100,000. This "top-coding" of high incomes understates the incomes of very wealthy families and thereby understates inequality. Aside from indicating even greater inequality, more accurate data would not change any of the broad conclusions discussed below. For a discussion of the limitations of the CPS data, see Lindert (2004).

6. Deficits do play a role in countering the business cycle. Presidents Reagan and Bush cut taxes below the amounts needed to fund long-term government expenditures, which created huge deficits designed in part to put pressure on welfare state expenditures.

7. The losses are even smaller when expressed as a share of market income—only 18 percent for the top group. Expressing the gains to those at the bottom as a share of market income makes those gains even bigger—indeed, the percentage gains to the bottom fifth in several countries approach infinity because market incomes are zero or close to zero.

8. Ordering of mixed cases was as follows: elders (persons 65 and older) who are living with children are counted among families with children (age under 18); elders are only elders without children. The remainder have neither elders nor children, and are the childless non-aged.

9. Note, however, that both childrearing and retirement encompass broad age ranges, which means that the redistributions across income class portrayed for the aged and families with children contain some life-cycle distribution. The elderly population in each country ranges in age from 65 to over 100. On average, the older the elderly person is, the lower is their income and taxes paid and the greater their health costs. Amongst the elderly, incomes decline with age because the longer one lives the more likely it is that savings will need to be used, and because the younger old earned higher wages during their working years and therefore have higher pensions. Similarly, amongst families with children, the age range of the parents is from below 20 to over 60. Exactly how much of welfare state redistribution is life-cycle redistribution versus redistribution across income classes is very difficult to tease apart because there is such a strong relationship of income to age. Falkingham and Hills (1995) do the most careful analysis and find that old-age pensions in the UK in the early 1990s had a large element of both life-cycle and cross-class redistribution.

10. Furthermore, the data in Table 5.1, in the next chapter, are misleading in that they do not take into account the tax subsidy for owner-occupied housing in the US income tax. We omit housing tax benefits from the table because our ultimate goal in this chapter is to make international comparisons and comparable data for other nations are not available. But, as noted in Chapter 3, US housing tax benefits are distributed very unequally. For families with children, benefits range from practically zero in the bottom quintile to $450, $1,660, and $2,700 for the lower-middle, middle, and upper-middle quintiles, to $10,920 for the top quintile. When these benefits are added to those displayed in panel A, what emerges is a U-shaped distribution of total welfare state benefits. By way of contrast, benefits for the elderly, except for the slight dip between the first and second quintiles, increase steadily with income.

11. These analyses rely on the LIS data described in the Appendix. The LIS data for Ireland, Italy, and Spain severely undercount cash income relative to administrative and national accounts data. Non-cash benefit information was also difficult to obtain for these three nations and Norway. We believe that the sample of nations we do include is indicative of the results one would find for these four nations, were they to be included.

12. For example, in the US in 1991 only 13.7 percent of women age 45 or more are childless, while in Italy, in 1995, the percentage is 9.2 percent.

13. The data actually understate very high incomes in the US (see note 5) and therefore overstate the percentage reduction in the incomes of the top fifth.

14. Atkinson, Rainwater, and Smeeding (1995); Hacker, Mettler, and Pinderhughes (2005); Kenworthy (2004); Smeeding (2005, 2006a).

15. Purchasing Power Parity (PPPs) were used to convert other currencies to US dollars.

16. Some indicators suggest that the growth in poverty levels is less than in proportion to the average growth in income, while others suggest that it is greater. One indicator of the citizenry's definition of poverty is the amount of spending on public assistance to the poor relative to income. As demonstrated in Figure 5.1 in the next chapter, this indicator has gone up much more than proportionally to income in every rich country, including the US—increasing on average fourfold in the last 100 years. Another indicator is the public assistance benefit level relative to average earnings. Lebergott (1976) finds that over the period 1850 to 1903 the benefit level increased less rapidly than income.

17. The theoretical and empirical importance of valuing in-kind benefits has been understood for nearly a quarter-century (Smeeding, 1982). Conceptually, it is clear that these benefits are worth some non-trivial amount to beneficiaries. Similarly, indirect taxes reduce the living standards of households no less than direct taxes. Thus, from a theoretical point of view, a measure that counts in-kind transfers and indirect taxes is superior to the conventional measure of cash-disposable income as a measure of a household's standard of living

(Atkinson and Bourguignon, 2000). The only cross-national study of inequality to incorporate health and education (Smeeding et al., 1993) found just small changes in cross-national differences, with the exception of Great Britain. However, these researchers used data from 1980 when health care played a much smaller role than it does now; it also did not incorporate indirect taxes, and relied upon national experts to conduct separate country analyses, rather than utilizing a common cross-national simulation analysis.

18. The LIS survey data contain all items needed to compute disposable income, but, as noted earlier and described in detail in the Appendix, we had to estimate the value of the in-kind transfers (predominantly health and education) for each individual household.

19. Smeeding and Thompson (2008) show that taking account of wealth in the US substantially increases inequality. The increase is probably greater in the US than other countries because wealth is bigger relative to income and more unequally distributed in the US than most other rich nations.

20. Future research could overturn this result. As mentioned above and described in the Appendix, we distribute education benefits equally across income class in all nations. We have pretty good evidence that this is not true in the United States, where empirical research indicates that education expenditures per child are, depending upon the study, a little to a lot lower than average in the bottom income quintile. If the expenditures were a lot lower, and if expenditures in other nations were really equal across income class, the full income picture for families with children would look like the disposable income picture, with the US being a world apart. Unfortunately, we do not know how education expenditures are actually distributed by income class in other rich nations. But we strongly suspect that benefits in other countries are distributed unequally. One study conducted in the United Kingdom by Julien Le Grand (1978) indicates that upper-income families used the British National Health Service more than lower-income families, despite having better health. Even nominal entitlement to equal expenditures does not guarantee actual equality. The actual distribution of not just education, but health and other in-kind benefits, by income class is an important area for research.

21. This finding reinforces the large group of scholars who have challenged the validity of the concept of three worlds of welfare capitalism. Feminist scholars of the welfare state have been particularly effective critics of the three-worlds view. See, for example, Orloff (1993a). For more general critiques and overviews of the debate, see Pierson (2000) and Arts and Gelissen (2002).

22. Arguably, labor markets are as important as welfare state transfers for promoting opportunity.

23. Pre-primary spending: OCED avg = 0.5% of GDP, US = 0.4%; Tertiary: OECD avg = 1.4%, U.S. = 2.9% (source: OECD Ed at a glance, 2006b).

24. The source for high school and college attainment is the *OECD Handbook for Internationally Comparative Education Statistics*, 2004. Upper secondary educa-

tion is equivalent to a US high school degree and upper tertiary education is equivalent to a US college degree. The OECD data come from representative surveys of the country populations in 2001. The estimates for 1970, therefore, are based upon adults who are 55–64 in 2000 and would have been 25–34 in 1970. Because some adults age 25–34 in 1970 will have died before 2001, the figures are only approximations. But since survival rates conditional upon reaching age 25 do not vary substantially across countries, the estimates do convey an accurate relative picture of differences in attainment. See OECD (2002d) and World Bank (2007).

25. Data from the US National Hospital Discharge Survey report 160,000 primary hip arthroplasty procedures in 1998, which is the equivalent of 60 per 100,000 residents (American Academy of Orthopedic Surgeons, 2003). The US has lower rates of primary THR than other developed countries. Scandinavian countries and France have some of the highest rates of incidence, between 90–135 operations per 100,000 inhabitants. Lower rates are evident in Australia, Ireland, and England, ranging from 63–73 procedures per 100,000 inhabitants (Merx et al., 2002).

26. Some sociologists also use the term "mobility" to refer to income growth. See Beller and Hout (2006).

27. Opportunity to earn more or less might still be greater than zero. But opportunity to advance relative to one's parents would be zero.

28. Studies also differ on ages at which fathers and sons are compared; sample sizes and measurement error; and sample selection. For instance, when comparing fathers and sons, almost all studies drop sons where the father is absent or where his earnings are not observed in the proper period, thus eliminating a large group of children from unmarried single-parent units where the chances of success are low. Recent studies by Lee and Solon (2006), Mazumder (2005), and Grawe (2004), have helped clarify measurement biases and aided understanding of subtle differences in how mobility interacts with equality of opportunity and outcome. See also high-quality volumes by Bowles et al. (2005a) and Corak (2004), as well as thoughtful papers by Roemer (2004), Jencks and Tasch (2005), and Solon (2004), to understand subtle differences in how mobility interacts with equality of opportunity and outcome.

29. For a recent short review of mainly the economist perspective, see Piriano and Haveman (2006), and also Corak (2004, 2006). For the sociological side, see Breen and Jonsson (2005), or Erikson and Goldthorpe (2002). Recently, Wilson, Smeeding, Haveman, and Miller (2006) have presented fresh results for several types of measures, focusing on income, earnings, SES, and occupational prestige.

30. LIHEAP also includes cash distributions, but the amount is relatively small such that considering LIHEAP as a 100 percent in-kind benefit does not make a significant difference in the micro-simulation.

31. According to OECD, 16–86 percent of ALMP is redistributed as other in-kind benefits. This includes transfers to service providers, such as salaries of teachers, salaries of the supervisors on make-work programs, and associated buildings, materials, and management.
32. The actual allocation of the benefit to households with children is less than 100 percent. The relative amount is small and does not significantly change the results in the micro-simulation.

5

A Short American-centric History
of Welfare State Programs
and Outcomes

In the previous two chapters, we described current welfare state programs and their outcomes. In this chapter, we present a brief history of these programs and their outcomes in currently rich countries. Because enactment of welfare state programs is always heatedly contested, every country's development of its own welfare state depends on its own history of earlier policy fights. Thus, a short history cannot possibly do justice to any one country's history, let alone to the histories of all rich countries. Similarly, the exploration of differences and similarities in historical outcomes must be limited.

To simplify the analysis, we address one major question: do current similarities and differences in welfare state programs and outcomes across rich nations go back a long way or are they of relatively recent origin? In particular, we focus on what ways and for how long the US has been exceptional. In the first part of the chapter, which deals with program development, we ask: has the US always been a laggard in providing public assistance and social insurance, and both a leader and laggard in providing mass education? In the second part of the chapter, which deals with outcomes, we ask: has the US always had more income inequality, worse health and education outcomes, and less intergenerational opportunity than the other rich countries? In this chapter, we take the approach of Detective Joe Friday in the American TV series *Dragnet*, whose mantra was "Just the facts, please."[1] Establishing the facts is one key to understanding. The other key, addressed in Chapters 6 and 7, is putting the facts together into a coherent story that explains the facts.

For two reasons, we do not try to extend backwards all the measures that we have examined in Chapters 3 and 4. First, in some cases, such as achievement test scores, the data are not available. Second, doing so would overwhelm the reader with facts and defeat our purpose of being reader-friendly. Where we had choices, the measures we chose were representative and interesting.

I. Welfare state program development

In the first part of the chapter, we go back to 1800 and show that the US has always been a laggard in providing cash relief and social insurance and that it was, until the last quarter of the twentieth century, a leader in providing mass education. The lags in cash relief and social insurance are reflected by spending trends and by the dates of program enactment respectively. Leadership in mass education is measured by enrollment rates. While dates of enactment and enrollment rates are of interest in themselves, they cannot be readily compared. Thus, we also look at the welfare state as a whole from the beginning of the twentieth century, through the lens of total social welfare spending, and conclude that at the beginning of the twentieth century the US was neither laggard nor leader, but closer to leader in total social welfare spending relative to GDP. As late as 1960, the US was close to the middle of the pack but, by the end of the century, it clearly lagged.

Relief for the poor

The oldest welfare state program is poor relief. As feudalism gave way to capitalism in Western Europe, the state supplanted the feudal lord and the Church in bearing responsibility for aiding the poor. Capitalism and public poor relief developed together, first in Great Britain and the Netherlands. Providing public aid to the poor was a big, hotly contested step, and even though the principle of public responsibility became increasingly less controversial, the nature of the aid to be provided continues to this day to be a subject of great debate.[2] Because the US came into being as colonies of Great Britain, it provided public relief for the poor throughout its history.

Figure 5.1 depicts the share of national income (percent of GDP) spent on public relief (what is known colloquially in the US as *welfare*) by all levels of government in 10 currently rich nations—Ireland, the UK, and the US; Belgium, France, Germany, and the Netherlands; and Denmark,

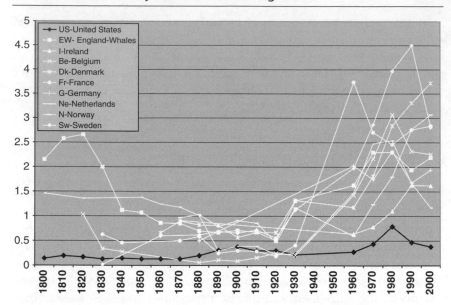

Figure 5.1: Percentage of GDP spent on public assistance, 1800 to 2000

Source: See footnote 3.

Norway, and Sweden—from 1800 to the present.[3] Despite some huge gaps in the data, as signified by the straight lines between the Xs or Os and other symbols that denote both the country and the year of data, this picture clearly depicts several important facts. In all countries, the share of national income spent on public relief (measured from bottom to top in the figure) has grown over time. The biggest increases in spending occurred during the last 40 years of the twentieth century.

All countries have also experienced big fluctuations in spending over time, some of which are driven primarily by unemployment. When unemployment goes up, so does public spending on relief. But GDP goes down. The combination of an increase in spending and a decrease in GDP leads to spikes in the percent of GDP devoted to public relief, as exemplified by the Swedish spike in 1990.

Most interesting, in terms of American exceptionalism, is how far back its low provision of cash relief goes. Amongst the nations we study, the US has always been the lowest or near-lowest spender. In percentage terms, the differences are large. Today, the US spends less than half of what the next lowest country spends and only about one sixth of what the most generous spends. In short, throughout its history, compared with other rich nations, the US has had a particular aversion to public relief.

Though Figure 5.1 is full of other interesting facts, we call attention to only one other. The UK stands out as being the early leader in providing public relief for the poor and is above average in spending until at least 1970. Clearly, the US did not inherit its special aversion to cash-relief benefits from the mother country. What accounts for the difference between the US and other rich nations is taken up in the next chapter.

Social insurance and other cash benefits

Social insurance came into being in the late nineteenth century in Germany and gradually spread through the rest of the rich world throughout the twentieth century. The US lagged behind the European nations both in terms of when it enacted these programs and in how much it spends on them. In this section, we focus on dates of enactment because they present new and interesting information (spending would be similar to the information presented in Figure 5.1). Figure 5.2 indicates the dates when each country enacted the laws creating its various social insurance programs. The countries are grouped by rows into the familiar three groups: English-speaking, continental European, and Scandinavian. Each column in the table represents a particular program, including work-injury compensation, work sickness insurance, old-age insurance, unemployment insurance, survivors' insurance, disability insurance, family allowances, health insurance, and paid family leave. The date each country enacted each program is entered into the appropriate row and column. Work-injury compensation is the oldest program; National Health Insurance and paid family leave are the newest. Health insurance came into being for the most part after World War II. Child or family allowances are also of relatively recent origin—for the most part a near mid-twentieth-century phenomenon.

Besides the steady spread of programs among the rich nations throughout the century, two other features are worth noting. First, leadership differs depending on the program in question. Germany led in work-injury compensation, Denmark in old-age insurance, France in unemployment insurance, Belgium in family allowances, Spain and the Netherlands in health insurance, and Spain and Sweden in paid family leave.

Second, throughout the twentieth century, the US has lagged behind other rich nations in enacting social insurance programs. It was the last nation to adopt workers' compensation, which is, even now, a state rather than a national program in the US. Not until 1935 did the US enact old-age and unemployment insurance. The US still lacks universal health insurance, work sickness insurance, family allowances, and paid family leave

Figure 5.2: Years when first laws of social security programs were enacted

	Work Injury	Sickness	Old Age (1)	Unemployment	Survivors	Disability	Family Allowances	National Health Insurance	Maternal Leave
English-Speaking Countries									
Australia	1902a	1948	1908	1944	1942	1908	1941	1975	1994
Canada	1908	1957	1927	1940	1952	1955	1944	1957	1985(3)
Ireland	1897	1911	1908	1911	1935	1911		1957	1994
UK	1897	1911	1908	1911	1928 (18)	1911		1948	1994
USA	1897	None	1935	1935	1939	1956	None	1965b	1993
Continental-European Countries									
Belgium	1903	1894	1900	1920	1967	1944	1930	1945	1971
France	1898	1928	1910	1905	1949	1975	1932	1945	1946
Germany	1884	1883	1889	1927	1911	1889	1954	1962	1986
Italy	1898	1943	1919	1919	1919	1919	1936a	1978	1971
Spain	1900	1942	1919	1919	1919	1919	1938	1936	1929
Netherlands	1901	1931	1901	1949	1959	1966	1939	1941	1966
Scandinavian Countries									
Denmark	1898	1892	1891	1907		1921	1952	1970	1989
Finland	1895		1937	1917	1956	1937	1948	1964	1946
Norway	1894	1909	1936	1906	1936	1936	1946	1967	1946
Sweden	1901	1891	1913	1934	1913	1913	1947	1955	1931

Source: Social Security Programs Throughout the World: Europe, 2006, 2004; Social Security Programs Throughout the World: Asia and the Pacific, 2004; Social Security Programs Throughout the World: The Americas, 2003, 2005; M. S. Gordon (1988), Social Security Policies in Industrial Countries: A Comparative Analysis. Cambridge: Cambridge University Press; Sheila B. Kamerman and Alfred Kahn, eds (1991), Child Care, Parental Leave, and the Under 3s: Policy Innovation in Europe. New York: Auburn House.

a. First state or province law.

b. For the aged only.

programs.[4] Putting Figures 5.1 and 5.2 together, we conclude that the US has not only had a particular aversion to cash relief, but that it has also consistently lagged behind other rich nations in providing cash and social insurance benefits.

Public education

Public education began in some Prussian counties, in the Northern US states, and in Canada in the first half of the nineteenth century. By the end of the century, it had become near universal at the elementary level in leading countries. Figure 5.3 uses data compiled by Lindert to display the growth in public school enrollment rates in our 14 nations for three different years during the course of the nineteenth century—1830, 1870, and 1900. Enrollment rates are measured by the number of children enrolled in public elementary schools as a percentage of the population ages 5–14.[5] For each country and each year, enrollment rates are displayed by bars. The longer is the bar, the greater is the enrollment rate.

Although data for a few years are missing, several clear patterns emerge from Figure 5.3. First, over time, enrollment rates went up in all countries.

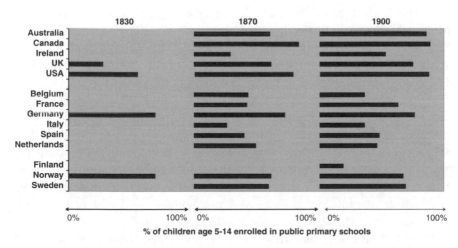

Figure 5.3: Percentage of children age 5–14 enrolled in public primary schools in 1830, 1870, and 1900

Source: P. H. Lindert (2004), *Growing Public*, Vol.2, *Further Evidence: Social Spending and Economic Growth since the Eighteenth Century*. New York: Cambridge University Press.

Note: 1830 data for the following are missing: Australia, Canada, Ireland, Belgium, France, Italy, Spain, the Netherlands, Finland, and Sweden. 1870 data for Finland is missing.

Although well under half of all students were enrolled in elementary school in most countries in 1830, by the end of the century, well over half were in school in most countries, and in the leading countries the share was close to 90 percent.

Second, leadership changed over time. In 1830, though US enrollment rates were among the highest, Germany's rates were even higher. But enrollment in Germany grew very little. By 1870, the US and Canada were the leaders and they maintained that leadership throughout the rest of the century.

Third, in education, there is no hint of the Esping-Anderson three worlds of welfare capitalism. The commitment to public education varied enormously within the English-speaking countries, with the UK and Ireland being education laggards and the US, Canada, and Australia being leaders. On the continent, Germany stood out as a clear leader. By the end of the nineteenth century, Norway and Sweden were in the middle of the pack and Finland was at the bottom.

One pattern not displayed in the figure is worth noting. The US averages obscure quite large regional and racial differences. After slave uprisings during the 1820s, all the Southern slaveholding states made it illegal to educate slaves, and public education even for whites developed much more slowly in the South than in the North (Kaestle, 1983).

At the beginning of the twentieth century, most American children attended primary schools, but few attended secondary or high schools and only a minuscule share attended college. This pattern changed dramatically during the first half of the twentieth century as the US leadership in mass education widened. Figure 5.4 depicts the growth in enrollment rates in secondary education between 1900 and 1930. The enrollment rate—the ratio of the number of secondary students to the number of children age 5–14 in each country—is not ideal for our purposes, but it still accurately reflects underlying differences.[6] What is striking is that the US rate is nearly double that of the next closest country, Germany, and three to six times higher than most of the other countries. Similarly, the proportion of children graduating from colleges and universities was much higher in the US than other nations.

The wide American lead in secondary and college education persisted past mid-century, at least until 1970, but by the century's end was much reduced. The length of the bars in Figure 5.5 depicts the share of adults age 25–34 in each country who have attained the equivalent of US high school and college degrees (in panels A and B) for two years—1970 and 2000.[7] The figures for 2000 are repeated from the previous chapter to facilitate com-

Figure 5.4: Secondary school (public and private) students per 1,000 age 5–15 children in 1900 and 1930

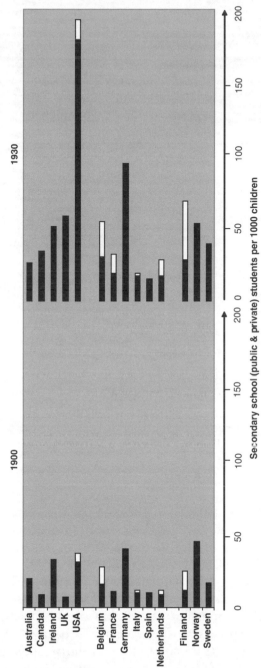

Source: P. H. Lindert (2004), *Growing Public, Vol.2, Further Evidence: Social Spending and Economic Growth since the Eighteenth Century.* New York: Cambridge University Press.

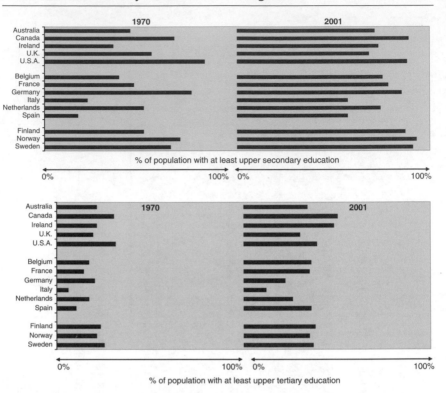

Figure 5.5: Percentage of the population that has attained at least upper secondary and upper tertiary education in 1970 and 2001

Source: *OECD Education at a Glance* (2002). Table A1.2 and Table A2.3.

Note: Year 1970 data is from 2001 in age group 55–64 (equivalent to 25–34 in 1970). Data in 2001 is from 25–34 age group.

parisons. As shown in panel A, in 1970 the US, at 83 percent, had a clear lead in the share of adults who had completed high school. Only Germany, at 76 percent, was close. In most countries, less than half of adults had the equivalent of a high school degree. By 2000, the picture had changed dramatically. Except for the US and Germany, which already had high rates, the share in all other countries increased substantially. The three Scandinavian countries and Canada had caught up to or surpassed the US. The other countries were not far behind.

Panel B, which depicts the share of each country's population that has attained at least the equivalent of a US college degree (upper tertiary

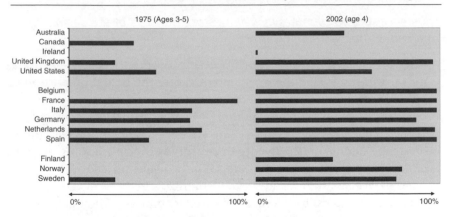

Figure 5.6: Percent of children enrolled in pre-primary education, in 1975 and 2002

Source: OECD Education Database (2005); OECD (1984); Kamerman (1976).

Note: The data refer to pre-primary education, which is limited to organized center-based programs designed to foster learning and emotional and social development in children age 3 to compulsory school age. Day structured and developmental activities may not be included in these data. For 1975 data, all rates are for 3–5 years, with the exceptions of Italy (3–6), the Netherlands (4–6), and the UK (3–4). 1975 data is missing for Australia and Norway. Sweden data is 1976.

education), tells much the same story. In 1970, the US together with Canada had a clear lead. By 2000, most of the other countries had caught up or nearly so, and Canada and Ireland were notably ahead. In short, since the 1970s, the US has been losing its big lead in educational attainment.

Finally, Figure 5.6 depicts how the US fell increasingly behind in early childhood education between 1975 and 2002. The bars for 2002 are repeated from Chapter 4 and show the share of four-year-old children in each country enrolled in early childhood education. Unfortunately, the data for 1975 are not exactly comparable as they refer to the share of children age three to five in most of the countries. Still, the difference between the two years is quite large. In 1975, the US is in the middle of the pack. By 2002, early childhood education is quite common and the US is clearly behind.

In sum, the US went from being one of the world leaders in mass education at the beginning of the twentieth century to being, by midcentury, far and away, the world leader. During the last quarter of the twentieth century, however, the other rich nations substantially closed or eliminated the gap in high school and college enrollment and attainment and surged ahead in early childhood education.

Differences across countries in welfare state transfers at the beginning and end of the twentieth century

As the nineteenth century ended and the twentieth began, Australia, Canada, and the US led the world in educating the largest proportion of their children, while Germany led the world in enacting social insurance programs—work-injury compensation, sickness insurance, and old-age pensions. Labeling the US as a welfare state laggard as of the beginning, or even the middle of, the twentieth century is thus misleading. A more accurate assessment would put the US as a leader in education and a laggard in cash assistance and social insurance.

What about leadership in terms of the welfare state as a whole at the dawn of the twentieth century? As we have seen already, the simplest way to put together the disparate domains is to compare social welfare spending in all domains as a percentage of GDP.[8] Figure 5.7 does just that. The part of the bars colored in black represents spending on education at all levels—elementary through university.[9] The part of the bars colored in white represents spending

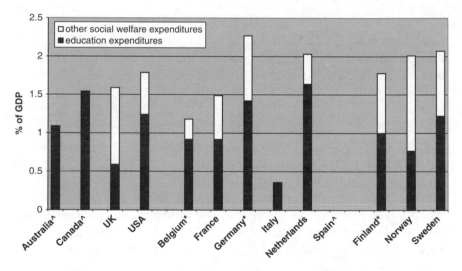

Figure 5.7: Gross size of the US and other welfare states in 1900

Sources: P. Lindert, Revised Data Set, "The Rise of Social Spending, 1880–1930." P. Lindert (2005), *Growing Public: Social Spending and Economic Growth since the Eighteenth Century*, Vol.2, Appendix C, Table C.3 Public expenditures, all levels of education, 1850–1910.

Notes: *Belgium's and Finland's education data and Germany's other SWE data are missing. The missing data have been substituted per following: Belgium = France; Finland = average of Sweden and Norway and Germany.

^Australia's and Canada's other SWE and all of Spain's expenditures are reported as zero.

Figure 5.8: Gross size and composition of the US and other welfare states in 1960, 1970, 1980, 1990, and 2001

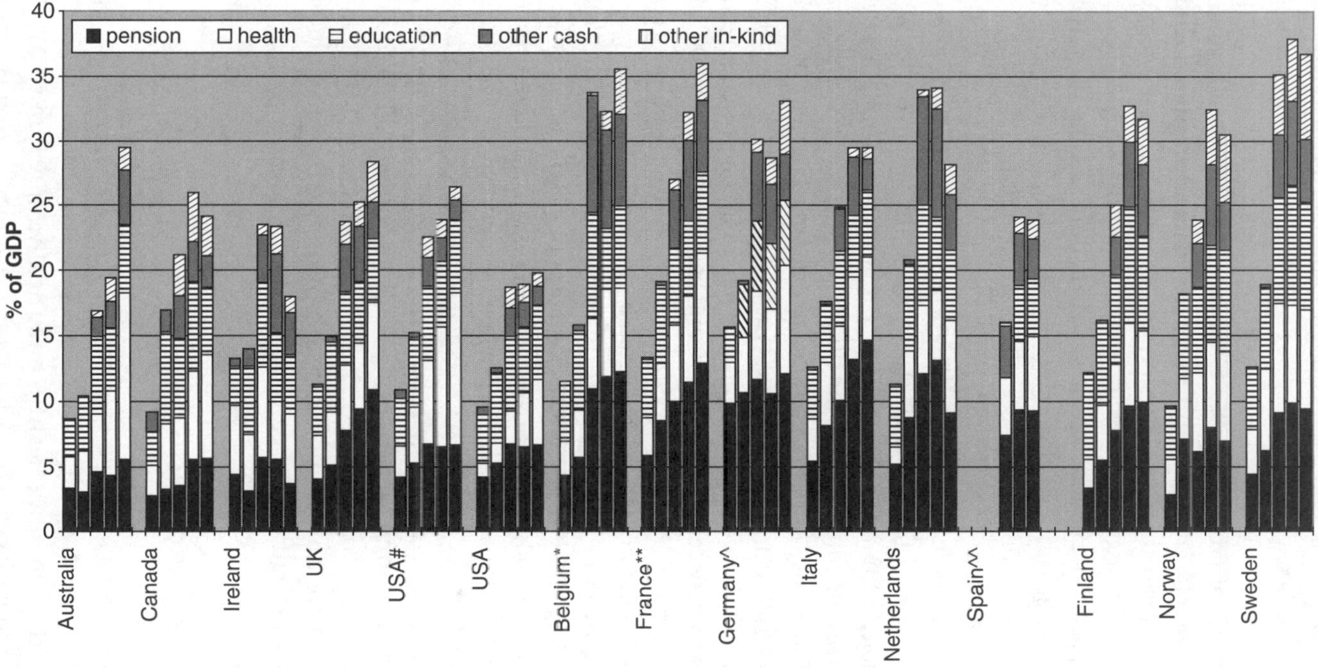

pension
health
education
other cash
other in-kind
% of GDP
0
5
10
15
20
25
30
35
40
Australia
Canada
Ireland
UK
USA#
USA
Belgium*
France**
Germany^
Italy
Netherlands
Spain^^
Finland
Norway
Sweden

Source: OECD Statistical Database.

Notes: # Includes employer-provided health insurance.

* 1960 pension estimated by 1964 data.

** 1960 education estimated by 1975 data; 1970 education estimated by 1975 data.

^ Data for 1960 to 1990 are from Western Germany; data for 2001 are from the United Federal Republic of Germany.

^^ Data for 1960 and 1970 are unavailable.

on all other social welfare domains. Though some data are missing, the big picture is very clear. Social welfare transfers are still quite a small percentage of GDP in all of the countries, ranging from below 1 percent of GDP to at most about 2.5 percent of GDP. With the clear exception of the UK, and the possible exception of a few other countries where data are missing, spending on education is larger than spending on all other welfare state programs. With respect to rankings, if we exclude education, the US stands in the middle of the pack. If we include all social welfare transfers, the US is neither laggard nor leader but is much closer to the leaders than the laggards.[10]

Consistent cross-national data on social welfare spending in all domains are not available between 1910 and 1960, but become available from 1960 onwards for nearly all domains.[11] Figure 5.8 displays transfers by domain for each nation for 1960, 1970, 1980, 1990, and 2001, the latest year for which data are available.[12] A number of interesting patterns emerge from this figure.

The overwhelming impression is the huge growth in social welfare transfers in all rich nations. Transfers grew from around 10 percent of GDP in 1960 to between 25 percent and 35 percent of GDP in 2001. Most of the growth took place during the 1960s and 1970s. In all countries, spending grew more slowly between 1980 and 1990 and between 1990 and 2001 than between 1960 and 1980. Between 1990 and 2001, in nearly half the countries, transfers as a percentage of GDP actually declined.

US spending in 1960 tended toward the low end, but not particularly low. The UK, Belgium, and the Netherlands spent about the same as the US, and Australia, Canada, and Norway spent less. (If employer-provided health insurance is not counted, the previous sentence would be changed only by moving Norway from below to equal to the US.) By 2000, however, US spending was more decidedly toward the low end. Only Ireland and Spain transferred less and, not counting employer-provided health insurance, only Ireland transferred less. What also set the US apart is the tremendous growth in spending on health insurance between 1960 and 2001—from 2.4 percent to 11.6 percent of GDP.

II. Welfare state outcomes

In this part of the chapter, we examine historical trends in outcomes examined in Chapter 4: inequality and poverty, human capital (as measured by education and health), and, finally, opportunity. We find that the US became a laggard only during the last quarter of the twentieth century.

Income inequality and poverty

Income inequality is much greater in the US today than in other rich nations. Has America always been much more unequal than other rich nations? Emmanuel Saez and Thomas Picketty have harmonized (made comparable for the purposes of cross-national comparisons) tax return data from 10 currently rich nations for most of the twentieth century.[13] Figure 5.9 displays the share of market income of the richest 1 percent in each country over the twentieth century. (The picture would be similar but less dramatic if we used the share of the top 10 percent rather than the top 1 percent of the population.) The big picture is crystal clear. Inequality dropped dramatically in all countries during the first part of the century.[14] The share of income going to the top 1 percent in the US fell precipitously, from 21 percent to 11 percent, between 1928 and 1944, the years of the Great Depression and of World War II when Franklin Delano Roosevelt was president. Between 1945 and 1973, the so-called Golden Era, most countries including the US became even more equal. Finally, during the last quarter of the twentieth century, inequality increased modestly in all nations, but it increased much more in the US and, to a lesser extent, in the UK and Canada.

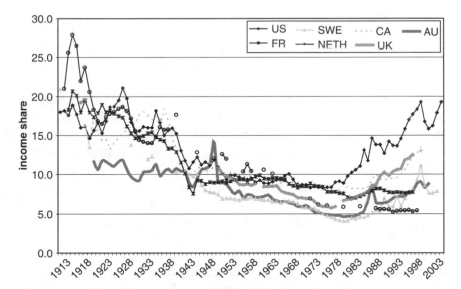

Figure 5.9: Top 1% share of income—selected countries, 1913–2005

Sources: Figure 7 in Roine and Waldenstrom (2006); Sweden (Roine and Walderstrom, 2006), Australia (Atkinson and Leigh, 2006), Canada (Saez and Veall, 2005), France (Piketty, 2003), the Netherlands and the UK (Atkinson and Salverda, 2005), and the US (Piketty and Saez, 2003).

Two other features of the figure are worth noting. First, until the last quarter of the twentieth century, there was nothing particularly distinctive about the US pattern. In other words, until the 1970s, the US was not a world apart in terms of inequality. Second, since 1980, the increases in United States income inequality have been huge.[15] At 19 percent, the share of the richest 1 percent is nearly as high as it was during the Roaring Twenties and is 1.5 times higher than the next closest country, the UK.[16] Finally, inequality in the US continued to widen during the first eight years of the twenty-first century. A 2007 Congressional Budget Office Report finds that the *change* in the income share of the top 1 percent of Americans from 2003 to 2005 ($524.8 billion) *exceeds the entire income share* of the bottom 20 percent in 2005 ($383.4 billion). It is clear that the very rich are doing increasingly well in the United States compared to other nations (Johnston, 2007).

In short, the US became distinctly and increasingly more unequal than other rich nations only during the last quarter of the twentieth century.

What about poverty? Recall from Chapter 4 that current US poverty rates are much higher than those in other rich nations if the poverty measure includes only cash or near cash transfers and is relative: differences in poverty rates across nations are quite small and the US no longer has the highest poverty rate if either the poverty measure is absolute or if in-kind transfers are included. Recall also that relative poverty measures inequality in post-tax, post-transfer income in the bottom half of the income distribution. Unfortunately, because the LIS extends back only to 1965 for two countries and to 1974 for five countries, we can only make inferences about how far back in time these differences and similarities go.[17] Piecing together several different facts convinces us that these patterns extend back to the beginning of the twentieth century.

The US standard of living has been higher than that of other rich nations throughout most of the twentieth century. Inequality in market income was not higher in the US until the 1970s. Together, these facts suggest that absolute poverty rates were never distinctly higher in the US than in Europe during the twentieth century and may actually have been lower until the 1970s. Similarly, because the US has been a long-term leader in education, we hypothesize that the US would not stand out as being more unequal at the bottom of the income distribution than other rich nations at any time during the twentieth century, if in-kind transfers were included in the measure of economic well-being.

On the other hand, because the US has been a laggard in the provision of cash benefits throughout its history, even though the US became notably more unequal in market income in the last quarter of the twentieth century, we hypothesize that relative poverty has been higher in the US throughout most of the twentieth century. This is because cash benefits raise the disposable income of those at the bottom of the income distribution, bringing them closer to the average. For two reasons, however, we also suspect the differences in the first part of the twentieth century were much smaller than in the last half of the twentieth century. First, cash welfare state transfers were much smaller in the first half of the century. Second, the distribution of market income was not notably more unequal in the US than in other rich nations until the 1970s.

Human capital: education and health

As discussed in Chapter 4, the single best indicator of educational attainment is probably achievement test scores. Unfortunately, good comparative data on achievement test scores in rich nations does not extend back before the 1970s, so it is not possible at this time to say whether the current US lag in this measure is new or old. The share of the population that has completed secondary and tertiary education is another measure of educational attainment, but population data on this outcome across countries unfortunately also extends back only to 1970. Still based on enrollment data, we can infer that US high school and college completion rates were much higher than those of the other rich nations throughout most of the twentieth century. Thus, we conclude that not only was the US a programmatic leader in education, but it also had a more educated populace throughout most of the nineteenth and twentieth centuries. Yet, during the last quarter of the twentieth century, the other rich nations substantially closed or eliminated the attainment gap and US students fell behind on early education enrollment and on adolescent achievement tests.

As described in Chapter 4, on the best single indicators of health early and late in life—infant mortality and life expectancy at age 60—the US has worse outcomes than most other rich nations. Figure 5.10 depicts long-term trends in infant mortality rates in 14 nations. (Except for larger improvements in all rich countries in recent years, the trends for life expectancy tell the same story.) While the US had the highest rate in 2000, what is most striking about Figure 5.10 is the huge drop in mortality rates during the twentieth century in all currently rich nations. Rates dropped from between 100 and 220 infant deaths per thousand at the beginning of the century to less than 10 per thousand at the end.

117

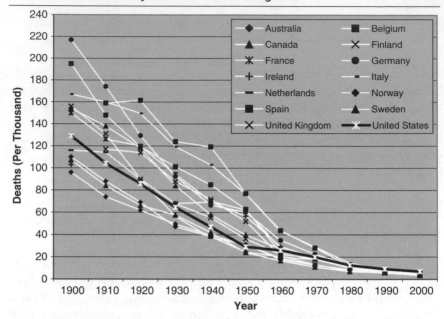

Figure 5.10: Infant mortality, 1900–2000

Sources: Preston and Haines (1991); Corsini and Viazzo (1997); Haines and Steckel (2000); Australian Bureau of Statistics; OECD Source.

Differences across nations were also much bigger at the beginning of the century than at the end. Finally, leaders and laggards changed over time. At the beginning of the century, Germany had the highest infant mortality rate and Norway the lowest, and the US was in the middle of the pack. The US remained in the middle until close to the end of the century. Most important, in the big picture, differences across rich nations were pretty small.

Opportunity

Intergenerational mobility rates in the US, as we saw in the last chapter, are no higher and may even be lower than mobility rates in other rich nations. Most Americans, who have been taught from childhood that the US is "the land of opportunity," will be surprised by this finding. Is American "opportunity," then, simply a myth? As anyone familiar with US history knows, for most of that history opportunity was surely a myth for blacks, one-tenth of the American population. Are blacks an exception? Or is the belief in opportunity more generally a myth? Five facts suggest that American opportunity is not a myth. After reviewing these facts, we return to the issue of opportunity for black and other minority-group Americans.

First, for nearly 200 years, renowned international scholars have viewed America as a nation offering great opportunity. *Democracy in America,* written by Alexis de Toqueville in 1835, first established the reputation of the US as the land of opportunity.[18] Later, in assessing the possibilities for socialism in the US, Karl Marx and Friedrich Engels attributed the relative weakness of unions and working-class parties in the US to the greater opportunities available to the common man.[19] The most comprehensive and best study of the United States since Toqueville's, *An American Dilemma: The Negro Problem and Modern Democracy,* was written by the Nobel Prize-winning Swedish economist Gunnar Myrdal, and published in 1944 in the midst of World War II. It too found the US the land of opportunity, even though it examined the nation through the lens of its most abused and disadvantaged group—its formerly enslaved black population.

Second, these qualitative assessments are supported by several recent quantitative studies. Alberto Alesina and Edward Glazer review the evidence and conclude grudgingly, and understating the difference, that the US had "somewhat" more mobility than European nations.[20] Joseph Ferrie (2005), who has done the best original research on historical cross-national differences in mobility rates to date, finds that, compared with both France and the UK, the US had substantially greater mobility in the mid-nineteenth century, but that increases in mobility in the UK and France in the late nineteenth century closed part of the gap, while decreases in mobility in the US at the end of the twentieth century closed the rest.

Third, intergenerational mobility is not the only indicator of opportunity. In the US, as of 1958, a member of the upper occupational class was five times more likely than a member of the lower occupational class to attend a university. In the UK, the relative chance was 8 to 1; in Sweden, 26 to 1; and in Germany, 61 to 1.[21] This indicator suggests that greater access to secondary and university education in the US increased equality of opportunity.

Fourth, for more than 200 years, millions of people from all the currently rich nations and from Eastern Europe found America the land of opportunity, as indicated by high rates of immigration. Today, eight times more people of Irish extraction live in the US than in Ireland. Likewise, nearly as many Norwegians, almost half as many Germans and Swedes, and about a quarter as many Italians and Poles, live in the US as in their native lands.[22]

Fifth, millions upon millions of the children, grandchildren, and great-grandchildren of American immigrants can now testify from their own family histories that they are the proud upwardly mobile products of the land of opportunity. Research confirms these stories of mobility. Descendants of the Irish, Italian, Jewish, and Chinese immigrants who were once the poorest of Americans are now on average among the wealthiest (Sowell, 1978, 1983; Greeley, 1976, 1988; Lieberson and Waters, 1988). None of the other rich countries, with the possible exception of Canada, has experienced this kind of immigration and upward mobility among descendants of immigrants. To ignore this uniquely American record of immigrant mobility is a fatal omission when one is seeking to ascertain whether the US has an exceptional history of equal opportunity.

An equally fatal omission would be to ignore the uniquely American record of racial oppression.[23] Blacks came to America not as immigrants seeking new opportunities, but as slaves. When slavery was effectively abolished with the end of the American Civil War, in 1865, the ex-slaves were at the bottom of the US income distribution, and there they remain today.

Proposals by radical Republicans to give the freed slaves 40 acres and a mule were rejected by the US Congress. Instead, soon after Reconstruction (the military occupation of the South) ended in 1876, the vote and civil rights more generally were taken away from blacks in every Southern state. Though all the former slave states finally adopted free universal public education after the Civil War, they also established separate schools for blacks, a so-called separate but equal system that the Supreme Court approved in 1896 in the *Plessy* v. *Ferguson* case, even though spending on the black schools was widely known to be nowhere near equal to spending on white schools. More generally, blacks were segregated, subjected routinely to discrimination, and terrorized. Between 1882 and 1955, more than 3,000 blacks were lynched.[24] Slowly but surely, blacks moved from the farms to cities, and from the South to the North, to seek better opportunities. Like other migrants, they found that moving improved their lot. But, wherever they went in large numbers, whether to cities in the South or the North, the overwhelming majority of blacks were invariably confined to the bottom rungs of the economic ladder. There were exceptions, of course, such as Joe Louis, the black heavyweight boxing champion of the world, who in 1938 knocked out Max Schmeling, the champion from Nazi Germany. That Louis was black was a source of great pride not only to black, but also to white Americans. His victory helped set the US apart from the racist ideology espoused by Hitler and the Nazi regime. Unlike today, however, the number of exceptions was very small.

Writing in 1944, Myrdal begins the *American Dilemma* as follows:

There is a "Negro problem" in the United States and most Americans are aware of it, although it assumes varying forms and intensity in different regions of the country and among diverse groups of the American people. Americans have to react to it, politically as citizens and, where there are Negroes present in the community, privately as neighbors.

To the great majority of white Americans the Negro problem has distinctly negative connotations. It suggests something difficult to settle and equally difficult to leave alone. It is embarrassing. It makes for moral uneasiness. The very presence of the Negro in America; his fate in this country through slavery, Civil War and Reconstruction; his recent career and his present status; his accommodation; his protest and his aspiration; in fact his entire biological, historical and social existence as a participant American represent to the ordinary white man in the North as well as in the South an anomaly in the very structure of American society. To many, this takes on the proportion of a menace—biological, economic, social, cultural, and, at times, political. This anxiety may be mingled with a feeling of individual and collective guilt. A few see the problem as a challenge to statesmanship. To all it is a trouble.

The American dilemma to which Myrdal refers in his title is how to reconcile the noble ideals expressed in the Declaration of Independence with the ignoble practice of legislated and socially enforced segregation and discrimination against Negroes. Myrdal correctly predicted that the US would in the not-too-distant future resolve this dilemma through a successful political appeal to the ideals of the American Creed. The revolution in civil rights and its consequences for American politics are described in more detail in Chapter 7. Here, we simply note that the civil rights revolution, like the abolition of slavery, was a huge and long-overdue step forward for democracy and equal opportunity in the US. Jackie Robinson did not break the color bar in baseball until 1947. Not until 1954 did the Supreme Court find that "separate but equal" had in practice proved to be inherently unequal, reverse *Plessy* v. *Ferguson*, and declare legal segregation of schools to be unconstitutional. Not until 1965, in response to the civil rights movement led by the Reverend Martin Luther King Jr, was President Lyndon Baines Johnson able to persuade the US Congress to enact the Voting Rights Act, restoring the right to vote to the majority of the black population that still lived in the South.

Today, though legal discrimination has been eliminated and the harsh de facto discrimination endured by blacks has declined, though the gap in education and income between blacks and whites has narrowed throughout most of the twentieth century, though some blacks now even benefit from affirmative action, and though a majority of the country voted to elect Barak Obama as president, discrimination against blacks is still severe. Young black men are being imprisoned to an unprecedented extent, and progress in narrowing the black–white income gap appears to have stalled.[25]

One of the best and most recent studies documenting contemporary discrimination against the black population was conducted by Devah Pager, a sociologist at Princeton University, who designed an experiment to measure the existence and severity of discrimination against men with criminal records and against black men in the labor market today (2003). She randomly assigned matched pairs of black and white young men to apply for jobs that were advertised as requiring no more than a high school education. White and black applicants had identical résumés. Half in each group had criminal records and half did not. The criminal records, like the résumés, were identical for blacks and whites. The share of applicants called back for whites with no criminal record was 34 percent. The share of whites with a criminal record called back was 17 percent. The share of blacks without a criminal record was 14 percent. In other words, the penalty for being black was a bit bigger than the penalty for having a criminal record.

Since the 1970s, young black men in the US have experienced an epidemic of crime and imprisonment. The US prison population exploded from 300,000 in 1972 to 2.2 million in 2005, or from 143 for every 100,000 Americans to 738 for every 100,000 (Harrison and Beck, 2006). That imprisonment rate, the highest in the world (Hartney, 2006), is nearly 5.5 times higher than the average among the European Union. And the men (and women) imprisoned are disproportionately black. Though blacks are only a bit more than one-tenth of the total US population, they are about 40 percent of the incarcerated population. In 1995, nearly one in three black males aged 20–29 was under some form of supervision by the criminal justice-system, in prison or jail, or on probation or parole. "A black boy born in 1991 stood a 29 percent chance of being imprisoned at some point in his life, compared to a 16 percent chance for a Hispanic boy, and a 4 percent chance for a white boy" (Mauer, 1999). More than half of unwed black fathers living in large cities with children age five have been imprisoned (Lewis, Garfinkel, and Gao, 2007). While black men are statistically more likely to commit crimes, the criminal justice system also systematically treats blacks more harshly than whites (Fagan and Davies, 2003; Weich and Angulo, 2000). For example, in the juvenile justice system, youth of color are more likely than white youth to rely on the indigent defense system, and youth represented by that system are more likely to be convicted (Hoytt, Schiraldi, Smith, and Zeidenberg, 2001). In the adult court, for several decades the penalties for crack cocaine, the form of cocaine most used by blacks, were dramatically more severe than penalties for pure cocaine, the form most used by whites. Only recently did a Supreme Court decision rectify this longstanding imbalance, which had led to higher incarceration rates and longer sentences for black drug users.

Finally, black progress slowed during the final two decades of the twentieth century (Derek Neal, 2006). There is also some evidence that the intergenerational progress of recent immigrants of Hispanic origin has not kept pace with that of other twentieth-century immigrant groups (Borjas, 2006).

In short, throughout most of its history, the US was both leader and laggard in providing equality of opportunity, but is now simply a laggard.

Summary

As our brief factual history has shown, the share of national income devoted to welfare state transfers grew substantially throughout the twentieth century in all currently rich nations from a very low base. Leadership in welfare state provision among these nations has varied by domain and has changed over time. Although the US has been a consistent laggard in providing poor relief and social insurance, throughout most of the nineteenth and twentieth centuries, it was a leader in providing mass education. In the final quarter of the twentieth century, most other rich nations narrowed the gap in education. Some moved ahead of the US in secondary and higher education, and nearly all surged ahead in early childhood education.

Greater inequality in income is clearly a recent phenomenon and much greater relative poverty is very likely also a relatively recent phenomenon. Through the first three-quarters of the twentieth century, infant mortality rates in all rich nations, including the US, declined sharply. The US becomes noticeably worse only at the end of the century, when rates declined a little more slowly in the US than in other rich nations. Until recently, opportunity for upward mobility for citizens who were not black was also greater in the US than in most European nations. By the mid-twentieth century, at least some other rich nations, such as the UK and France, had caught up to the US. At the century's end, intergenerational mobility was lower in the US. The next two chapters offer an explanation of these facts.

Notes

1. For assembling the facts on both social welfare spending and mass education, we are greatly indebted to Peter Lindert's scholarship in his recent book, *Growing Public* (2004). At the same time, we caution the reader that, as described in notes and appendices, we not only put together data from different parts of his book but in some cases we also extrapolate from his data. While we are confident of our leaps, scholars should look closely at them, and Lindert should not be held responsible for any errors we may have made.
2. See Lindert (2004) for a discussion of the historical differences. More contemporary debates are also discussed in Lindert and in section 2.
3. Data for 1980–2000 come from "Lindert, P.H. (2004); OECD_1950–2001_annual," found at <http://www.econ.ucdavis.edu/faculty/fzlinder/OECD_1950–2001_annual1.xls> (Source 1).

   Data for 1975–9 come from "Lindert, P.H. (2004); OECD_1975–1996_annual series," found at: <http://www.econ.ucdavis.edu/faculty/fzlinder/ Lindert percent 20data percent 20CUP percent 20book/OECD_1975–1996_annual1.xls>. The data from this second source (2) overlap with data from Source 1 from 1980–1. We assume that the most recent data set is more accurate in the years of overlap, so we use Source 1. We also calculate a ratio of Source 1 to Source 2 in the years of overlap and multiply that ratio by Source 2 data to make them consistent with Source 1.

   For example, Source 1 states that US welfare spending was 0.73 percent of GDP in 1981, while Source 2 states that welfare spending was 0.87 percent of GDP. The ratio of these two numbers is 0.84. We construct a similar ratio for 1980, where the years overlap again. We average that ratio, 0.82, with the 1981 ratio, for an average ratio of 0.83. This number is then multiplied by Source 2 data from 1975–9 to create the best estimate for those years.

   Data for 1960–74 come from "Lindert, P.H. (1993) OECD_1960–1981_ annual series." This data set can be found at: <http://www.econ.ucdavis.edu/ faculty/ fzlinder/ Lindert percent 20data percent 20CUP percent 20book/ OECD19601981annual.xls>. These data, Source 3, overlap with Source 1 data from 1980–1. Again, assuming the latest data set is more accurate in the years of overlap, we calculate two ratios between Source 1 and Source 3 in 1980 and 1981, average them, and adjust the data in Source 3 with the average ratio to make them consistent with Source 1.

   Data for 1880–1930 come from "Lindert, P.H. (1992) Benchmark_data_1880–1930," located at: <http://www.econ.ucdavis.edu/faculty/fzlinder/ Lindert percent 20data percent 20CUP percent 20book/Benchmark_data_1880–1930.xls>.

   Data for 1780–1880 for all countries except the US comes from "Lindert, P.H. (1998). Poor relief before the welfare state: Britain versus the continent, 1780–1880. *European Review of Economic History*, 2, 101–140."

Data for 1800–70 for the US come from "Lindert, P.H. (2004) *Growing Public*, Fig. 3.4, p. 59." This source provides US data for 1850–70 and only Philadelphia data for 1800–40. An 1850 ratio of US to Philadelphia expenditures is calculated and applied to the 1800–40 data and is used as an estimate for the US as a whole.

4. Of course, as we have noted repeatedly, saying the US lacks a universal health insurance program does not mean that most Americans lack health insurance. As we have seen, the opposite is true. The overwhelming majority of Americans have health insurance. Similarly, the partially refundable income tax credit for children in the US tax code would be economically equivalent to a universal child allowance if it were made fully refundable. While some large employers and a few states provide some benefits, Americans are much further away from having universal sickness insurance and paid family leave.

5. In a few instances, enrollments were available for only the sum of public plus private enrollments. By the end of the century, private enrollments were a small portion of the total in all rich nations.

6. It would be preferable to have the percentage of children of secondary school age—say 14–18—who were enrolled in secondary schools, but these data are not available. Unless there were drastic changes in cohort sizes, however, using the 5–14 year old group will accurately reflect differences in secondary enrollments across countries over time.

7. To measure educational outcomes, we use the share of the population that has completed secondary and tertiary education—roughly the equivalent of US high school and college degrees—and is enrolled in pre-school education programs. We use OECD data that is designed to make completion rates comparable in terms of attainment across nations.

8. Fortunately, Lindert has again compiled the data, which we draw from "The Rise of Social Spending, 1880–1930," in Lindert, P. (2004), *Growing Public: Social Spending and Economic Growth since the Eighteenth Century*, Volume 2. Appendix C, Table C.3 Public expenditures, all levels of education, 1850–1910.

9. Excluding university education does not change the big picture. It reduces spending a bit in all countries.

10. Alesina and Glaesar (2004: 20), relying on Tanzi, Schuknecht (2000) paint a very different picture, showing the US seriously lagging behind continental Europe since 1870. The biggest difference is that they omit education. It is also not clear how they handled missing data, since the data for many components of spending in many countries do not extend back to 1900, let alone to 1870.

11. The OECD database provides education spending by all levels of government on all levels of education, as well as government spending not allocated by education level, in local national currency. These numbers were then converted to a function of GDP based on OECD GDP measures, also reported in local national currency. But, the education data are somewhat inconsistent for different periods. From 1960–81, education data are taken from *OECD, Social Expenditure 1960–1990* (as are the other domains' spending) and include spend-

ing on pre-primary, primary, secondary, and tertiary education, as well as spending on education affairs and subsidiary services to education (OECD 1985: 75). Later data on education are based on two primary sources, all computed from OECD records. Data between 1985 and 1991 are based on the National Center for Education Statistics' "International Education Indicators," and include spending on direct expenditures for primary, secondary, and higher education, but exclude indirect expenditures such as student loans or subsidies to families.

Data between 1992 and 2001 are based on the authors' computations from the OECD statistical database.

12. Data on tax expenditures and employer provided pensions are available for 2001 but not for earlier years and are therefore omitted for all years. This has the effect of making expenditures as a percent of GDP in 2001 a bit smaller than the percentages reported in Chapter 3. Employer-provided health insurance in the US is included in all years.

13. Andrew Leigh (2006) finds that the pre-tax income shares estimates compiled by Emmanual Saez and Thomas Picketty and others from tax data, are highly correlated with and track trends in post-tax, post-transfer measures of inequality both within and across countries in the LIS data. Leigh also shows this measure of income inequality is highly correlated with Gini coefficients.

14. Inequality in the US and all the other currently rich nations increased as the nation industrialized and shifted from farming to manufacturing. But, in all countries, the rise in inequality in the nineteenth century was followed by a decline in inequality in the twentieth century. The rise and fall in inequality has been referred to as the Kuznet's curve, after the Nobel Prize-winning economist Simon Kuznets, who first described this phenomenon.

15. Smeeding (2005) shows that the more inclusive the income concept, the greater the change. Counting capital incomes and the increasingly lucrative pay of top executives in the United States, coupled with regressive income tax policy that has reduced taxes on capital incomes, has led to a mushrooming of inequality.

16. The calculation is made for the last year where there is comparable data in the chart. As compared to Canada, in the last year with comparable data, the top 1 percent share in the US is 1.8 times higher.

17. The pattern for relative poverty rates in 1974 looks similar to that for 2000. The US at 16 percent stands out as having the highest poverty rate, though Canada at 14 percent is a very close second. In the UK, only 9 percent are poor and in Sweden and Germany only 7 percent are poor. In 1965, the poverty rate was much higher in Sweden—11 percent—and much lower in the UK—6 percent.

18. Unfortunately, De Toqueville because of an agreement with M. Gustave De Beaumont, his good friend and collaborator in the study of America, does not deal with slavery, race, or American Indians, topics covered by Beaumont's book, *Marie, or Slavery in America*. The two friends were both French civil

servants who made the trip to the US ostensibly to investigate prisons, but intending all along to grapple with the great question that European aristocrats had of America—how has this democracy so far failed to descend into the rule of the mob?

19. For a discussion of their views and a broader discussion of why socialism failed in the US, see Lipset (1977).

20. Alesina and Glaeser (2004) go on to say, "but the differences are not overwhelming, especially given the problems with the data. One would hardly expect an 8 percent gap in upward mobility rates between the US and Germany to produce such massive differences in beliefs about the determinants of income and such massive differences in redistribution" (p. 67). While Alesina and Glaeser dismiss these differences as being too small to matter, their reporting is misleading and their logic is faulty. The gap which they label as "only 8 percent" is more accurately described as an 8 percentage point gap—with the US at 24 percent and Germany at 16 percent. In other words, the US measure is 150 percent not 8 percent higher than the German rate. The reason they give for rejecting the 8 percentage point difference—the poor quality of the data—is simply wrong. Poor-quality data understates rather than overstates differences. Thus, the fact that virtually all studies indicate the US had more mobility, even though the data is poor, suggests that the real differences are most likely even bigger than the data is detecting.

21. Heidemheimer and Layson (1982: 149).

22. OECD (2007c) provides country populations and the US Census Bureau (2004) provides ancestry populations.

23. The text focuses on blacks and mentions Hispanics, but ignores Asians entirely, not because the latter have not suffered from discrimination and oppression, although it was less systematic and long lasting, but because they are less central to the story of the American welfare state. The internment of the Japanese-Americans during World War II, and the Civil Liberties Act of 1988 apologizing and paying indemnities to those unjustly interred, illustrate a broader theme. Like slavery and Emancipation, restriction of voting rights and the 1965 Voting Rights Bill, the internment and the apology reflect the worst and best of the USA.

24. The Tuskegee Institute Lynch Report last issued in 1959 counted as lynching all illegal murders that were racially motivated and involved at least three or more perpetrators. The Institute documented 3,437 black lynchings as well as 1,293 lynchings of "whites" who appear to have been predominantly Mexicans, Native Americans, and Chinese.

25. For the classic study of blacks in the US, see Gunnar Myrdal's *An American Dilemma* (1944). For evidence of long-term narrowing of the education and wage gap between blacks and whites, see Smith and Welch (1989), and Fischer and Hout (2006). For a discussion of affirmative action in historical context, see Katznelson (2005).

6

Explaining American Exceptionalism: Laggard in Public Relief and Social Insurance—Leader in Education

In this chapter we explore why the US has been a consistent laggard in providing poor relief and social insurance and, until the last quarter of the twentieth century, a consistent leader in providing mass education. One large group of scholars of the welfare state has sought to explain why the US lagged in developing social insurance.[1] Another group has sought to explain why the US led in providing mass education.[2] We build on these mostly separate literatures and seek to explain both—not just why the US lagged in making available cash assistance and social insurance, but also why it led in providing education. If the lead and the lag are related, to tell the story of one without the other is to omit more than half the story.[3]

We refer to the combination of the lead in education and lag in poor relief and social insurance as American exceptionalism. In the first part of this chapter, we address the American lead in education and lag in poor relief, and argue that both stem from a combination of several unique aspects of the nation's history, institutions, culture, and politics—Protestantism combined with religiosity, capitalism unencumbered by a feudal past, early democratization and a revolutionary heritage, twin traditions of immigration and migration to a frontier, and, finally, racial, ethnic, national, and religious diversity.

Protestantism privileges education and stigmatizes poor relief. And because Americans have been, from their beginnings, a deeply religious people, their Protestant heritage has been more influential in shaping their political institutions than it has been in other countries. Similarly, the nation's tradition of capitalism has led it to take a positive view of education and a negative view of poor relief. The absence of a feudal legacy (except in some respects in the South) promoted a belief in social mobility and spared the nation of the power of landed aristocrats who viewed mass education as a threat to social order. The US commitment to self-government, evident from its colonial origins, together with its Revolutionary War for Independence, fostered democracy and education. Democracy presupposes an educated citizenry and also arms the lower classes with the ballot. Leadership in democratization and education also promoted equality of opportunity and result. All increased political support for education and probably undermined support for public relief. Similarly, both the early frontier experience and the successive waves of immigration promoted social mobility and strengthened the value of self-reliance, again privileging education and stigmatizing cash relief. Finally, America's radically diverse population has depressed poor relief. But, though the institution of slavery hampered the development of public education in the South, the religious, ethnic, and national diversity of the North tended to promote it.

The early and continuing successes of capitalism, democracy, and public education in the United States weakened the appeal of socialism for white Americans and, in combination with the phenomenal diversity of the population, prevented the emergence of a strong labor movement and a majority socialist party. In the second part of this chapter, we argue that in most currently rich nations, the threat of socialism spawned social insurance, whose spread was hastened by the electoral success of left-wing, mostly socialist, parties. The relative weakness of the political left in the US throughout the twentieth century accounts for the American lag in social insurance.

America's lead in education and lag in cash relief are of long standing, dating back to the beginning of the nation's history. That beginning is where the explanation of American exceptionalism is likely to be found.

I. The lead in education and lag in public relief

Protestantism without a state Church and with religiosity

The US was settled initially by Protestants, many of whom, like the Pilgrims and Quakers, were small sects whose religious dissent was central to their identity. Though some Catholics, Jews, and Muslims immigrated to the US quite early in its history and the US reputation for religious tolerance predates the American Revolution, the US was overwhelmingly

Protestant until the mass immigration of the Irish following the potato famine of the mid-nineteenth century. At the beginning of the twentieth century, about 80 percent of the population was still Protestant. Even today, 60 percent of the US population is Protestant.

Literacy was an essential skill for Protestants because it enabled them to read their own Bibles. As Figures 5.3, 5.4, and 5.5 in the previous chapter made clear, until the end of the twentieth century, all the countries that have led in providing public education have been Protestant or Protestant-dominated (the same holds true for literacy, though the data on literacy is not displayed (Cipolla, 1969)). The Catholic nations—France, Italy, Ireland, and Spain—have been consistent laggards. Prussia, the predominantly Lutheran Protestant region of Germany, was the earliest leader in literacy along with Lutheran Norway. By the beginning of the twentieth century, the US had taken the lead. In view of the historic link between Protestant-ism and education, Catholic Ireland's emergence as a leader in providing college education at the end of the twentieth century is remarkable.

Protestantism also discouraged support for cash relief and redistribu-tion. As the familiar term "Protestant work ethic" suggests, Protestants have traditionally regarded hard work as a moral virtue and poverty as linked with a moral failing. Some Protestant sects took the view that the poor were able to save themselves with a renewed commitment to right behavior and hard work. Others, like the Calvinists, saw wealth and pov-erty as outward signs of a person's preordained destination, either heaven or hell. For all, regardless of which perspective they favored, the experi-ence of being so poor as to have to request public assistance would have been humiliating evidence of personal moral failure.

By itself, however, the dominance of Protestantism cannot explain US exceptionalism. Protestantism, after all, is common to many rich nations, including those in Scandinavia that led the way in providing social insur-ance. What sets the US apart from all other currently rich nations is the absence of an established state Church and the singular importance of religion in the nation's life. The lack of an established Church strength-ened religion in two ways. First, it forced churches to compete for mem-bers. Second, state churches everywhere have long been associated with the status quo. As a consequence, as the labor movement and socialist parties gained strength in other nations during the twentieth century, many people left state churches on political grounds. In the US, although many religious leaders have been aligned with parties in power (as the religious right currently undergirds the Republican Party), leading reli-gious figures and churches in the US have also been aligned with such democracy-promoting causes (Myrdal, 1944) as extending the franchise and abolishing slavery. More recently, the Reverend Martin Luther King Jr. led the civil rights movement.

De Toqueville and Myrdal were both struck by the importance of religion in the nation's past, and modern scientific survey research confirms the continuing and unique centrality of religion in American life. Close to 80 percent of Americans, but only 45 percent of Europeans, view religion as important in their lives.[4] Nearly 30 percent of American adults attend church at least once a week, which is slightly more than twice the average in other rich nations.[5] In short, although Protestantism is not unique to the US among rich nations, the importance of religion is. As a result, Protestantism has been and continues to be a stronger force in the US than in other rich countries.

A critic might object to our claim that Protestantism stigmatizes relief. As Peter Lindert shows in *Growing Public*, the early leaders in poor relief were England and the Netherlands, the post-war leaders in transfers to the poor are again somewhat Protestant, and, on average in European history, Protestant countries relative to Catholic countries used government to transfer more, both for education and for poor relief. These historical facts are not inconsistent with our claim that Protestantism as a belief system stigmatizes relief. We do not argue that Protestantism by itself is determinative. Rather, our argument is that one cultural/historical element that sets the US apart is Protestantism combined with religiosity. Other factors besides religion also affect the provision of cash assistance. England and the Netherlands were early leaders in cash assistance because they were the first countries to industrialize.

Capitalism and the absence of feudalism

Capitalism and education, as discussed in Chapter 2, are complementary. Capitalists and employer groups in the US have traditionally been strong supporters of public education. But capitalism was common to all currently rich nations by the end of the nineteenth century, when social insurance programs began to emerge. Thus, like Protestantism, capitalism by itself cannot explain US exceptionalism. But, unlike most of the other currently rich nations, the US never experienced feudalism. Neither, of course, did Australia and Canada, both of whom (especially Canada), as we have seen, at times resemble the US in being leaders in education and laggards in cash relief.

During the long feudal histories of the currently rich European nations, the landed aristocracy generally opposed mass education as a threat to social order. The plantation slave-owning elite in the US South did the same. Three contemporary observations make the point. A landed conservative in German Silesia commented in 1800:

"Our forefathers never had occasion to quarrel with their illiterate serfs: an illiteracy which did not prevent fields from being cultivated at least as well as they are today, and manners being unquestionably purer... And [is it not true that] the lords experience far more difficulty in maintaining authority over their serfs than they did when the latter were still illiterate?... The most uncouth and ignorant peasant will invariably make the best soldier. He can be treated as if he were a machine, and when he is so treated one can rely on him absolutely." (Lindert, 2004)

A Tory member of the British House of Commons, in 1807, voiced opposition to a proposal to provide publicly financed elementary schools:

"Giving education to the labouring classes of the poor... would... be prejudicial to their morals and happiness; it would teach them to despise their lot in life, instead of making them good servants in agriculture, and other laborious employment to which their rank in society had destined them; instead of teaching them subordination, it would render them factious and refractory...; it would enable them to read seditious pamphlets, vicious books, and publications against Christianity; it would render them insolent to their superiors." (Lindert, 2004)

And William Harper, a pro-slavery lawyer from South Carolina, saw things this way:

"The Creator did not intend that every individual human being should be highly cultivated... It is better that a part should be fully and highly cultivated and the rest utterly ignorant." (Kaestle, 1983)

In short, if you educate the common people, "how are you going to keep them down on the farm?" The absence of a feudal past and a landlord class tilts politics in the direction of education.

Feudalism also left a legacy of class, hierarchy, and social distinctions in the European nations (and Japan) that the US, outside the South, was spared. The feudal legacy was fertile ground for a belief that status is inherited and upward mobility impossible. And, if status is inherited, education is worth less, and cash redistributions more, to beneficiaries. The aristocratic landlord class in the UK favored poor relief not only out of a sense of *noblesse oblige*, but also because it provided a way to keep a low-wage labor force available for seasonal farm work. The early nineteenth-century spike in the UK provision of poor relief that was shown in Figure 5.1 is partly attributable to fear generated by the French Revolution, but it was landlords' domination of parliament that led to enactment of the famous Speenhamland system of outdoor cash relief for able-bodied poor. Not long after the British business classes got the vote and took dominance away from the landed aristocrats, they passed the Welfare Reform of 1834, severely restricting the Poor Law, abolishing outdoor relief for the able-bodied poor, and requiring the poor to enter the Workhouse as a test of need.

Unlike landlords, capitalists have generally supported public education. Throughout American history, employers have played leading roles in promoting mass public education (Katz, 1971, 1987; Bowles and Gintis, 1976; Kaestle, 1983). Capitalists supported education in the belief that educated workers are more productive and adaptive, and that education promotes rather than undermines social order. Karl Kaestle, in his book *Pillars of the Republic,* puts it simply and most generally, "Capitalism is a world of literacy and numeracy."

Similarly, business groups were supportive when the US took the lead in secondary education during the early twentieth century (Bowles and Gintis, 1976; Goldin, 1998). Today, the Committee for Economic Development (2002), which represents big corporations, has endorsed universal public pre-school.

Democracy, the American Revolution, and the American Creed

Democracy in America far pre-dates the American Revolution. In fact, it is no exaggeration to say that democracy spawned the Revolution. The Virginia Company, which promoted the first US settlement at Jamestown in 1618, introduced English common law, due process, private property, and a representative assembly with the power, subject to Company veto, to pass local laws. As Captain John Smith, said, "No man will go from hence to have lesse freedome there than here." Plymouth Colony too had strong democratic elements from its inception in 1620, as embodied in the Mayflower Compact, which the men on board signed in assent to obey laws that they themselves enacted.[6] The town hall meetings that quickly grew up in Massachusetts and other New England colonies were democratic assemblies of town members. And, long before the War of Independence, all the colonies had elected assemblies in addition to the Crown's appointed representative.

Benjamin Franklin, printer, writer, publisher, businessman, scientist, civil servant, and revolutionary leader—the best-known and probably most influential American of his time—was proud to be a British subject as well as an American colonist (Brands, 2000; Isaacson, 2003). He tried his best to work out acceptable compromises between the colonists and the Crown. "No taxation without representation" seemed like a reasonable demand to Franklin and his compatriots. From the colonists' point of view, as educated British subjects accustomed to governing themselves, their cause was simply an extension of the British tradition of rule by law and the more recent supremacy in lawmaking of a representative body—parliament.

But, in terms of democracy, the US took a giant leap ahead of the British as a consequence of the War of Independence and the American Revolution. On July 4, 1776, the American Declaration of Independence was signed by all members of the Continental Congress. The most famous and important words in the document appear in the second paragraph:

We hold these truths to be self-evident, that all men are created equal, that they are endowed by their Creator with certain unalienable Rights, that among these are Life, Liberty, and the pursuit of Happiness. That to secure these Rights, Governments are instituted among Men, deriving their just powers from the consent of the governed.

These two sentences embody the core of what Gunnar Myrdal has called "the American Creed." In 1776, and even today, these are radical words.

Myrdal's description in 1944 of the American Creed and its role in American history up to that point remains unsurpassed as description and prophecy.

These ideals of the essential dignity of the human being, of the fundamental equality of all men, and of certain inalienable rights to freedom, justice, and a fair opportunity represent to the American people the essential meaning of the nation's early struggle for independence. In the clarity and intellectual boldness of the Enlightenment period these tenets were written into the Declaration of Independence, the Preamble of the Constitution, the Bill of Rights, and into the constitutions of several states. The ideals of the American Creed have thus become the highest law of the land. The Supreme Court pays its reverence to these general principles when it declares what is constitutional and what is not. They have been elaborated upon by all national leaders, thinkers, and statesmen. America has had, throughout its history, a continuous discussion of the principles and implications of democracy, a discussion which, in every epoch, measured by any standard, remained high, not only quantitatively but also qualitatively. The flow of learned treatises and popular tracts on the subject has not ebbed, nor is it likely to do so. In all wars, including the present one, the American Creed has been the ideological foundation of national morale.

The American Creed is important because it both unites the American people and makes the struggle for democracy the central theme of American history. Unlike other nations, Americans do not share a single nationality or religion. Instead, the American Creed serves as a shared, secular religion. As Myrdal notes, the Creed is propounded by American public schools, in which all schoolchildren read the famous excerpts from the Declaration of Independence. Like a religion, the Creed specifies a high set of ideals. In practice, people and institutions fall short of those ideals. But, like religion at its best, the American Creed is also a force for moving behavior and practice closer to the ideal. If, "all men are created equal" and governments "derive their just powers from the governed," advocates of extending the franchise asked, how can the vote be limited to those with property, or to men, or to whites? If all men are created equal, asked the abolitionists, how can we have masters and slaves? The early extensions of democracy in America, like extensions of the right to vote, were soon accepted and eventually celebrated, further reinforcing the centrality of democracy and the American Creed. Ending slavery and racial oppression were far more difficult (indeed the latter battle is ongoing), but here too the American Creed played a critical role. Today, Abraham Lincoln is considered by most Americans to be, except for George Washington, the greatest American president. And Martin Luther King Jr. is honored by a national holiday.

Democracy and public schooling developed together in the United States. Indeed, public schooling was one of the earliest manifestations of self-governance. Throughout the colonies, citizens at the local level organized schools that were financed by a mix of local taxes, in-kind contributions, and fees paid by parents. In rural communities, where most of the population lived, one school would serve everyone. The older students helped teach the younger ones. Teacher quality was low and teacher turnover high. As cities grew, so did the number of schools. In many cities, charitable organizations established free schools for the poor.

Democratization promoted mass education both by increasing the upper classes' interest in educating the lower classes and by giving the vote to the middle- and lower-income classes who gained the most from it. Support for education came not just from the employers, but from workers as well (Kaestle, 1983; Katznelson and Weir; 1985; Katz, 1987; Bowles and Gintis, 1976).[7] Working-men's groups in New York and Massachusetts in the 1820s and 1830s were opposed to separate schools for the poor and were strong supporters of the common school movement—publicly funded schools. As the editors of the *Mechanics Free Press* put it, "Give us our rights and we shall not need your charity." They advocated a common school system, "where the children of the rich and the poor shall

135

receive a national education calculated to make republicans and banish aristocrats."[8]

When American elementary public education spread throughout the North before the Civil War, both major parties—Whigs (predecessors of the Republicans) and Democrats—favored expansion of public education (Kaestle, 1983; Ravitch, 2000). The disagreement between the parties was principally about the degree of centralization and professional control of the curriculum. Ironically, given today's politics, it was the Democrats who favored local control. The Whigs, most of whom were to become Republicans, were the centralizers.

Outside the US, working-class parties and leaders also agitated for free public schools. Free public schools were the 10th plank in the famous 1848 Communist Manifesto. But, unlike workers in the US, the lower classes in the European nations did not have the vote. Lindert (2004) presents convincing statistical evidence that among 24 currently rich and a few middle-income nations between 1880 and 1930, when the right to vote was being extended, the degree of democratization accounts for variations across countries and over time in the spread of mass elementary and secondary education.

In the US democratization, the American Creed and public education were intimately linked in another fashion. Franklin, Jefferson, and others were strongly in favor of self-governance, though, steeped as they were in Greek and Roman history, they were also acutely aware that democracy can deteriorate into mob rule. Both Franklin and Jefferson organized schools. As governor of Virginia, Jefferson proposed free schools in the state in 1779. He asked Virginia to adopt a three-tiered system: free local elementary schools, free tuition to secondary regional academies for selected boys, and support at William and Mary College for the 10 best and needy students. In the preamble to the Bill, Jefferson explains his rationale: widespread education is essential to the survival and well-being of the new republic. Without it, citizens will be unable to choose their leaders wisely.[9]

It is clear how the American Creed, with its emphasis on equality of opportunity and self-governance, privileges education. Perhaps less obviously, it also stigmatizes relief. If opportunity is available, the poor must be responsible for their own plight. Modern public opinion polling indicates that Americans even today are much more likely to voice this belief than are Europeans. According to the World Values Survey, only 29 percent of Americans as compared to 60 percent of Europeans (European Union) believe that the poor are trapped in poverty, 30 percent of Americans as compared to 54 percent of Europeans believe that luck determines income, and 60 percent of Americans as opposed to 26 percent of Europeans believe that the poor are lazy. (Alesina and Glaeser, 2004: 184).[10] Although scientific public opinion polling is a twentieth-century phenomenon, there is good evidence that American leaders, beginning with Franklin and continuing through Presidents Roosevelt and Johnson, embraced education and were deeply suspicious of poor relief. Franklin said of the British Poor Law:

The day you passed that Act you took away from before their eyes the greatest of all inducements to industry, frugality and sobriety, by giving them a dependence on somewhat else than a careful accumulation during youth and health for support in age and sickness. . . . I think the best way of doing good to the poor is not making them easy in poverty, but leading or driving them out of poverty.[11]

Even though, as president, Franklin Roosevelt persuaded Congress to provide federal poor relief on an unprecedented scale and enacted three new permanent federal cash relief programs, he too was deeply distrustful of poor relief, likening it once to a narcotic. The distaste for poor relief is also evident in the following excerpt from the report of the 1938 Advisory Council on Social Security, which proposed expanding the recently enacted Old Age Insurance System to provide Survivors' Insurance:

While public assistance is now being provided to a large number of dependent children in this country on a needs-test basis, the arguments for substituting benefits as a matter of right in the case of children are even more convincing than in the case of aged persons. A democratic society has an immeasurable stake in avoiding the growth of a habit of dependence among its youth. The method of survivors' insurance not only sustains the concept that a child is supported through the efforts of the parent but affords a vital sense of security to the family unit.[12]

Similarly, President Lyndon Johnson, who was responsible for the biggest expansion of the American welfare state since Roosevelt, declared when he proposed his War on Poverty that the program was designed to provide a "hand up" not a "hand out."

Immigration and the American frontier

Two closely related aspects of American history—immigration and the frontier experience—reinforced the preference for education over poor relief and social insurance. The United States was from the outset, and continues to be today, a nation of immigrants. By definition, immigrants are mobile.

Whatever their motive for moving—religious freedom, economic opportunity, political freedom—American immigrants were more willing to move than the family, friends, and neighbors who stayed behind. And Americans still move about much more than their European counterparts do. Though geographic mobility is hardly equivalent to social mobility, people who are willing to migrate to improve their conditions are more likely to believe in self-reliance, in taking their fate in their own hands, in the efficacy of taking advantage of opportunities. These views do not preclude valuing cash redistributions to achieve more equal outcomes, but they are more consistent with valuing education as promoting opportunity and meritocracy.

Furthermore, the continuing flow of immigrants encouraged native-born Americans to favor public education as a means of Americanizing the newcomers. Diane Ravitch's (2000) history of the development of public education in New York State vividly illustrates the importance to native-born Protestants of appropriately schooling the newly arrived Irish Catholics.

Similarly, the frontier experience shared by all the earliest Americans also reinforced the values of self-reliance and independence. Surviving on the frontier made such values imperative. The option of moving West provided a safety valve for discontent, the opportunity to start over. The existence of the frontier also meant that land was cheaper and wages higher in the US than in Europe, resulting in greater opportunity to raise one's absolute standard of living, still another form of mobility.[13]

Diversity

Being an immigrant nation also made the US an extremely diverse nation. Indeed, with the possible exception of Canada, no other rich nation is nearly so diverse in terms of religion, nationality, language, and race.[14] Diversity, or what Alesina and Glaesar (2004) term "fractionalization," reduced social solidarity and thereby reduced public support for poor relief and social insurance. It also weakened the development of left-wing institutions—labor unions and a socialist party—thereby indirectly retarding the development of social insurance. The effects of diversity on support for education are less clear-cut.

There is ample historical, statistical, and even experimental evidence that differences in religion, nationality, language, and race reduce social solidarity (Putnam, 2001). Current and past religious, linguistic, national, and race-based wars are perhaps the starkest evidence of diversity's negative effect on social solidarity. American racial and ethnic diversity reduced solidarity and weakened organized labor. (Lipset, 1995; Hill, 1996). We cited and discussed in the previous chapter the experimental evidence of continuing racial discrimination in the US. Several research studies that take into account income and other differences across US states and cities provide statistical evidence that the greater the share of blacks in a population, the lower spending is on welfare benefits and other public goods (Orr, 1976; Alesina, Baqir, and Easterly, 1999). Most directly relevant, in "Fighting Poverty in the US and Europe," Alesina and Glaeser (2004) not only give an historical account of the importance of race prejudice in American history, but also conduct a quantitative analysis of the importance of diversity. They find, after controlling for differences in income, age structure, and other factors, that the more racially diverse a nation is, the lower is its spending on poor relief and social insurance. Indeed, they estimate that greater fractionalization in the US accounts for about half the difference between US and European spending levels. This estimate is huge and almost certainly too large.

American diversity is, as Alesina and Glaeser and others including Quadagno (1994) and Lieberman (1998) argue, clearly an important factor in accounting for the weakness of the American left and the American lag in public relief and social insurance. By itself, racial diversity in the US would have led to the lags. But, as we have argued, the same is true for other unique aspects of American development. US leadership in democracy, in mass education, and, except for its black population, in economic opportunity, also made it more difficult to organize unions and weakened the appeal of socialism. Attributing all of the lag to diversity, therefore, overstates its importance.[15]

How racial diversity affects education has not been systematically studied. As we have seen, racial diversity reduced support for public education in the American South. Other kinds of diversity, on balance, actually may have increased US support for public education. As noted in the previous section on immigration, native-born Protestants in the US were positively disposed to funding public education because they thought it important to imbue immigrant Irish Catholics with American values. In this instance, it appears that diversity had a positive effect on the development of mass public education. More generally, we expect that, under capitalism, the dominant group will prefer to provide education, rather than cash transfers, to the poorer minority groups not only because it is more skill-enhancing, but also because it encourages their adherence to the dominant value system. This preference for education over cash transfers should apply to racial as well as religious and national diversity. But, to date, no evidence supports this hypothesis.

Decentralization: a skeptical note

Self-governance in America began at the local level. The Articles of Confederation, ratified by the 13 former colonies in 1781 following victory in the War of Independence, provided for extremely weak central government. The US Constitution, adopted seven years later, set in place a much stronger central or federal government, but state governments retained a far larger role in governance than in any of the other rich nations, with the possible exception of Switzerland. The Constitution also included multiple checks and balances designed to restrain government action. The three branches of government—executive, legislative, and judicial—are separate. The president is chosen independently of the legislative branch, which itself consists of two independent bodies, the Senate and the House of Representatives. The president appoints Supreme Court justices with the Advice and Consent of the Senate, but, once appointed, the justices serve for life and the Supreme Court is the ultimate arbiter of what is constitutional. Many welfare state scholars, such as Alesina and Glaesar (2004) and Iverson and Soskice (2005), believe that the decentralization of the US political system is an important explanation for why the US provides less cash assistance and social insurance.

While the argument that decentralized government reduces government involvement has intuitive appeal, Peter Lindert, in *Growing Public*, argues convincingly that an often overlooked but critical factor in early educational leadership was decentralization. What the education leaders—Prussia, the US, and Canada—had in common was decentralized responsibility for funding education. By way of contrast, the United Kingdom, with centralized responsibility for financing education, was an education laggard. Decentralization allowed wealthier and more enlightened localities to forge ahead and not be held back by communities less able to afford, and less interested in, education. Within the US, the difference between development of education in the North and South illustrates the importance not only of race, but also of decentralization. Had public education been a national rather than a state responsibility in the US, the existence of a slave-holding rural elite in the Southern states would have slowed its growth considerably.

Lindert also notes in *Growing Public* that the famous 1834 reform of England's Poor Law, which severely restricted relief, involved centralization of responsibility for poor relief. Similarly, as discussed in detail in the following chapter, the severe cutback in US relief was associated with a federal law, the 1996 PRWORA, which involved some decentralization of authority to the states, but, more important in terms of restricting assistance, required all states to adopt work requirements and limit assistance to families to a maximum of five years. More generally, just as decentralization allowed wealthier and more enlightened localities to forge ahead and not be held back by communities less able to afford, and less interested in, education, in principle decentralization could have the same effect on public relief and social insurance.

II. The lag in social insurance: the critical role of the left

The idea of social insurance dates back to radicals in the late eighteenth-century Enlightenment, including Antoine-Nicolas de Condorcet, the French philosophe and author of *A Sketch for the Progress of the Human Mind*, and Tom Paine, the author of the American Revolutionary War pamphlet *Common Sense*.[16] Social insurance programs in Germany, the UK, the US, and other countries, however, were enacted by conservative and liberal, not socialist, parties. Indeed, craft unions of skilled laborers such as printers initially provided insurance to their own members and opposed public programs. Industrial unions of less-skilled workers, however, could not afford to provide such benefits, and eventually, as industrial unions grew in strength, the labor movement and socialist parties became advocates of social insurance programs.[17] That conservative and liberal parties enacted the earliest social insurance programs does not, however, mean that the strength of left-wing institutions did not play a critical role in their enactment.

Fear of the left, or the need to compete with it, helped spur early conservative and liberal expansions of poor relief and social insurance. In this section, we explain the social conditions that gave rise to the socialist left and to the fear of it, and then we discuss the historical circumstances surrounding innovations in social insurance in three countries—Germany, Great Britain, and the United States—by non-socialist parties.

By the second half of the nineteenth century, capitalism and the Industrial Revolution were leading to increasingly rapid changes in all 14 currently rich nations. Individuals and families moved from the country-side to cities and shifted from farm work to industrial work, such as mining, manufacturing, and transportation—building and maintaining ships and ports, canals, railroads, and highways.

Capitalism and industrialization were making these countries rich. At first, the increase in wealth was accompanied by an increase in inequality, as most of the increase in wealth went to only a relatively small group, epitomized by successful entrepreneurs and bankers. Extreme fortunes were accumulated by an even smaller group, some of the most illustrious members of which—Carnegie, Rockefeller, Mellon—were known in popular parlance in the US as robber barons. That many of these so-called robber barons later devoted large portions of their fortunes to public purposes—Carnegie founding and funding public libraries and museums in cities throughout the country, and Rockefeller buying land and donating it to the government—is noteworthy, indeed praiseworthy, now.

But reality for the vast majority of the populations in currently rich nations during the nineteenth century was grim, with the threat of becoming worse. In his 2005 book, *The Escape from Hunger and Premature Death*, Robert Fogel, a Nobel Prize-winning economic historian, reports that, although the real wages of the working class increased over the course of the century, two more basic measures of health and well-being—life expectancy and height—were stagnant or declining. Working conditions in the factories and living accommodations in the cities were often terrible. Between 10 and 20 percent of the populations in the cities were homeless.[18]

The gulf between the great wealth of company owners and the poor conditions of their workers spurred the growth of the labor movement, a vast number of strikes in all nations, and, in some, insurrections and revolutions. In Germany in 1848 and France in 1870, communists led revolts attempting to overthrow the government, but the governments put down the uprisings and the revolutionaries who were not killed or imprisoned hid from the authorities and, in many cases, fled their countries.

At mid-century, no European nation was a full democracy with universal suffrage. Indeed, universal suffrage was one of the principle demands of the newly emerging socialist parties. Over the course of the second half of the nineteenth century, however, the franchise was extended to an increasing share of the male population. Women did not win the right to vote in any country, except New Zealand in 1893, until the twentieth century. As the right to vote spread, socialist parties gained strength. While socialists in the US never achieved much support on the national level, in some states, such as Wisconsin, they played an important role and indirectly helped shape national policy. Within all the other rich nations, however, socialist parties emerged during the second half of the nineteenth century and the early twentieth century as the main opposition party and eventually, beginning in 1930 in Sweden, as sole governing parties. As they gained electoral strength, the socialist parties eventually shed their revolutionary agenda and adopted reformist or evolutionary aims. But the process was gradual, and, though this happy outcome may appear in hindsight to have been inevitable, during the late nineteenth and early twentieth centuries the increasing strength of socialist parties, together with growing industrial strife, appeared threatening to old and new elites and to many common people as well. The Communist Party takeover in Russia in 1917, and unsuccessful insurrections in Austria and Belgium, heightened fears and led to a Red Scare in the US.

Fear of socialism in the late nineteenth century was especially strong in Germany and with good reason. Germany was the birthplace of Karl Marx and the Communist Party, and home to the failed revolution of 1848 and the strongest Socialist Party in the world. Under the leadership of the Conservative Chancellor Bismarck, during the 1880s, Germany initiated the first social security programs—work injury, sickness insurance, and old-age pensions. Isabella Mcarcs in *The Politics of Social Risk,* published in 2004, tells a compelling story of how the combined efforts of large export-oriented employers and civil servants played a critical role in enacting these social insurance programs. Before the enactment of work-injury laws, employees who were injured on the job could be compensated for the injury only if they sued their employer and proved that the employer was at fault. Although workplace injuries were common, employees rarely had the resources to win their cases in court and consequently were often represented by unions. But, eventually, large employers realized that the old fault-based system inevitably pitted employees and their union representatives against employers in a zero-sum game in which one side won and the other lost. Seeking to minimize class conflict, a federation of German employers, led by those who already provided the best benefits, first proposed the enactment of work-injury insurance.[19] Capable Prussian civil servants worked with both employer groups and labor groups to develop a proposal that would be satisfactory to most employers. That capitalists split on the enactment of social insurance and that civil servants played a key role in developing social insurance in

Germany does not mean that the strength of the left was unimportant. In the broader historical picture, Bismarck, like the large employers, promoted social insurance to reduce class conflict and promote social stability. By compensating the working-class victims of the capitalist system, Bismarck was able to steal the thunder of the German Socialist Party. With that party growing fast and still committed to revolution, the accomplishment was no mean feat.

In Great Britain, the Liberal Party defeated the Conservative Party in the election of 1906 and swept into power with the help of 29 Liberal-Labour representatives and a mandate to enact reforms. Winston Churchill, who began and ended his career as a Conservative Member of Parliament, had abandoned the Conservatives and joined the Liberal Party in 1904, and he led the way in designing the unemployment insurance program enacted in 1911. Even then a master of words, Churchill observed, "Insurance brought the miracle of averages to the rescue of the masses." But the Liberals and Churchill were not only responding to the threat of the emerging Labour Party on the left, they were also implementing the proposals of the leading socialist thinkers in Great Britain—the Fabian Society. The Fabians were "a little band of intellectuals"—highly educated, well-respected, and influential people such as Sidney and Beatrice Webb and the playwright George Bernard Shaw—who were appalled by the excesses of capitalism.[20] Unlike the Marxists, the Fabians were evolutionary socialists who believed in achieving socialism through persuasion and the vote. Sidney Webb was a civil servant who drafted the unemployment insurance law for Churchill.

The United States, during the Progressive Era at the beginning of the twentieth century, also enacted more generous poor relief programs for the aged and widows with children, and its first social insurance program—workmen's compensation—but at the state rather than the federal level. It was no coincidence that Wisconsin, the first state to enact workmen's compensation, had one of the strongest socialist movements in the nation. Milwaukee elected a socialist representative to the House of Representatives in 1910 and again in 1918, as well as three different socialist mayors who governed most of the time from 1910 to 1960: 1910–12; 1916–40, and 1948–60. Governor Lafollette's principal economic advisor, Richard T. Ely, the founder of the American Economic Association, was a Christian Socialist.

As Theta Skocpol (1992) argues so persuasively, however, the US lag in social insurance is attributable not only to what the US lacked—a strong labor movement and socialist party—but also to what the US had, namely, the Civil War Pensions Program. In 1862, the US Congress enacted the first federal income transfer program in the history of the United States. It was a program of federal pensions for Union men disabled in the war, and pensions for widows and children of Union men killed in action. Eligibility did not depend on income. This program was substantially liberalized in 1890 to provide pensions to disabled and retired Union veterans regardless of whether their disability occurred during service, and also pensions to widows and children of deceased Union veterans regardless of whether the men died while in the service. Ann Orloff estimates that nearly half of native, male Northerners had received these pensions by 1900.[21] Because the Civil War pensions provided benefits to such a large proportion of the aged and widows in the North, social insurance programs that provided protection against the risks of old age and widowhood appealed to a smaller constituency. Thus, ironically, the generosity of this welfare state program contributed to the US lag in social insurance.

It was not until the 1930s that the US enacted federal social insurance programs. Though the landmark Social Security Act of 1935, which created the federal Old Age Insurance Program, the federal/state Unemployment Insurance program, and three federal/state relief poor relief programs—Aid for the Aged, Blind, and Dependent Children—was initiated by a liberal Democratic president rather than a socialist party, all historians are agreed that the Great Depression moved the US to the left.

The Great Depression, which began with the Stock Market Crash in late 1928 and lasted throughout most of the 1930s, spurred a big increase in welfare state programs in all rich nations. Depressions had come and gone throughout the history of capitalism. But none, before or since, had lasted so long or been so severe. In the US, so many people were unemployed and unemployment lasted for so long—an average of 18 percent of the labor force was jobless from 1930 through 1940—that virtually everyone in the country either knew someone who had suffered from the Depression or was personally affected. These dire circumstances made it difficult to blame the poor for their impoverished conditions. Undoubtedly, the Depression also convinced many people that their own chances of becoming poor were higher than they had previously thought. Finally, so many people who had been accustomed to managing on their own could no longer do so without help that the general faith in self-reliance was shaken. The Republican president, Herbert Hoover, who became identified with the position that the government should let the Depression take its natural course, while the Depression kept worsening, was soundly defeated in the election of 1932 by the Democratic candidate, New York's Governor Franklin Delano Roosevelt.

The US labor movement gained strength during the 1930s. The Congress of Industrial Unions organized unions on an industrial rather than craft basis, tripled union membership, and led the autoworkers in the famous sit-down strikes of 1936–7. The Roosevelt administration, and eventually the US Congress, supported the increase in unionization. The socialist and communist parties in the US also gained strength from the Great Depression. But neither came close to gathering a mass following, and both remained marginal forces. Father Charles Coughlin and Senator Huey Long, however, did attract mass followings. Long championed the common man, invoking the slogan, "Every Man a King," and proposed a "Share the Wealth Program," which would have heavily taxed corporations, put a cap on personal incomes, and distributed cash benefits to all American households. By 1935, his Share the Wealth Society had 7.5 million members in 27,000 clubs across the US. Father Coughlin began his radio broadcasts in 1926 and by the early 1930s, at the peak of his popularity, a third of the nation tuned into his weekly broadcasts. Although Coughlin endorsed Roosevelt in the 1932 election, by 1935 he had turned against Roosevelt and endorsed Long's Share the Wealth proposals. FDR and the architects of the US Social Security system viewed social insurance as more in keeping with such traditional American values as thrift and responsibility, and with capitalism, than the purely redistributive schemes of Long and Coughlin.

Though the 1935 Social Security Act finally initiated federal old-age social insurance, the depressing effect of racial diversity on transfers was present in ways big and small. First and most important in the long run, because of the weakness of the left in the US, the Roosevelt administration had to compromise with the right more than the left to succeed legislatively. Though the Economic Security Commission that designed the landmark Social Security Act in 1935 included both a National Health Insurance program and a permanent work relief program in their blueprint for a fully developed Social Security system, neither was included in the president's proposal to Congress because of his judgment that including them would jeopardize the entire Social Security Act (Witte, 1963). More directly, to get enough votes from Southern Democrats to enact the Bill, Roosevelt had to agree to exclude agricultural and domestic workers— the two most common occupations of black men and women in the South—from Old Age Insurance coverage altogether (Lieberman, 1998). Not until 1950 were agricultural and domestic workers covered by OAI.

III. Summary and conclusion

The American combination of capitalism, democracy, and diversity is remarkably contradictory. Until 1865, capitalism in America was accompanied by slavery. The US led the world throughout the nineteenth century in extending the vote from landowners to the business, professional, and working classes, and at the dawn of the twentieth century it was the second nation to give the vote to women, but, except for the brief period of Reconstruction following the Civil War, it denied the vote to the overwhelming majority of its black citizens until 1965. The US led the world in mass education throughout most of its history, but forbade educating slaves and, until this day, provides segregated and inferior education to the bulk of its black children. As Myrdal (1944) said, "the history of the USA has been a struggle within the soul of Americans—an attempt to live up to the ideals of the American Creed." All the other currently rich nations have struggled to break down class divides and provide greater opportunities for those at the bottom. A few have struggled, as did Germany, with its mixture of Catholics and Protestants and a small Jewish minority, to live with religious diversity. Some, like Switzerland, with its combination of German, French, and Italian sections, have struggled to cope with national diversity. But only the US has struggled not just with national and religious, but also racial, diversity. Slavery and racial discrimination are shameful aspects of America's history. The abolition of slavery and the elimination of legal discrimination against blacks are glorious historic achievements. To understand America's role as both welfare state laggard and leader, one must come to terms with these American contradictions.

Though the relative importance of the different sources of American exceptionalism is difficult to discern, it does seem clear that the lead in education and the lag in poor relief and social insurance stem from common causes and are related. Protestantism and religiosity, capitalism in the absence of a feudal past, early democratization and the Revolutionary heritage, immigration and the frontier, and national, religious, linguistic, and racial diversity all contributed both to the lag in poor relief and to the lead in education. All also contributed to the relative weakness of the left-wing institutions—labor unions and socialist parties—that promoted social insurance.

Notes

1. Lipset (1996) and Alesina and Glaesar (2004) both emphasize the diversity of the American population and the consequent weakness of the American left. Lipset also emphasizes American leadership in democracy, which Alesina and Glaesar ignore, and American leadership in opportunity, which Alesina and Glaesar deny. Skocpol (1992) emphasizes American leadership in democracy and the consequent laggardship in state bureaucratic capacity, as well as the negative role that Civil War pensions played in the development of Old Age Insurance. Katz (1996) emphasizes the strength of capitalism and opposition of employers.
2. Kaestle (1983) and Lipset (1996) take the broadest approach. Their explanations for American leadership in education include, most importantly, Protestantism, the absence of a feudal landlord class, the emergence of capitalism and the support of employers, American leadership in democracy, the decentralized political structure, and diversity of the American population. Lipset (1996) attempts to explain American exceptionalism, of which leadership in education is a critical part, whereas Kaestle is concerned only with explaining American leadership in mass public education. Ravitch (2000) focuses on diversity. Lindert (2004) focuses primarily on democracy and decentralization, but also acknowledges the importance of Protestantism. Bowles and Gintis (1976), and Katz (1971), focus on capitalism and the strength of employers.
3. Unfortunately, this is a shortcoming of most of the best of the cross-national welfare state literature, including Kamerman and Kahn (1978), Esping Anderson (1990), and Alesina and Glaeser (2004). Peter Lindert (2004) comes closest to a satisfactory answer to the question of why the US led in education and lagged in cash and social insurance, but unfortunately he stops just short of explicitly explaining US exceptionalism. Seymour Martin Lipset (1996), one of the post-World War II giants in sociology, tackles the subject explicitly in his book *American Exceptionalism*, but, unfortunately for our purposes, his focus is much broader than the welfare state. While we build on the work of all of these scholars, we are particularly indebted to Lindert and Lipset.
4. Lipset, p. 62.
5. Other rich nations refer to the other 13 nations described in Chapter 3. The data are reported in the World Values Survey, Official Integrated File (4-wave aggregate), <www.worldvaluessurvey.org, downloaded 2/18/2008>.
6. For a description of the importance of self-governance in these early settlements, see Samuel Eliot Morrison, The Oxford History of the American People," pp. 86–95.
7. Though Katz and Bowles and Gintis reject the idea that the emergence of public education in the US was the result of the successful struggle of the working class, and argue instead that capitalists and capitalism were the dominant players, they do concede that workers generally supported free public schools.

8. Quoted in Kaestle (1983: 138).
9. The Virginia legislature did not pass the Bill in 1779 or during the 1790s when Jefferson repeatedly reintroduced it, or in 1817 when he last reintroduced it. Sadly, like the other slaveholding states, Virginia did not adopt a statewide free school system until after the Civil War—in Virginia's case not until 1870.
10. Alesina and Glaeser, p. 184.
11. Quoted in Mencher (1967), *Poor Law*, p. 96.
12. *Final Report of the 1937–38 Advisory Council on Social Security, in* 50th Anniversary Edition of *The Report of the Committee on Economic Security*, pp. 17–18.
13. Frederick Jackson Turner in his 1893 paper on the "Significance of the Frontier in American History", and his book in 1921, *The Frontier in American History*, argues that frontier experience is the dominant force in American development and accounts for American uniqueness.
14. Canada is less diverse racially but more diverse overall, according to Alesina and Glaeser's measure of fractionalization.
15. The US lag in poor relief and social insurance, and lead in education, was due not only to incredible diversity but also to Protestantism combined with religiosity, capitalism without a feudal past, and leadership in democracy and opportunity. These differences in history are not and cannot be controlled for in Alesina and Glaesar's analyses. In the US, at least, such differences are correlated with both diversity and expenditures, and absent their inclusion in the analysis they will be reflected through the diversity measure. In short, in technical terms, their estimate is too high because of omitted variables bias.
16. For a description of the proposals of Condorcet and Paine and an account of their intellectual history, see Gareth Stedman Jones (2004), *An End to Poverty*. Jones argues their ideas were not at first taken up by, and indeed seem to have been forgotten by, the left advocates in the labor movement and socialist parties.
17. Isabella Mares (2003), *The Politics of Social Risk*.
18. Fogel (2004: 41).
19. Isabela Mares (2006).
20. For a description of the Fabians, see Anne Fremantle (1960), *This Little Band of Prophets*. The Webbs played a critical role in the development of the British welfare state. They were arguably the most influential power couple of their day. Invitations to their dinners were highly prized by up-and-coming politicians such as Churchill, and even by ministers and Cabinet ministers (see Jenkins (2001), *Churchill: A Biography*). The Webbs were experts on poverty and the British Poor Law. Beatrice was from a very wealthy industrial family, while Sidney was from a humble background but had been identified as talented and supported through high school and college with scholarships. Sidney was a civil servant who drafted the unemployment insurance law for Churchill. Beatrice was appointed a member of the Royal Commission on Poverty and, with Sydney's assistance, wrote the dissenting Report to the Royal

Commission Report issued in 1904 or 5. While the Majority Report recommended minor reforms in the Poor Law, the Minority Report rejected the Poor Law as the principle means of providing cash assistance to the poor and recommended instead that the masses be aided via social insurance programs. Their agenda for reform was adopted first by the Fabians, and then by the Labour Party, and became the basis of British reform for the rest of the century.

21. See Ann Shola Orloff (1993b), *The Politics of Pensions: A Comparative Analysis of Britain, Canada and the United States, 1880–1940*.

7

Explaining US Divergence in the Last Quarter of the Twentieth Century: The Long Swing Right

Why, during the last quarter of the twentieth century, does the US lose its wide lead in education, fall behind in early education and in achievement test scores, experience a decline in mobility rates from higher-than-average to lower-than-average, fail to adopt universal National Health Insurance, and allow its health-care costs to outpace those in all other rich nations, and, finally, experience an exlosion of inequality greater than that in any other rich nation?

In a nutshell, the answer is that, soon after President John Fitzgerald Kennedy inspired hope for change and President Lyndon Baines Johnson led the nation to expand the welfare state and secure the vote and other civil rights for blacks, the short sharp swing left in US politics was followed by a long swing right. Beginning in 1968, with the election of a Republican, Richard Nixon, to the presidency, the US swung haltingly but steadily to the right for more than 30 years. In 2002, for the first time since 1928, the Republican Party seized simultaneous control of the White House, the Senate, and the House of Representatives. Other developments were also at play. The increase in inequality, for example, stems partly from the vast new sources of wealth generated by the computer and Internet revolution—that is, capitalism, nourished by sound government, at its best. Similarly, Americans shifted to the right during this period in large part, but not only, because of a backlash against the civil rights revolution. To be sure, it was the war in Vietnam, not the civil rights revolution that brought Johnson down and helped elect Nixon in 1968. And both the stagflation of the 1970s that beset the economy after the oil crisis in 1972 and the Iranian Revolution that led to the US hostage crisis

151

in 1979 helped elect Ronald Reagan as president in 1980. The rise of the religious right also played an important role. But race and the backlash against the gains of the civil rights movement were also pivotal in the long swing right.

The 2006 election, in which Democrats took back both Houses of Congress, and the 2008 election, in which the Democrats won the presidency and widened their leads in both Houses of Congress, both mark the end of the long swing right and portend a swing back to the left. The possible future consequences of a new swing left are discussed briefly at the end of the following and concluding chapter.

In the first three parts of this chapter, we present a narrative history. In the first and second parts, we describe the American short swing to the left during the 1960s followed by the long swing right. In the third part, we analyze the origins and consequences of President Clinton's move to "end welfare as we know it" and show it to be, in larger context, a move both left and right. In the fourth, and final part, we address skeptical reservations about whether the long swing right was key to the US loss of its standing in education, social mobility, health, health insurance, and equality among other rich nations during the final decades of the twentieth century. We also summarize briefly the statistical evidence that confirms the narrative story of the importance of the strength of the left wing. That the size of welfare state transfers depends not only on long-term commonalities and differences among nations, but also on the shifting political strengths of the left and right wings suggests that, over time, differences among the rich nations will both grow and shrink, depending on the changing political fortunes of left and right wings in different countries.

I. The short swing left

During the 1930s, under Franklin Roosevelt, the United States had swung left. Arguably as early as 1937 and certainly by the time Roosevelt died in office in 1945 and Vice President Harry Truman succeeded him, the swing left had come to an end.[1] After World War II ended, the United States enjoyed a period of great prosperity. Truman narrowly won re-election in 1948, proposed a National Health Insurance program, which got nowhere in the Congress, and retreated to a proposal for National Health Insurance for the aged, which also got nowhere. In 1952, Americans chose the Republican candidate and war hero, General Dwight D. Eisenhower, as their president, and then re-elected him in 1956. In terms of the welfare state, the swing right was not dramatic. The Eisenhower administration accepted the basic architecture of the American welfare state constructed by Roosevelt and even agreed to Congressional initiatives that strengthened the system. Having enacted a federal disability assistance program in 1950 under President Truman, Congress next enacted a federal disability insurance program in 1956 under Eisenhower.

Just as the Great Depression had led to a swing to the left during the 1930s, a combination of events led to another move left during the 1960s. In 1960, Senator John F. Kennedy became the nation's first Catholic president. During the presidential campaign, he championed National Health Insurance for the aged, which he called Medicare. Despite the excitement that Kennedy's election stirred, his electoral victory was the narrowest of the century, and the Democrats made no gains in either the House or Senate. While the Democrats had large majorities of 262 to 174 in the House and 65 to 35 in the Senate, nearly half of the Democratic majority was from the South. Conservative Southern Democrats joined Republicans to stymie attempts to pass Medicare and other progressive policies proposed by the Kennedy administration.

Kennedy did persuade Congress to establish the Peace Corps and a social services program for welfare recipients, but his most notable accomplishment was to spur economic growth by reducing federal income taxes. With federal revenues at that time growing faster than projected spending, it was clear that without either greater spending or a cut in taxes, the fiscal surplus would become a drag on the economy and lead to a recession. Those on the left within the administration who argued that there were plenty of worthwhile ways to spend the money were defeated by the practicality argument: Kennedy believed increased spending was not politically feasible. Bob Dylan's folksong, "The Times They Are a-Changin," was at once a plea for this coalition of obstructionists and, more generally, the older generation to step aside and a prophetic description of the momentous changes ahead.

Though Kennedy was unable to move the Congress, the Reverend Martin Luther King Jr. and his organization, the Southern Christian Leadership Conference (SCLC), along with other civil rights groups such as the National Association for the Advancement of Colored People (NAACP), the Congress of Racial Equality (CORE), and the Student Non-violent Coordinating Committee (SNCC) were moving the nation. In 1954, NAACP attorney Thurgood Marshall convinced the US Supreme Court that separate but equal was inherently unequal and unconstitutional.

King arrived on the national stage soon after, with his successful leadership of the Montgomery bus boycott, which began in December 1955 when Rosa Parks refused to give up her seat to a white man and move to the back of the bus. The boycott ended in December 1956 after the Supreme Court declared Alabama's racial segregation laws for buses to be unconstitutional, and Montgomery passed a city ordinance that eliminated racial segregation on its buses. In the interval, King's house, as well as the house of Ralph Abernathy, the co-leader of SCLC, and four black churches had been fire-bombed. King was arrested, put on trial, and convicted of interfering with the public's right to transportation. Montgomery set the pattern for a series of campaigns led by King and the SCLC.

The personal bravery and eloquence of King inspired first his own people and then the whole nation to end legal discrimination and guarantee civil rights, including the right to vote, to blacks and more generally to come closer to living up to the American Creed that "All men are created equal." King, as a Christian minister, was inspired by Jesus. As an oppressed Christian, he was inspired by Mahatma Ghandi, who had used non-violent civil disobedience to unjust laws to win independence for India. American blacks and whites, especially students and clergy, in both the North and the South, were engaging, in steadily increasing numbers, in non-violent protests. In August 1963, at least a quarter-million people came to Washington from all over the country in response to a call from all the major civil rights organizations to attend a March for Jobs and Freedom, where King, arguably the ablest American orator of the twentieth century, gave his famous "I Have a Dream" speech. A few of his words that day are worth quoting to convey the power of his oratory—his succinct description of racial oppression, his appeal to the American Creed, and his faith in the American future.

Five score years ago, a great American, in whose symbolic shadow we stand, signed the Emancipation Proclamation. This momentous decree came as a great beacon light of hope to millions of Negro slaves who had been seared in the flames of withering injustice. But one hundred years later, we must face the tragic fact that the Negro is still not free. One hundred years later, the life of the Negro is still sadly crippled by the manacles of segregation and the chains of discrimination. One hundred years later, the Negro lives on a lonely island of poverty in the midst of a vast ocean of material prosperity. One hundred years later, the Negro is still languishing in the corners of American society and finds himself an exile in his own land.

When the architects of our republic wrote the magnificent words of the Constitution and the Declaration of Independence, they were signing a promissory note to which every American was to fall heir... Instead of honoring this sacred obligation, America has given the Negro people a bad check; a check which has come back marked "insufficient funds." But we refuse to believe that the bank of justice is bankrupt...

I say to you today, my friends, that in spite of the difficulties and frustrations of the moment I still have a dream. It is a dream deeply rooted in the American dream. I have a dream that one day this nation will rise up and live out the true meaning of its creed: "We hold these truths to be self-evident—that all men are created equal." I have a dream that one day on the red hills of Georgia the sons of former slaves and the sons of former slaveowners will be able to sit down together at the table of brotherhood. I have a dream that one day even the state of Mississippi, a desert state sweltering with the heat of injustice and oppression, will be transformed into an oasis of freedom and justice. I have a dream that my four little children will one day live in a nation where they will not be judged by the color of their skin but by the content of their character.

While the civil rights movement was increasing Americans' awareness of social injustice and the political power of the poorest segment of American society, the post-World War II economic prosperity was reinforcing traditional American confidence. The assassination of President Kennedy in 1963 gave new life to his languishing legislative programs, and then his vice president and successor, Lyndon Baines Johnson, an older and far more experienced politician than Kennedy, boldly extended them.

Johnson, as described in the first three volumes of Robert Caro's engrossing biography, was unusually tall and smart, with a dominating presence. From the outset of his political career, whenever he entered a room, he invariably became the center of attention, even in the presence of more politically powerful men, toward whom he quickly gravitated. Johnson had begun his political career in 1931 as the administrative assistant to a Congressman from Houston, Texas. Soon after arriving, he organized and became the leader of the administrative assistants in the House. He became a favorite of Sam Rayburn, also a Texan and the Speaker of the House. Through Rayburn, Johnson met and became a favorite of President Roosevelt. In 1935, he was appointed by the administration to run the National Youth Administration program in Texas. He ran for and was elected to the House in 1937, and the Senate in 1948. In 1955, he became Senate Majority Leader, and in 1957 as "Master of the Senate"— the title of the third volume of Caro's biography—Johnson engineered the first civil rights legislation since Reconstruction.

Quickly, after assuming the presidency, Johnson mastered that office as well. Although the Congress had for three years repeatedly stymied

Kennedy's efforts, it began enacting Johnson's legislative initiatives within the first year. A few months after assuming the presidency, Johnson proposed a War on Poverty and in 1964 Congress established the Office of Economic Opportunity to lead the war. Echoing themes from the New Deal, Johnson promised a Hand Up, not a Hand-out. In June 1964, Congress, at Johnson's behest, also passed the Civil Rights Act, which outlawed discrimination in schools and public places and established the federal Equal Employment Opportunity Commission to enforce anti-discrimination laws.

In 1964, the Republicans nominated Senator Barry Goldwater as their candidate for president. An old-fashioned Western Republican Conservative, Goldwater believed so fervently in limited government that he rejected not just Johnson's recent initiatives, but also Social Security, which, following Milton Friedman's advice, he campaigned to repeal and to replace with a negative income tax. Goldwater also threatened to bomb Hanoi, thus enabling Johnson to emphasize the risk of having Goldwater's finger on the nation's nuclear trigger. Johnson led the Democrats to a landslide victory, winning 61 percent of the popular vote and enlarging the Democratic majorities in the House and Senate. In a stunning series of successful legislative initiatives, he led the country leftward.

Most important, President Johnson embraced the civil rights movement. During the summer of 1964, more than 1,000, mostly white, students from across the country responded to the request from the Student Non-violent Coordinating Committee to go to Mississippi to promote voter registration. Two white students from New York City, Andrew Goodwin and Michael Schwerner, along with a local black student, John Chaney, were kidnapped and killed. In early 1965, King and SCLC joined forces with SNCC and called for a national March for Voting Rights from Selma, Alabama, to the state's capital, Montgomery. Once more, students, clergy, and others from all over the country responded to the call and joined the mostly local black marchers. When Governor George Wallace sent state troops to stop the march, the local forces of law and order, mobs, and the Ku Klux Klan responded once more with violence, kidnapping and murdering two marchers. When the violence perpetrated by police was captured on film by television journalists and broadcast to the nation, calls arose for Johnson to send federal troops to restore law and order, as Eisenhower had done when Little Rock was integrating its schools in 1956, and as Kennedy had done in 1963 when James Meredith, the first black to be admitted to the University of Mississippi, had tried to enroll. At first, Johnson deferred, allowing the calls for troops to mount. As the violence grew worse, Governor Wallace requested a meeting with

President Johnson. On leaving the long meeting, Wallace agreed to the need for federal troops and muttered that if he had stayed any longer Johnson would have tried to make him a believer in civil rights. Two days later, Johnson sent the troops. At the same time, Johnson championed a federal voting rights Bill in a nationally televised speech to a special joint session of Congress:

I speak tonight for the dignity of man and the destiny of democracy...What happened in Selma is part of a larger movement which reaches into every section and state in America. It is the effort of the American Negroes to secure for themselves the full blessings of American life. Their cause must be our cause too. Because it is not just Negroes, but it is all of us who must overcome the crippling legacy of bigotry and injustice.

At that point in his speech, Johnson paused and, quoting from an old Baptist hymn that had become the anthem of the civil rights movement, said, "We shall overcome." Less than five months later, the Voting Rights Act had passed both Houses of Congress and been signed into law by the president.

In 1965, Johnson also persuaded Congress to enact Medicare, a program of National Health Insurance for the aged, and Medicaid, a program of federal and state health assistance for the poor. That same year, Johnson proposed and Congress enacted the Elementary and Secondary Education Act, under which the federal government provided funding to states and school districts to improve the education of children from economically disadvantaged families. Finally, at his request, Congress also increased Old Age Insurance payments. Congress went on to substantially increase Old Age Insurance benefits four more times in the next seven years, and, in 1974, Congress tied future benefits to increases in earnings, thereby ensuring that the higher benefit levels would not erode over time.

Alongside the largest expansion of the welfare state since the 1930s and the revolution in civil rights, the women's rights movement in the US— inspired by *The Feminine Mystique* (1963) by Betty Friedan, and by Gloria Steinem, founder of *Ms.* magazine, and many others—focused on unfair treatment of women and promoted gender equality of opportunity. Many feminists refer to the 1960s and 1970s as the second wave of feminism— the first being the suffragette movement of the nineteenth century that succeeded in gaining women the right to vote in 1920. Though women's labor-force participation rates had been steadily expanding from a very low base throughout the twentieth century and had shot up during the Second World War (1941–5), after the War, women, especially mothers, were once again encouraged to give up work outside the home. Work, before marriage and children and after the children were grown, was acceptable and many women did go to work then. But, upon marriage and childbirth, women were expected to be mothers and housewives, and before the 1960s most women accepted this role. So much has changed since then, that it is worth recalling the differences.

In 1960, only 19 percent of mothers with children under age six worked. As of 2006, the percentage was 63 percent. In 1972, only 4 percent of lawyers and 10 percent of doctors were women. In 2007, the percentages were 33 and 30. In 1960, of the 437 members of the US House of Representatives, only 17 were women and of the 50 Senators only 2 were women. In 2008, the numbers are 77 and 16.

This "economic emergence of women" (the title of Barbara Bergman's book)—accelerated by the women's movement—plays a critical role in welfare state development because, as discussed in the first chapter, welfare states socialize family functions. The socialization reduces gender inequality and in many rich nations, including the US and Sweden, women have played a critical role in the development of welfare state institutions. The critical role of women in the development of the welfare state in the US and Sweden runs from the famous and nationally or even internationally influential, such as Jane Adams, Frances Perkins, and Eleanor Roosevelt in the US, and Alva Myrdal in Sweden, to the voting behavior of the women. The stories regarding the fights for gender equality are as interesting and compelling and ultimately more central to welfare state development in general than the US story about the fight for racial equality, but they are not as germane as race to the difference between the US and the rest of the rich world.

II. The long swing right

The move left during the 1960s was powerful, but short-lived. By themselves, the successes of the civil rights and women's rights movements and the expansion of the welfare state might have been enough at some point to provoke a successful reaction, but the backlash was abetted by a more general fear that America was out of control. The fears extended beyond those who simply objected to blacks and women not knowing their place, and were fed by race riots in 1965 and 1968 in cities across the nation, by the war in Vietnam and the growing anti-war protests, and by the cultural revolution in drugs and sex. By 1968, the war in Vietnam had grown very unpopular and become a political liability for the Democrats. Opposition to his war policies by a large and rapidly growing minority of Democrats persuaded Johnson that he might be vulnerable to defeat in the election. As a consequence, on March 31, he announced on television his decision not to run for re-election. Then, on April 4, Martin Luther King was assassinated. Race riots once again broke out nationwide. On the eve of his victory in the June 6 California Democratic Party primary for the 1968 presidential nomination, Senator Robert Kennedy too was assassinated. The Democratic Party Convention that nominated Vice President Hubert Humphrey that summer was itself a riotous affair, with Yippee protesters outside the convention hall being mauled by cops, and Dan Rather, a CBS national correspondent, being punched in the stomach on the convention floor by Mayor Richard Daley's men. Richard M. Nixon, the Republican candidate for president, benefited from and played to the growing fear of disorder, and claimed to have a secret plan for peace in Vietnam. He successfully adopted the Southern strategy as described by Kevin Phillips, in the *Emerging Republican Majority* (1969), and was elected president, signaling the beginning of the end of the Democratic Party's long dominance. In retrospect, it also signaled the beginning of another era of Republican Party dominance, an era that was to continue until 2006, when the Democrats took back the House and Senate.

The political momentum created by the civil rights movement and President Johnson's blizzard of progressive legislation, however, drove social welfare spending substantially higher throughout Nixon's first term. Indeed, Nixon hired Daniel Patrick Moynihan, an assistant secretary of labor during the Kennedy administration, to run his domestic policy office, and in 1969 Nixon proposed a Family Assistance Plan (FAP) that would have provided a nationwide non-categorical cash minimum welfare benefit. Under the US Social Security law, the federal government paid for 50 percent of the state costs of providing safety-net assistance to the aged, blind, or disabled, as well as to families with dependent children—those living with a single mother. Unless the father was blind, disabled, and, in some states, unemployed, poor two-parent families were not eligible. Experts from across the political spectrum agreed that assistance should be extended to two-parent families, and most united under the banner of a Negative Income Tax.[2] The rationale was twofold—equity and efficiency. Not only was it equitable to treat poor one- and two-parent families alike, but it also reduced the incentive to create single-parent families. Though Nixon trumpeted FAP as a way to reduce long-run welfare costs, by slowing the growth of one-parent families, the immediate effect of extending

159

eligibility to two-parent families would have doubled costs. Although FAP did not pass, the Supplementary Security Income Program, a national Food Stamp Program, and the Earned Income Tax Credit all emerged from the debate and process. The SSI program, enacted in 1972, established a federal minimum benefit for the poor who were aged, blind, and disabled. The Food Stamp program was extended in legislation in 1972 and 1974 to establish a federal minimum food-stamps benefit for all low-income residents. In 1974, Congress enacted the Earned Income Tax Credit, which supplements the earnings of low-income workers by giving them a federal income tax credit. In 1974, Congress also created the federal child support enforcement program, which is described below.

But the Nixon administration was also a restraining force. Most important, in 1971, Nixon vetoed legislation that would have established a federal childcare program.

President Nixon was re-elected in a landslide in 1972, but the Republican ascendance was slowed dramatically by the Watergate hearings that revealed Nixon had approved illegal acts to further his election and conspired with his top advisors in a cover up. Under a threat of impeachment that had broad bipartisan support, Nixon was forced to resign the presidency in disgrace. The Watergate Scandal led to election in 1976 of the Democratic Party candidate, Jimmy Carter, who promised to restore honesty and dignity to the presidency. Though Carter also proposed extending eligibility for the federal safety net to two-parent families, Congress rebuffed his proposals, and Carter was defeated in a relatively close election in 1980 by the Republican governor of California, Ronald Reagan. Though apparently not personally a racist, Reagan began his presidential campaign with a speech declaring his support for state's rights in Neshoba County, Mississippi, where the three young civil rights workers had been killed in the summer of 1964.[3] Southern white support played the critical role in Reagan's election and re-election.

Though Ronald Reagan had, as a young man, supported President Roosevelt, the New Deal, and unions, and indeed entered politics by becoming the president of the Screen Actors Guild, in one of his first acts as president, he busted the Airline Controller's Union by firing its striking workers. He also proposed and Congress enacted huge cuts in the federal income tax. The tax cuts reduced the progressivity of the tax system and, combined with a huge expansion of military spending, led to increasing budget deficits. In every budget proposal to Congress, Reagan also proposed cuts in spending for a wide variety of safety-net social welfare programs, including AFDC, food stamps, Medicaid, public housing, and the Women, Infants, and Children (WIC) program. Except for the last, Congress enacted cuts, though invariably smaller than those suggested by the president. The president seemed to reserve special venom for the AFDC program, referring to its beneficiaries as "Welfare Queens." The term appealed to racist stereotypes that welfare mothers were unmarried, promiscuous, fecund black women living high off the hog because of their many babies.

President Reagan, who had begun his national career in the Barry Goldwater presidential campaign in 1964 as an opponent of Social Security, presided over the first cut ever in Social Security benefits, though he was able, at the same time, to take credit for saving Social Security. In response to accusations that the program was fiscally unsound, Reagan appointed Alan Greenspan to chair a bi-partisan committee to recommend solutions to the president and Congress. The Greenspan Commission recommended that the long-run shortfall between benefits promised and taxes obligated be made up by a combination of increased future taxes and decreased future benefits, including a gradual increase in the retirement age. The president and the Congress embraced the proposal, and together claimed credit for saving Social Security.

By the end of his second term, President Reagan was very popular, primarily because of his foreign policy achievements. As his first term began, he challenged the Soviet Union, calling it the Evil Empire, and embarked on a huge defense build-up. By the end of his second term, Reagan and Mikhail Gorbachav, the new reformist head of the Soviet Union, were friends and allies in dismantling the Communist Party dictatorship in the Soviet Union. Reagan's vice president, George H. W. Bush, was elected president in 1988. After one term, Bush was opposed for re-election not only by the Democratic Party candidate, Arkansas Governor William Jefferson Clinton, but also by a billionaire Republican, Ross Perot, whose main campaign issue was fiscal responsibility. Perot won almost 19 percent of the popular vote, allowing Clinton to win the presidency with only 47 percent of the popular vote. Two of Clinton's major campaign promises were to "make work pay" and to "end welfare as we know it."

III. Ending welfare as we know it: moving right and left

The Aid to Families with Dependent Children program, commonly known in the US as "welfare", was always a small program. At its most generous peak in 1975, when it provided assistance to more than half of all single-mother families, its spending made up less than 3 percent of total social welfare transfers.[4] Despite its small size, it was long the most controversial part of the American welfare state. Indeed, the most controversial, best-known, and most misunderstood reform of the US income maintenance system in the last quarter of the twentieth century is the 1996 Personal Responsibility and Work Opportunity Reconciliation Act (PRWORA), which replaced the AFDC program with the Temporary Assistance to Needy Families (TANF) program. While some have decried PROWRA as a great retreat from the welfare state (Edelman, 1997), others have hailed it as an unparalleled success (Haskins, 2006). It was neither.

Like AFDC, TANF provides assistance primarily to families with children headed by single mothers. The 1996 law establishing TANF required mothers to work in return for assistance. It also strengthened requirements for non-resident fathers to pay child support, limited total federal lifetime eligibility for TANF to five years, and eliminated federal cost-sharing (hitherto Washington had funded at least half of state costs of public assistance), substituting instead federal block grants equal to a state's AFDC spending in previous years.[5] The shift from cash to work relief began long before 1996 and reflects a gradual reclassification of poor single mothers from a group not expected to work to a group expected to work. Similarly, the move to strengthen child support enforcement began long before 1996 and reflects changes in the causes of single parenthood and dependence on AFDC—from widowhood to divorce and non-marriage. The federal requirements to time limit assistance and to enforce work and child support, reflect the enforcement of traditional values at a national level and a restriction of poor relief. The long-run decentralization of funding responsibility achieved by substituting block for matching grants had little effect on aid in the short term because the initial level of funding for the block grants actually entailed increases in federal funding.

But, while federal requirements to time-limit assistance and enforce work and child support severely restricted cash assistance, these reforms in TANF were also part of President Clinton's broader reform agenda to provide assistance outside welfare in order to make work pay. The make-work-pay reforms, as a whole, more than doubled assistance to single mothers and their families.

When AFDC was created in 1935, most married mothers with children did not work. As the Report of the Committee on Economic Security that designed the Social Security Act makes clear, its purpose was to enable poor single mothers to emulate the practices of the middle classes by staying home to raise their children. The benefits were "designed to release from the wage earning role the person whose natural function is to give her children the physical and affectionate guardianship necessary, not alone to keep them from falling into social misfortune, but more affirmatively to rear them into citizens capable of contributing to society."[6] But the childrearing practices of the middle class were changing. The revolutionary increase in women's labor-force participation described by Barbara Bergman in *The Economic Emergence of Women* was already well under way by 1930, but the huge percentage increases that had already taken place did not receive a lot of attention because the base proportion was so low. After 60 years of steady growth in the number of women who worked outside the home, by the 1960s more than half of all married women with children worked. Conservatives fretted about, and liberals and feminists applauded, the continuing trend.

In 1962, President Kennedy proposed and Congress enacted amendments to the AFDC program that provided social services to help single mothers work and achieve independence from welfare. In 1967, Congress and the Johnson administration concluded that social services had been ineffective and enacted incentives to entice welfare mothers to work. But AFDC caseloads grew substantially and work increased only trivially. By the early 1970s, politicians on both ends of the political spectrum were advocating policies that included work in the marketplace for single women with no pre-school-age children. Some division remained on whether to encourage or to require work, but few observers advocated the Progressive and New Deal views that mothers who head families should be given sufficient income to stay home and rear their children. So, in 1972, for the first time in the 70-year history of mothers' pensions and AFDC, Congress required women with no children under six to register for work. In practice, however, the work requirement was never effectively enforced because Congress never authorized enough funding for the work registration program to provide services for all the AFDC recipients who wanted them. In 1988, a large bi-partisan majority led by Senator Daniel Patrick Moynihan passed the Family Support Act (FSA), which again reinforced work and gave states more flexibility to try alternative methods to increase work. During the 1980s and 1990s, states obtained waivers from federal requirements to experiment with different kinds of work requirements and supports. By 1996, several states, including most notably Wisconsin, had already enacted and successfully implemented strict work requirements.

163

Child support enforcement was not an issue when AFDC was first created in 1935 because the overwhelming majority of the single mothers aided by the program were widows.[7] As described above, the architects of the Social Security Act sought to minimize dependence on this public assistance program by enacting the Survivors' Insurance program. They did not anticipate the huge increase in divorce and non-marital births that fueled the growth of AFDC caseloads. By the 1990s, less than 10 percent of families aided by AFDC were headed by widows.

In response to the changing nature of the caseload, Congress enacted a few minor reforms during the 1950s and 1960s and then in 1974, in the first major reform, established the federal child support enforcement program. Before 1974, enforcing child support was strictly a state and local matter characterized by local judicial discretion. The old system condoned parental irresponsibility, was rife with inequity, and contributed to the poverty and welfare dependence of single mothers and their children. Most non-resident fathers paid no child support. Though a few were thrown in jail for non-payment, most suffered no consequences. The wages of delinquents could be and were occasionally garnished, but court officials were reluctant to use a tool that stigmatized fathers. Establishing the paternity of unwed fathers required a jury trial and blood tests were admissible as evidence only if they proved the accused could not be the father. Only 10 percent of unwed fathers had paternity established. The support that fathers were required to pay their children was determined by judges in the context of vague and contradictory state guidelines on a case-by-case basis. The 1974 federal legislation, however, established the federal office of child support enforcement, required all states to establish state enforcement offices, and provided funding for three-quarters of state costs for enforcing child support. The 1974 Act passed by a narrow majority with support from one part of the women's movement (Cassetty, 1978). After funding for non-welfare cases became permanent in 1981, a torrent of legislation, passed with overwhelming bi-partisan majorities, followed. Between 1981 and 1999, Congress enacted new amendments in all but three years.[8]

The legislation wrought a revolution in the US system of child support enforcement: away from local judicial discretion toward the state and national administrative regularity characteristic of social insurance (Garfinkel, 1994, 2001). All states now have numerical child support guidelines for determining child support obligations, require employers to withhold child support payments from paychecks from the outset of the obligation, require employers to report the Social Security numbers of all new hires, suspend drivers' and professional licenses of delinquent payers, charge interest on delinquent payments, provide voluntary paternity establishment programs in hospitals, and use DNA to establish paternity in contested cases. Most of these changes in child support enforcement predated the 1996 PRWORA.

Some analysts have asserted that the enforcement of work and child support within AFDC was driven primarily by prejudice. As the AFDC caseload shifted from predominately widowed to predominately divorced, separated, and never-been-married, and from predominately white to predominately black and Hispanic, the argument goes, the caseload attracted less sympathy, so support for the program diminished. Prejudice may have been the primary driver. Though the US has no monopoly on racial prejudice, it has played a big role in American history and social welfare policy. Thus, that interpretation is plausible. But, although prejudice undoubtedly played a role, it may not have been as fundamental as some believe. First, independent of racial prejudice, there were good reasons, consistent with traditional American values, to enforce work and child support. Second, the expectation that single mothers should work and non-resident fathers should pay child support is not confined to the US. Indeed, although the other English-speaking countries have lagged behind in this matter, they have all moved in the same direction. And Sweden, with no racial or ethnic minority, has long expected single mothers to work and fathers to pay child support (Garfinkel and Sorensen, 1982).

Accompanying the expectations that single mothers work, and non-resident fathers pay child support, was the belief on the left that public policy should supplement the incomes of poor single mothers outside the welfare system in order to make work pay. Child support enforcement is one way to supplement the incomes of poor single mothers. The idea of supplementing income outside the welfare system was a return to the original vision of the architects of the Social Security Act: although it is important to relieve poverty through public assistance, it is even more important to prevent poverty and dependence on public assistance. The ideas of making work pay and making cash assistance temporary were popularized by David Ellwood (1988) in his book *Poor Support*.[9] In the 1992 presidential campaign, Bill Clinton adopted these ideas and promised to "end welfare as we know it."

To fulfill his pledge to make work pay, President Clinton proposed, and the Congress passed as part of its budget Bill in 1993, a huge increase in the earned income tax credit. In addition, over the course of the next several

165

years, Congress substantially increased childcare and Medicaid funding and enacted a new child health insurance program. Clinton also proposed converting AFDC to a temporary cash assistance program to be followed by work relief for those who failed to find work on their own. But after the Republicans won control of the Congress in 1994, they passed a far more stringent Bill, with lifetime limits for any kind of assistance, stringent work requirements, and the end of the federal guarantee of assistance to all who were eligible. After vetoing the Bill twice, Clinton finally signed it in 1996. Between 1988 and 1999, welfare assistance (AFDC or TANF) fell from $24 billion to $13 billion, but federal funding to supplement the incomes of working low-income families grew from $11 billion to $67 billion. The increase in federal spending to supplement the earnings of low-income families dwarfed the decrease in spending on welfare assistance.[10]

Having increased 27 percent between 1990 and 1994, welfare caseloads then fell an unprecedented 56 percent during the following six years. During the same six years, the labor-force participation rates of single mothers increased 10 percentage points. The poverty rates of single mothers fell 11 percentage points, from 44 percent to 33 percent. Incomes of single-mother families in all quintiles increased during both 1993–5 and 1997–9, except for the poorest fifth of single mothers, who lost income in the post-PRWORA period. Even the lowest income group experienced gains in consumption, and the share of families reporting hunger fell between 1995 and 1999.[11] There is, however, evidence that a small share of single mothers lost assistance because their mental health problems made them unable to comply with work requirements, or that the sanctions they received for failing to comply led to mental health problems (Reichman, Teitler, Garfinkel, and Garcia, 2004; Reichman, Teitler, and Curtis, 2005).

The dramatic declines both in welfare caseloads and in poverty rates of single-mother families were attributable to a combination of three factors: (1) the increase in assistance outside welfare that made work pay; (2) the longest peacetime economic expansion in the nation's history; and (3) the enactment of TANF. Analysts have focused more on the decline in welfare caseloads than on the decline in poverty rates. Strong statistical evidence indicates that all three factors were important in reducing caseloads, but to date it has not been possible to isolate the independent effect of each because all three were moving in the same direction and reinforcing each other.[12]

The question regarding poverty rates is less ambiguous. Rebecca Blank (2002), in a superb review of research on the effects of welfare reform, takes particular note of differences in research experiments that only implemented strict work requirements and experiments that supplemented earnings in addition to requiring work. Experiments that required work without supplementing earnings led to a big drop in welfare receipt and a big increase in employment but no increase in total income, whereas experiments that required work and supplemented earnings not only led to big drops in welfare receipt and increases in employment, but also to big gains in income and declines in poverty rates. From these experimental results, one can infer that TANF alone would not have led to declines in poverty. This is not to say that TANF had no effect. It is possible, even likely, that the reductions in poverty would have been smaller if there had not been a push to leave welfare from the conversion of AFDC to TANF. But, without the pull of better employment opportunities and higher benefits outside welfare, there would have been no poverty reductions.

In summary, considered in the broader context of other policies that encouraged work and reduced poverty, PRWORA alone accomplished much less good than is commonly asserted. To be sure, PRWORA cut welfare assistance. But the declines in caseloads, increases in employment, and reductions in poverty that followed are attributable not to PRWORA alone, but also to the most vibrant economic expansion in US history and a doubling of total assistance to poor single mothers and their children. Without the increase in benefits and the economic expansion, there would have been no reductions in poverty. US leadership in this area is worth both emulating and avoiding.

IV. Long swing right and recent departures: how closely connected?

We have argued that the long swing right politically accounts for US departures in education, health, income transfers, inequality, and opportunity, but a skeptic could easily raise questions about all of these connections. In this part we step back from the historical narrative, raise the skeptical questions, and consider the causal connections explicitly for each of these areas. The section ends with a brief description of the statistical evidence of the strong relationship between the strength of the left and the proportion of GDP devoted to social welfare transfers within rich nations during the final 30 years of the twentieth century.

Skeptical questions addressed

As we saw in Chapter 5, in the final third of the twentieth century, the US lead in education shrank and the lead in opportunity turned into a lag because other rich countries imitated, caught up with, and surpassed the US. Obviously, the imitation of other rich nations cannot be attributed to the American turn right politically. So, how can we claim a role for the turn right? The answer is that if the US had not turned right politically, the nation would not have stood in place as other nations caught up and surged ahead. This is most obvious in the case of the American lag in early childhood education and care. Head Start was a big step forward for the poorest part of the American population, but it was a program for the poor alone, and it has never been funded generously enough to serve adequately even the poor. It remained an inadequately funded program for the poor only because America moved right soon after its founding. A larger federal role in child-care was stymied by President Nixon's veto and more generally by Christian fundamentalist and other right-wing traditionalist opposition to women working. The connection in higher education is strong as well. Since 1970, the share of Americans with high school and college degrees has remained stagnant. Other rich nations caught up or nearly caught up, and Canada and Ireland now have a higher percentage of students with advanced degrees than the US. In 1978–9 Pell scholarship grants for poor students were equal to 77 percent of average cost of attendance at a public university. In 2007, because the value of the grants has increased only slightly, while college costs have soared, Pell grants were equal to only 32 percent of costs.[13]

Health insurance is a different story. Here, the turn right reinforced pre-existing tendencies. Jacob Hacker, in *The Divided Welfare State*, traces the failure of the US to develop a universal National Health Insurance system in the final third of the twentieth century to a number of historical factors that set the US on the path toward employer-provided health insurance. These factors include the opposition of doctors to health insurance, the development of voluntary state hospital insurance plans (so-called Blue Cross) plans, the general anti-statist stance of US employers and the public more generally, the encourage-ment of employer-provided health insurance by the US tax code, and the weakness of the left. Once the US started down the path of private insurance companies and employer-provided benefits, it became increasingly difficult to enact a government-run program because the existing programs created powerful constituencies such as the Blue Cross insurance companies and private insurance companies. Even unions that were able to negotiate good insurance deals gained a vested interest in the status quo. More generally, employer-provided health insurance undermined the attraction of a govern-ment-run health insurance program simply by providing health insurance to most workers. That a large and increasing number of employees were covered by employer-provided insurance is one reason that Democratic presidents Truman, Kennedy, and Johnson focused on health insurance for the aged. But recall, from Figure 5.2, that nearly all rich nations introduced National Health Insurance after World War II. In the broader international context, therefore, the US was not far behind during the 1960s. Achieving National Health Insurance for the aged was also quite a political achievement. What might have happened had there been no war in Vietnam and had the US continued moving left? It is conceivable that the US would have adopted universal National Health Insurance. But this is speculative. What we know is that in the midst of an intense but short move left, in the 1960s, the US adopted National Health Insurance for the aged and national health assistance for the poor, while, in the midst of the subsequent 40-year shift right, the US made little further progress to universal health insurance.

Inequality increased in almost all of the rich nations during the final part of the twentieth century, but increased the most in the US. Inequality increased for many reasons, including the development of new technol-ogy that increased the value of a more advanced education, globalization, and other forces that contributed positively to economic growth. Product-ivity changes were skill-biased, also favoring the well educated. Output grew most rapidly in the service industries, especially finance and com-puting, and with it the wages of the high-skill entrepreneurs and graduates who work in those industries. At the same time, the lowering of trade barriers opened new markets that were quickly exploited by US-based multinationals. Further, the opening of world capital markets and high stock-market returns (even after the brief recession of 2001) have increased the economic shares of capital at the expense of labor's share of national income. But changes in technology and globalization were at work in all of the rich nations.

To account for differences across rich nations in the degree to which inequality increased requires taking account of other differences across nations, including differences in education expansion, unionization, and income transfers and taxes. In the US, the demand for highly skilled workers was not matched by an increase in supply, so wages at the top rose. Higher education, as we have seen, expanded far more in other rich nations, restraining wage increases. Unions and union strength in the US, as compared with other rich nations, declined precipitously. The real value of the minimum wage also declined (Levy and Temin, 2007). Finally, most other rich nations did more than the US to counter increasing inequality in market incomes with social welfare transfers and taxes (Atkinson, 1997; Kenworthy and Pontussan, 2005). The long swing right in the US reinforced and widened pre-existing differences in social welfare transfers. Had the US further expanded access to higher education, the relative wages for the more highly educated would have been lower. Indeed, Goldin and Katz (2008) trace the decline in inequality in the first two thirds of the twentieth century to the expansion of high school and higher education, and the increase in inequality in the last quarter of the century to the failure of the US to further expand access to higher education. Had the US adopted a National Health Insurance system, health insurance would have been more equally distributed and the costs more equitably financed. Had the US not cut taxes on upper incomes and inheritances, inequality would not have grown quite so much. Finally, though this is harder to document, the long swing right probably also helped to increase social tolerance for inequality.

Ironically, the connection between the long swing right and the loss of US leadership in opportunity is the most questionable. The timing is wrong. Estimates of intergenerational mobility, which we, along with most scholars, have used as a measure of opportunity, indicate that the European nations caught up to the US in mobility by the 1970s. If the other rich nations had caught up to or surpassed the US in intergenerational mobility by the 1970s, the long swing right that begins in 1968 cannot have been responsible. But the timing is also wrong in another way. The US loses its lead in intergenerational mobility by the 1970s before it loses its lead in education—after 1970. This is puzzling because virtually all the scholars in this area agree that education is the driving force in promoting intergenerational mobility. We do not profess to have the answer to this puzzle, but speculate that perhaps the disastrously high European death rates in World War II increased mobility rates for the survivors. And we remind readers that intergenerational mobility is but one measure of opportunity. But it is also possible that, for reasons independent of education, the US lost its lead in mobility before the long swing right allowed the other rich nations to catch up in education.[14]

Statistical evidence from rich nations 1960–2000

Up to this point, the evidence for our argument that the long swing right in US politics accounts for US departures in education, health, inequality, and (less certainly) opportunity has come from a narrative history of the US. In this last part of the final section, we examine statistical evidence of the relationship between the strength of the left and social welfare transfers between 1960 and 2003, first for the US and then more broadly for rich nations.

Social welfare transfers are measured as before as a proportion of GDP. How to measure the strength of the left wing is less clear, and different scholars conducting cross-national research have utilized different measures, including indicators based on popular voting percentages, cabinet percentages, and proportion of the labor force that is unionized (Huber, Evelyn, Ragin, and Stephens, 1993; Huber and Inglehart, 1995; Cusack, 1997; Huber and Stephens, 2001; Iverson and Soskice, 2005; Bartells, 2007). None of these measures adequately captures the unique decentralization of political power at the federal level in the US. Thus, we devise a simple new measure that captures, no doubt imperfectly, this decentralization. The measure gives a large weight to controlling each of the three elected branches of government, additional weight to controlling all three branches of government, and smaller weights to the degree of dominance of each institution.

Democratic control of each elected branch of government increases the score by approximately a half-point: Controlling all three branches increases the score an additional half-point. Republican control of each branch decreases the score by approximately a half-point, with an additional decrease of a half-point for control of all three branches. We use the term "approximately" because the exact increase or decrease is normally somewhat higher than 0.5, depending upon the strength of the majority control in each branch. The strength of control is measured by the proportion of representatives and senators in the House and Senate respectively, and the proportion of the vote for the president.[15]

This is a very imperfect measure of left-right strength in the US. A very obvious and important omission is composition of the Supreme Court. Similarly, political power at the state and local level is ignored. And control of the executive branch should probably be given greater than one third weight. Probably the most important omission is the failure to take account of the conservatism of Southern Democrats prior to the civil rights revolution of the 1960s. Still, it captures many elements of the uniquely decentralized nature of political power at the federal level and it does capture at least roughly the changing political fortunes of the left and right in the US over time.

Figure 7.1 displays graphically our measures of the strength of the US left and social welfare transfers as a percentage of GDP in the US from 1960 to 2003, the latest year for which we have data. (To be consistent with the comparative research discussed below, we do not include employer-provided benefits, but the trends are similar whether or not employer-provided benefits are included.) Consider, first, each of the trends separately. The strength of the left variable indicates that the political power of the left peaked in the 1965–9 period, when the Democrats controlled all three elective branches of the federal government and the president was elected by a very large majority, and bottomed out in the 2003–7 period, when the Republicans controlled all three branches. Though Democrats held the presidency twice more after 1969—from 1977 to 1981 and from 1993 to 2001—each time the overall strength of the left was weaker than the last. Each time the Republicans held the presidency, the overall strength of the right was stronger. In short, after 1969, there are ups and downs, but the overall picture until 2006 is a long trend right.

The trend in social welfare transfers is quite different. Transfers increase modestly between 1960 and 1965, and dramatically between 1965 and 1975, level off until the late 1980s when they increase a bit more, then level off again till a second small increase in the early 2000s.

The dramatic increase in transfers is clearly closely related to the peak strength of the left from 1965 to 1969. The continued growth from 1970 to

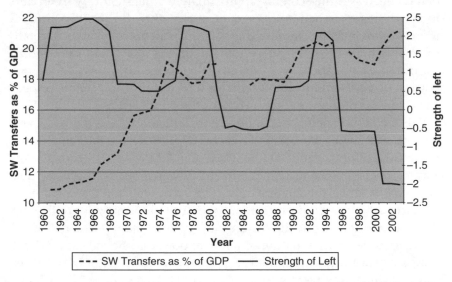

Figure 7.1: Strength of the left and social welfare transfers in the US, 1960–2003

1975 reflects the unfolding of programs enacted in that period, as well as the strength of the surge left in the 1965–9 period as reflected in the continued strengthening of old programs like Social Security and enactment of new programs, such as SSI and the EITC. The short swing left from 1976 to 1980—attributable to the election of President Jimmy Carter in 1976—had no discernible effect on social welfare transfers. The longer swing left, beginning in 1986 when the Democrats recapture the Senate and culminating in the 1992 election of President Clinton, does appear to closely track the small increase in social welfare transfers during this period. In short, the picture depicts a strong, but complicated, relationship between strength of the left and increases in social welfare transfers.

That transfers might not change instantaneously in response to a change in political power, upon reflection, especially after seeing the data, makes sense. Even if changes in programs lead to immediate changes in transfers, it takes time to enact legislation and to change administration of programs. Furthermore, not everything can be done at once. Finally, many policy changes increase or decrease future rather than present benefits. For example, Margaret Thatcher's cut in old-age pension benefits was arguably the largest reduction in welfare state benefits she achieved, but little of the drastic reduction in benefits achieved showed up in reductions in social welfare expenditures until years later because the big cuts were to the benefits of future retirees. In short, not only are there good reasons to believe that there are time lags between shifts in political power and political effects on transfers, but there are also equally good reasons for believing that the time lags for different changes in transfer programs will differ.[16]

Many distinguished scholars argue that a large part of differences in social welfare spending among rich nations is attributable to differences in the strength of the left. (Lipset, 1996; Hibbs, 1977; Korpi, 1985, Esping-Anderson, 1990; Castles, 2004; and Huber and Stephens, 2001) Even scholars such as Alesina and Glaeser (2004), and Iverson and Soskice (2002, 2005), who argue that differences in racial fractionalization or political institutions underlie differences in the strength of the left and are therefore more fundamental, agree that differences in welfare state spending are driven by strong left-wing parties.[17] We close this chapter by describing the statistical evidence for the importance of the strength of the left in accounting for social welfare transfers that comes from the recent historical experience of rich nations.

Evelyn Huber and John Stephens have done the most extensive statistical analyses of the impact of differences across rich nations in the last part of the twentieth century in the balance of left to right party power (2001; see also Iverson and Soskice, 2002, 2005; and Bradley et al., 2003). They measure the balance of political power across nations and over time by the percentage of Cabinet ministries held by right, center, and left parties. Each country and each year receives a score of 0 to 4, with 4 being the most left and zero the most right. Because length of time in power, as well as currently being in power, is likely to affect the generosity of social welfare provision, Huber and Stephens also construct a measure of cumulative time in power by the left wing by summing up all the values for each year beginning in 1946. They find that year-to-year fluctuations in power have little effect, but cumulative time in power has a very big effect on the proportion of GDP devoted to social welfare transfers. (While they code the left in power variable as zero for the US for all years, and do not include education in SWE, we found similar results when our measure of US left in power is substituted for theirs, and when education is included.) These results are consistent with both our more detailed examination of the US case above and with the common observation that the right seeks to reduce and the left to increase social welfare expenditures. When power shifts, if the shift is large enough and lasts long enough, transfers decline or increase, not necessarily instantaneously, but over time, the changes in transfers accumulate.

That the size of welfare state transfers depends upon the shifting political strengths of the left and right wings does not obviate our argument in Chapter 6 that enduring differences between the US and other rich nations account for some long-term differences in welfare state development, or our argument in Chapter 2 that long-term common problems and trends in rich nations are the fundamental driving force in the development of welfare state institutions. Recall, all these rich nations have large welfare states.

That the size of welfare state transfers depends not only on long-term common problems and trends in rich nations, as well as enduring differences among these nations, but also on the shifting political strengths of the left and right wings, however, does have at least two implications. Most generally, it suggests that over time differences among the rich nations will both grow and shrink, depending on the changing political fortunes of the left and right wings in different countries. Thus, it is not surprising that some studies find divergence and others convergence in the welfare states of rich nations (Castles, 2004). In particular, it suggests that the average differences between the US and other rich nations are likely to be at or near their maximum at the end of the long swing right in the US.

Notes

1. While some progressive legislation, including the Social Security Amendments of 1938 and the Murray-Wagner Labor Relations Act, comes in 1938, by the late 1930s the spate of progressive social welfare legislation came to an end. See Alan Brinkley in *The End of Reform: New Deal Liberalism in Recession and War* (1995). Similarly, Theodore Sorensen, in *Kennedy*, argues that since 1937, the Republican, Conservative Southern coalition blocked most progressive legislation. On the other hand, inequality continued to decline quite dramatically during World War II.
2. For a discussion of the triumph of the Negative Income Tax idea in policy circles and its influence on policy, see Garfinkel and McLanahan (1986: 111–15), and Moffitt (2003).
3. For an informative and lively discussion of Reagan's intent and motives from both sides of the political spectrum, see the *New York Times* op-ed columns by David Brooks, Robert Herbert, Lou Cannon, and Paul Krugman (November 2007): David Brooks, "History and Calumny," *New York Times* (November 9, 2007), p. A.27; Bob Herbert, "Righting Reagan's Wrongs?," *New York Times* (November 13, 2007), p. A.29; Lou Cannon, "Reagan's Southern Stumble," *New York Times* (November 18, 2007), p. 4.15; Paul Krugman, "Republicans and Race," *New York Times* (November 19, 2007), p. A.23.
4. We calculated this statistic by dividing 1975 AFDC expenditures by total 1975 social welfare transfers. AFDC spending was taken from the House of Representatives Committee on Ways and Means' *Green Book* (1994). Total social welfare transfers for 1975 were taken from the Social Security Administration's *Annual Statistical Supplement* (2002).
5. Under the welfare Act, only citizens and qualified immigrants are eligible for federal public benefits. The qualified immigrant category includes: lawful permanent residents (LPRs), refugees, asylees, and certain abused immigrants. All other immigrants, including those legally present in the US, are considered "not qualified." Immigrants who entered the US after the passage of the reforms are banned from SSI and other means-tested public benefits until they have been a qualified immigrant for at least five years. Post-enactment immigrants are subject to stricter "deeming" regulations. The income of the immigrant's sponsor will be deemed to be part of the immigrant's application for public assistance for up to 10 years (National Immigration Law Center, 2005).
6. Preamble to 1938 Act, p. 34.
7. For a fuller account, see Garfinkel (1992).
8. The federal legislation consisted of amendments to the portion of the Social Security Act and took the form of requirements imposed on the states as a condition for receiving federal funds for AFDC and, after 1996, TANF. In view of the fact that the new laws the states were required to adopt applied not just to AFDC or TANF cases, but frequently to all child support cases, this may be thought of as a case of the tail waving the dog.

9. In *Single Mothers and Their Children* (1986), Garfinkel and McLanahan developed similar arguments. The National Commission on Children (1991), appointed by President Reagan and chaired by Senator Rockefeller, adopted a similar agenda.
10. Blank (2002). Includes EITC, childcare, and Medicaid and Chip expenditures for those not receiving cash assistance.
11. Blank (2002).
12. See Blank (2002).
13. See Bryan J. Cook and Jacqueline E. King (2007). The figure for 2007 comes from Sandy Baum and Patricia Steele (2007).
14. Another puzzle—unrelated to welfare state transfers—is that in the midst of the long swing right and increasing income inequality, the US experienced increases in gender pay equality.
15. In two presidential elections—Clinton in 1992 and Bush in 2000—the victor got less than 50 percent of the popular vote.
16. From an econometric point of view, the importance of lags cannot be overstated. The existence of lags means that a contemporaneous measure of political power will be biased toward zero. But, because the lags will differ for different programs, the lags need not be the same across time period within countries or across countries. Thus, even lagged variables of political power will be biased toward zero. We thank Andrew Gelman, professor of statistics and political science at Columbia University for this critical insight. The existence of lags explains why the cumulative time in power variable does a much better job of explaining variations across countries than does a contemporaneous measure of being in power.
17. Alesina and Glaeser, Iverson and Soskice, and others who explain large current differences between the US and other rich nations by enduring differences, such as race fractionalization and majority versus proportional representation, overstate the importance of these particular enduring differences for two reasons. First, current differences in social welfare spending are temporarily unusually large because of the unusually large US swing right. Second, and more fundamental, as explained in section I in Chapter 6 of this volume, there are many other long-term differences besides race fractionalization and political institutions, such as early democratization and leadership in education and opportunity, that contribute to the weakness of the left in the US in the twentieth century. Failing to control for these other long-term differences attributes all of the current differences to the one long-term difference—fractionalization or proportional representation—examined. In technical terms, their estimates are subject to omitted variables bias.

8

The Future of the American Welfare State

We have explained why all rich nations have large welfare states. We have also described similarities and differences in welfare states in rich nations in size and structure and documented the degree to which welfare state programs reduce inequality and poverty and promote human capital and opportunity. And we have identified and explained both enduring and recent differences between the US and other rich nations.

In this final chapter, we look forward and ask how the United States can strengthen its welfare state. In particular, this last chapter addresses three specific challenges that confront the American welfare state: (1) making the old-age insurance program fiscally sound; (2) achieving universal health insurance and restraining the growth in health-care costs; and (3) restoring American pre-eminence in education, while making other productive and complementary investments in children. For more than a decade, the first has received by far the most attention, yet, compared to the second and third, successfully meeting the first challenge is the least of the problems we face. Tinkering with a mix of small benefit cuts and small increases in taxes will restore fiscal balance to old-age insurance.

Achieving universality in health care is challenging by itself, but, by itself, increases costs, just as an aging population also increases health-care costs. Costly and beneficial improvements in medical care will also drive up health-care costs. Restraining health-care costs is at least as daunting a challenge as is achieving universality in coverage.

The third challenge is the most important in terms of future wealth and productivity. Yet in the face of an aging population, which will inevitably drive up public sector costs and taxes, it may be the most difficult to achieve.

The most general challenge to welfare states can be posed as reducing poverty and inequality, while at the same time increasing efficiency and

177

growth. Although this exercise cannot be value free, scientific evidence plays a central role in our analysis. We place high value on achieving the traditional objectives of welfare state programs—economic security, poverty prevention and amelioration, opportunity and equality. At the same time, we believe that priority should be given to welfare state reforms that promote these objectives in ways that increase efficiency, economic growth and well-being. This priority points to investments in children, which is why the third challenge is the most important. But it also points to other reforms that are likely to improve both equity and efficiency. Though the specific proposals examined are limited to the United States, the challenges faced by our nation are not unique and therefore our analyses have implications for the welfare states of all rich nations.

I. Balancing taxes and benefits in old-age insurance

The Old Age, Survivors', and Disability Insurance (OASDI) program—popularly known as Social Security—once again faces financial difficulties. As described in the previous chapter, the 1983 Greenspan Commission recommended and Congress legislated to restore fiscal balance through a combination of benefit cuts and tax increases—increasing the age of retirement, taxing benefits, and increasing tax rates on workers. OASDI is financed primarily on a pay-as-you-go basis, with payroll taxes from current workers financing the benefits paid to current retirees. The payroll tax in 2009 equals 12.4 percent of the first $106,800 of earnings.[1] An additional 2.9 percent of payroll tax on all earnings finances the Medicare program (which we deal with separately below). Since 1983, payroll taxes have exceeded benefits paid so that future benefits for both programs could be financed from the accumulated trust funds. Payments to beneficiaries are projected to exceed payroll tax revenues, starting in 2017 for Social Security, and requiring redemption of trust fund bonds to support payments. The Medicare system began to draw down its reserves in 2007. Without a change in policy, the OASDI trust fund is projected to be depleted by 2040 (OASDI Trustees, 2006). At that point, payroll taxes are projected to equal only 74 percent of benefit obligations.

The Social Security actuaries project 75 years into the future. Their intermediate estimate of the OASDI financing shortfall is equal to about 2 percent of taxable payroll. Solvency over the next 75 years could be restored with an immediate 16 percent increase in the payroll tax, a 13 percent cut in lifetime benefits, or a combination of the two.[2] The projected deficit in OASDI is driven primarily by increasing life expectancy, and secondarily by decreasing fertility and the indexation of future benefits. Increases in life expectancy increase the number of retired workers to be supported, thereby increasing total benefits. Between 2010 and 2050, the population aged 65 and over is projected to more than double, from 40 million to nearly 87 million (US Census, 2004). Declining fertility decreases the relative number of potential workers who pay taxes. When Social Security was first implemented, the ratio of workers to retirees was 16 to 1. There are now 3.3 workers for each retiree; by 2040 that number has been projected to fall to as low as 1 to 1 (Ball, 2005).[3]

Since 1974, Social Security benefits have been indexed in two ways. Initial benefits at the point of retirement (or death or disability) are indexed to the average growth in earnings in the economy. Thus, if average US earnings grow by 50 percent between 2006 and 2040, the average retiree in 2040 will get benefits 50 percent higher than the average new retiree in 2006. Once benefits begin, they are indexed to increases in the cost of living as measured by the consumer price index. Earnings indexation is designed to make sure that the relative standard of living of the aged keeps up with improvements in the standard of living of the working population. Indexation to the cost of living assures that once a worker is retired, the real value of the Social Security benefit keeps up with inflation.

If the entire shortfall in benefits were financed by an increase in the payroll tax, the relative standard of living of the working-age population, as compared to the aged, would decrease. Similarly, if the entire shortfall were financed by a decrease in benefits, the relative standard of living of the aged would be diminished. This is not to say that the absolute standard of living of the aged would decrease. If retirees in 2040 received only 74 percent of what they are now promised, they would still receive higher inflation-adjusted benefits than current retirees do (Baker and Rosnick, 2005).

At least as important as the relative well-being of the average retired and working-age populations is the distributional effect *within* cohorts of alternative reforms. For example, the burden of raising the cap on taxable earnings from its current level of $106,800 would fall only on workers who make more than that. In 1983, when Congress established the cap, it was equivalent to 90 percent of earnings, but it is now equal only to 85 percent of wages because wage increases have outpaced inflation (Ball, 2005). To bring the cap back to the 90 percent level would entail raising it to $140,000. Higher contribution rates could entitle these workers to higher benefits, but based on current law only 15 cents are added for every dollar contributed. Eliminating the earnings cap completely would eliminate 93 percent, or virtually all, of the 75-year shortfall (Reno and Lavery, 2005). The primary objection to eliminating the earnings cap is that it will undermine support among very high earners for the Social Security system because so much of their additional contributions through the payroll tax (roughly 85 percent) will go to other, low-income retirees rather than to themselves in the form of higher benefits (Aaron and Reischauer, 2005). Similarly, increasing the proportion of Social Security benefits subject to the federal income tax from 50 percent in current law to 100 percent, would also distribute the burden progressively, but risks undermining support among high earners for Social Security.

Raising the age of retirement is a natural though not entirely neutral response to increases in health and longevity because the major source of the projected shortfall in revenues is due to more years being spent in retirement by larger numbers of elders who are living ever longer lives. Indeed, the largest fraction of deficit savings from the Greenspan Commission came from this source. But gains in life expectancy have not been uniform across the income distribution, and low earners tend to live fewer years into retirement (Steuerle and Bakija, 1994), while high earners and those with more education are the ones who are most likely to continue working because of their health and the value they place on work (Autor and Duggan, 2006). Thus, the burden of increasing the retirement age falls disproportionately on lower-income workers and retirees because they are more likely to be manual laborers and have physically demanding jobs that promote earlier retirement. However, as Mermin and Steuerle (2006) suggest, coupling higher retirement ages with a reasonable increase in the Social Security minimum benefit and with a more lenient Disability Insurance system for workers older than age 62 would allow us to raise the retirement age without increasing poverty rates.

Waiting another decade or two to address the solvency issue will require greater and more precipitous changes than if preventive action took place in the next several years. For example, revenues will be only 74 percent of promised benefits in 2040, necessitating a 26 percent cut in benefits or a comparable increase in payroll taxes. Whereas if we cut benefits now, balance would be achieved over the next 75 years with only a 13 percent cut in benefits or a 16 percent increase in payroll taxes. Precipitous cuts in benefits or increases in the age of retirement are especially inappropriate because they undermine the security objective of Social Security and planning for retirement. The single advantage of delay is that the longer we wait to address the solvency issue, the more confident we will be of the magnitude of the problem. Projections of the deficit rely on projections of trends in fertility, mortality, immigration, productivity growth, and labor-force participation, any one of which could turn out to be quite different over the next 30-plus years than the experts now expect.[4]

When Congress restores fiscal balance in the Old Age Insurance program, will it do so in a way that reduces rather than increases inequality? Despite the natural appeal of raising the age of retirement, in the near term Congress could rely minimally on changing the retirement age and maximally on increasing the wage cap and taxing benefits. In the longer term, if the health of the aged and longevity continue to increase, Congress could once again increase the age of retirement.

Adding security and efficiency to the system

President Bush proposed in 2003 to divert Social Security revenues to finance private savings accounts that would be invested in the stock market. Diverted contributions would reduce the guaranteed benefit that participants receive from Social Security, thereby decreasing benefit payments and reducing costs in the long term. Although increasing wealth and inheritances among the lower classes through private savings accounts is an attractive idea, doing so at the expense of the economic security achieved by social insurance is not a good idea, as the huge stock market decline in 2008 has clearly borne out. In practice, the Bush proposal would have led to little inheritable wealth among low earners as they would have been required to convert their private accounts into annuities. Moreover, the diversion of payroll taxes to private accounts would have exacerbated the Social Security revenue shortfall because the revenue diverted to private accounts would not be available to pay current benefits and would have to be raised from another source (Reno and Lavery, 2005). President Bush never explained how he would finance the increased deficit. For all these reasons, the proposal was deservedly a non-starter in Congress.

While private accounts as a substitute for Social Security are not desirable, private accounts as an *add-on* to Social Security may be desirable. The United States could go a long way toward helping low- and moderate-income families achieve a higher living standard in retirement by enacting a new 1.5–2 percent private retirement account administered by a Federal Reserve-like Board of Directors. These accounts, equivalent to a national mandatory IRA or 401k retirement plan, would be an "add on" to OASDI and would require new financing. They would have no effect on people with adequate private pensions, who would reduce contributions to current plans to compensate for the new OASDI add-on. But they would provide private retirement accounts to the 40 percent of Americans now lacking them, thus giving every family another leg to stand on besides OASDI when they reach retirement age, while also cushioning against any further reductions in OASDI benefits. Furthermore, private accounts as an add-on rather than a substitute for Social Security had bi-partisan support (Sperling, 2005). The precipitous drop in the stock market in 2008, however, is likely to diminish the attractiveness of private accounts even as an add-on to Social Security. Private accounts will contribute to security only if they can guarantee a safe investment vehicle, such as indexed government bonds.

One could add measurably to the security of the OASI as a failsafe system by introducing a minimum benefit for longer-term users, which is tied to the Supplemental Security Income (SSI) system for low-income and low-asset elders and which would be very inexpensive. The Canadians have managed to reduce elder women's poverty by means of such a system by raising benefits for elders who have nothing but OASI to rely on to poverty-line income levels (Smeeding, 1999; Estes, Glasse, and Smeeding, 1999). Together, these new pillars would increase both self-provision and security for all elders, especially the very old.

People are living longer in all rich nations. Indeed, as noted in Chapter 5, Americans do not live quite as long as citizens in other rich countries. Although differences in mortality are relatively small, birth rates in the United States are substantially higher than birth rates in most of the other rich countries. As a consequence, the problem of financing future retirement benefits is more serious in the other rich nations than in the United States. The financing problem in the United States is also more manageable because of its tradition as an immigrant nation. One way to finance the benefits of future American retirees is to allow more working-age immigrants into the country. Of course, this solution is only temporary, as the immigrants themselves will ultimately grow old and retire. But, as one generation of immigrants retires, more immigrants of working age can be admitted. Though other rich nations are now admitting more immigrants than they have in the past, most do not have the US tradition of being a nation of immigrants, and all remain far more homogeneous than the United States. Even in the United States, however, political resistance to continuing the large-scale immigration of the past 30 years is now growing.

II. Achieving equal access and restraining the growth of health-care costs

The US health-care system stands out from that of other rich nations in two negative respects. It has the largest inequalities in access to health care and is, by far, the most expensive system. On the positive side, it provides high-quality care for the most fortunate and best-insured segment of its population.

Is equal access to health care, like equal access to education, an essential element of equality of opportunity? First, we argue that it is, examine the extent to which the US measures up, and show that improving the situation will increase costs. Then we argue that constraining the growth in health-care costs is at least as important as achieving equal access. Ironically, restraining health-care costs may in time be the strongest argument for a publicly financed universal health insurance system.

Equal access and universal coverage

Health care, like education, is a fundamental determinant of human capital and well-being. At the most fundamental level, health care is often a matter of life and death. At a slightly less, but still fundamental, level, it is an essential ingredient to the productivity and quality of life. Because of vaccinations, children no longer die from or become crippled by chicken pox, diphtheria, measles, mumps, rubella, polio, smallpox, and tetanus. Eyeglasses allow children and adults with weak vision to see very well. Steroids, nasal sprays, and consistent care allow children and adults with asthma to control the disease and lead normal lives. Without hip replacement surgery, those who need it experience ever-increasing pain and disability. With hip replacement surgery, older citizens in all the rich nations lead normal pain-free lives. Equal access to personal health care is, in this sense, an aspect of equality of opportunity. R. H. Tawney, the Fabian socialist, made this point eloquently nearly 80 years ago in his classic book *Equality*. Nobel Prize-winning economist, Amartya Sen, makes essentially the same argument in his book *Inequality Re-examined* (1992). Virtually everyone in rich countries recognizes that health care is an essential ingredient to the productivity and quality of life and frequently to life itself. That conviction helps explain why large majorities in all countries favor equal access to health care and, along with the efficiency of community-provided health insurance, why medical care is

183

largely socialized in all rich countries. Even in the United States, most adults believe in equal access to health care,[5] and, as we have seen, health-care consumption is largely socialized.

But US practice diverges substantially from the ideal—not that the ideal has been achieved in many nations. In Great Britain, for example, where personal health care has been socialized since 1949, upper-class British citizens make better use of the National Health Service than do their lower-income compatriots (Le Grande, 1978). In the real world, perfection is unattainable. Elites will always find a way to secure better-than-average care. But other rich countries more closely approach equal access to health care. Britain comes closer. So do the Netherlands and Switzerland—which are viewed by some as possible models for the United States, and where privatized but heavily regulated insurers manage with government support to cover nearly all citizens. While the rich (the top 10–15 percent of the populations) in Europe can and do "buy up" with unsubsidized insurance to provide private rooms and quicker access to specialists, the "floor level" of health care is usually very high (OECD, 2006).

The OECD (2004c, Chapter 1) recently classified health-care systems in three ways:

1. *Public integrated model*: a one payer system with strong cost controls and publicly run hospitals. These systems offer less choice than do the other models, but stronger cost controls. They include Canada, UK, France and Sweden. In all except Canada, private insurance can be used to supplement public coverage.

2. *Public contract systems*, where public sector payers contract with private health-care providers. These systems offer more choice and are more responsive to patient needs, but do less well at cost control. These include Australia, Belgium and Germany.

3. *Private insurance /provider systems*, where private sector health insurers may have to compulsorily cover citizens (Switzerland, Netherlands) or voluntarily cover them (USA). These systems are most responsive to ability to pay and related consumer needs, but are least able to control costs.

In all three types of systems, cost-sharing arrangements for patients are present; but only one system does not provide a basic floor of coverage to all citizens, and that is the United States.

The United States is indeed different. The top 50 percent of the populace has full access to high-quality health care. Those receiving Medicare are almost as likely as the bulk of the employer-insured population to have access to high-quality care. Medicaid is a step below Medicare in terms of access and quality. Only the United States has a large uninsured population. The quality of care proceeds down across class lines. In a *New York Times* report, Janny Scott (2005) tells an interesting story of three people of the same age, each of whom has the onset of the same serious heart condition. The upper-class person immediately receives the best and most proper care. The middle-class person wrestles (figuratively speaking) with health-care providers and after a month or two also gets proper care. The lower-class person without health insurance is told she cannot receive the proper care as it is too costly; she fears for her life. The Institute of Medicine (2004) documents that the uninsured in the United States go without critically needed medical care because of the lack of insurance and estimates that as a result 18,000 Americans die prematurely.

Insuring the uninsured is a prerequisite for achieving equal access. By itself, achieving universal coverage, however, will increase costs. Gruber (2008) estimates that the costs would be between $105 and $125 billion per year. Moreover, universal coverage by itself would not achieve equal access. Reducing inequalities in health-care quality would bring the country closer to equal access, but equalizing up by raising the bottom and middle portions closer to the top (which we presume most of us would prefer), will also increase costs.

Constraining costs

1. WHY ARE COSTS SO HIGH AND GROWING RAPIDLY?

Constraining the growth in health-care costs is at least as important as achieving universal coverage. For the last 30 years, per capita health-care costs in the US have grown a bit more than twice as rapidly as the growth in per capita GDP—4.3 percent versus 2.0 percent. The Congressional Budget Office (CBO) has projected the consequences for the federal costs of Medicare and Medicaid as a percentage of GDP if health-care costs continue to grow so rapidly compared to GDP. Currently, Social Security, Medicare, and Medicaid amount to under 10 percent of GDP. By 2074, all three are projected to amount to over 25 percent of GDP! The increase in Social Security expenditures is trivial compared with the size of the needed revenues for health care for the aged and poor. The increase in Social Security costs are driven by the aging of the population. The increase in medical care costs are driven only secondarily by the aging of the population, but primarily by greater use of new technologies (CBO, 2008). The costs of employer-provided health insurance benefits, out-of-pocket medical care expenses, and state costs for Medicaid are not included in the CBO projections. If overall health-care costs increase in the next 60 years at the same rate in excess of GDP as they have increased in the last 30 years, total health-care costs will be equal to about one third of GDP!

One reason why health-care costs are so high and increasing so rapidly is that health care is very valuable and the value is increasing (Cutler and McClellan, 2001; Cutler, 2004). For that reason, as individuals become richer, they are willing to spend more for health care. In the United States, annual spending per person on health care increased from $700 per person in 1960 to $6,700 in 2005 (Catlin et al., 2007). At least half of that increase is due to increases in services rather than increases in price. Life expectancy also increased during this period by about seven years, and Cutler estimates that perhaps half of the increase is attributable to improvements in medical care. Indeed, Cutler's book *Your Money or Your Life* (2004), as discussed in Chapter 4, challenges the conventional wisdom of excessive spending. It provides convincing evidence that the benefits of just a few new medical care procedures exceed all of the recent increase in costs of medical care in the United States. That benefits exceed costs by such a wide margin, of course, does not address the issue of whether costs could be much lower with little or no diminution in benefits. Other rich nations have achieved the same or higher gains in life expectancy at much lower costs.[6]

Still, Cutler's evidence of very high returns to medical care spending should give pause to even the most enthusiastic advocates of health-care spending restraints.[7] Although there is good evidence that Americans pay higher prices for the same quantity of care received by citizens of other rich nations (Anderson et al., 2003; Anderson and Frogner, 2008) and have higher administrative costs, it would be naive to assume that, as health-care cost increases are restrained in the future, there will be no costs in terms of forgone improvements in the quantity and quality of medical care treatment. Restraining costs is likely to result in lower relative salaries for doctors and health-care administrators and lower provision of amenities and some kinds of medical care procedures. Cost increases in the USA and elsewhere are being driven by new technology in health care (CBO, 2008). For example, other countries provide much less kidney dialysis than does the United States and also fewer expensive diagnostic tests like CAT scans. Indeed, some economists, such as Fogel (2004) are quite sanguine about the prospect of spending one third of our income on health care, noting that for people in rich nations spending on more health care is probably more valuable than spending on more material possessions.

A second reason why health-care costs are also high and growing so rapidly in all rich nations is because they are largely socialized. Because most individual patients pay little of the costs of their medical care, they have little incentive to spend less on medical care. If all patients or their families had to pay the full price of medical care, they would no doubt spend far less on health care. Even though more than 50 million Americans are uninsured, health care in the United States today is for the most part paid for by health insurance or by charging insured patients more to make up for charity or below-cost reimbursed care. Thus, from the point of view of most patients, US health care is already largely socialized.[8]

The major reason why costs are so much higher in the United States is that US socialization is so decentralized. Government provision (centralization) of health insurance lowers costs in two ways. First, private provision of health insurance entails advertising, selling, profits, and other costs not incurred by government provision. Similarly, private insurance imposes substantially greater costs on doctors and hospitals than does a single-payer system. Woolhander, Campbell, and Himmelstein (2003) compare administrative costs in the US to Canada—31 percent versus 16.7 percent—and conclude that a sole-payer system in the US would save 14.3 percent of total health-care costs.[9] Private provision also entails attempts by insurers to weed out potentially costly patients, which not only increases administrative costs, but undermines insurance itself.

Second, and more important in the long run, when the government is the sole payer for health insurance, it restrains costs by limiting the total health insurance budget. When health insurance is part of the budget, an increase in health benefits requires an increase in taxes. While restraining costs through budgets is a blunt instrument, it is an effective instrument. Increases in cost in the USA and other rich nations are being driven by new technology in health care, a much more potent force than population aging for driving costs (CBO, 2008; White, 2007; OECD, 2004c). But a recent study shows that, controlling for economic growth, population aging, and other factors that differ across nations, health-care costs in rich nations with publicly financed systems grew 1.1 percent faster than national income from 1970 to 2002, while US costs grew 2.0 percent faster than national income over that same period (White, 2007). Switzerland has experienced almost as rapid excess-cost growth as has the United States. The Netherlands also experienced above average excess-cost growth. Both, like the US, have extensive private insurance and provision.

2. WILL UNIVERSAL COVERAGE REDUCE COSTS?

The Swiss and the Netherlands systems are worth describing in a little more detail because they provide the only country examples of universal National Health Insurance systems that are built around a vast private health insurance industry and rely on a nearly universal individual mandate for individuals to buy their own coverage on an open market from heavily regulated derivate insurers (Switzerland), or insurers and government agencies (the Netherlands), to reach universal coverage. To reach this goal all nations—ours and theirs—we need an effective regulatory enforcement mechanism to assure risk-pooling and heavy subsidies for the poor. The Dutch and Swiss cover nearly 100 percent of their people via a managed competition system that allows all to buy the same "standard" policy at the same rates regardless of age or medical condition. The standard policy covers all types of cost-effective care. Employers may purchase coverage for their employees at a 10 percent discount. Tax revenues from employers and the self-employed are used to subsidize the poor and to offset losses for companies which have a large portion of sick people. Those who do not purchase a policy are fined 130 percent of the premium they would have paid (UC Berkeley Center for Labor Research, 2007).

Adapting such a system to the United States with employer coverage would require heavy regulation of insurers, creation of risk pools for insurers with secondary insurance by governments, and perhaps even employer "play or pay" mandates with no exceptions for small-firm sizes, in addition to full mobility of policies from firm to firm so that insurance was separate from employment (Van de Water, 2008; Steuerle and Van de Water, 2007). Such a system for adults would also mesh well with Medicare for the elderly and a universal S-Chip type program for all children under age 25. But these systems, especially the Swiss and also to some extent the Dutch are worse than average in terms of cost containment (White, 2007). This suggests that even if clauses for pre-existing conditions and community rating are enforced, costs in private insurance systems will increase more than they do in single-payer systems.

3. WHAT'S THE MATTER WITH THE FREE MARKET SOLUTION?

Many free market economists also believe that the United States is spending too much on health care, but attribute the problem to excessive health insurance coverage for ordinary health-care expenditures. This view underlies President Bush's and the Republican candidate John McCain's proposal to limit the tax subsidy in the income tax for employer-provided health insurance benefits by counting the benefits as taxable income and their proposal for Health Savings Accounts (HSAs) and high deductible health insurance (Feldman et al., 2005; Owcharenko 2004). There is strong evidence from the Health Insurance Experiment (financed by the Office of Economic Opportunity and conducted by the Rand Corporation) that co-insurance and deductibles induce individuals to use less health-care services. Indeed, the plan with the highest co-insurance and deductibles reduced costs as compared to conventional employer-provided health insurance by 30 percent without any apparent compromise in health outcomes (Newhouse et al., 1993). That is a pretty big potential saving— about twice the saving in reduced administrative costs of a single-payer system. But economists such as John Cogan, Glenn Hubbard, and Daniel Kessler (2005), who use the health insurance experiment to make the case for the so-called free market solution, neglect to note the experiment also showed that at least as much could be saved by eliminating the fee-for-service reimbursement system which creates an economic incentive for physicians and hospitals to give the patient more services. Physicians are bound by the Hippocratic Oath to do all in their power for their patients. To reinforce this professional obligation with economic self-interest does not seem wise.

Furthermore, even if catastrophic insurance cut costs by 30 percent, it would not reduce the long-term growth rate in costs. Recall that it is costly new technology that is driving health-care costs. Costly new technology is exactly what catastrophic health insurance covers.

Finally, for several reasons, we doubt that in the real world the high deductibles implicit in the provision of catastrophic health insurance would have such benign effects as evidenced in the experiment. First, the experiment excluded the aged because they were already covered by Medicare. Thus, the results cannot be generalized to the most expensive per person part of the medical care system. Second, it is hard to reconcile such a big effect with a well-known fact regarding the remarkably uneven distribution of medical care expenditures. Though the concentration has declined somewhat, in 2003, one quarter of all medical care expenditures in the US in 2003 were accounted for by only 1 percent of the population, one half of all expenditures were accounted for by only 5 percent of the population, and 80 percent of all expenditures were accounted for by only 25 percent of the population (Zuvekas and Cohen, 2007). The bulk of health-care expenditures are very large or above the proposed deductible amounts. Ordinary health-care expenditures which would be affected by the deductibles make up only a small share of total health-care costs. Unless the deductible levels are high enough to eviscerate insurance, how can high deductible health insurance substantially reduce health-care spending without compromising health? But, if preventive care is not exempted and made free, which was not true in the health insurance experiment, high deductibles are likely to deter preventive care—such as periodic pre-natal visits, well visits, and annual checkups for older adults—especially among low-income families, and as a consequence are likely to compromise health. Third, a weakness of nearly all social science experiments is that they provide evidence on short-term micro rather than long-term macro effects (Manski and Garfinkel, 1992). In the case of the health insurance experiment, the study provides good evidence on the medical care expenses incurred by individuals, and their health-care outcomes, for up to three years for most of the sample and up to five years for the rest of the sample. It is possible that there were negative long-term health effects, especially in view of the fact that preventive services were not exempted. The absence of long-term follow-up seems particularly serious in the case of the health insurance experiment. Equally important and more certain, micro social experiments such as the health insurance experiment cannot detect long-run market effects, which are bound to dilute the cost-reducing effects of the catastrophic insurance. As technology makes medical care more expensive, an increasing share of medical care expenses will be catastrophic or covered. Moreover, medical care providers will have incentives to provide more of the covered, expensive services.[10] For all these reasons, we think it risky and unwise for the nation to pursue high deductible health insurance. As discussed below, however, in the context of a federal policy to encourage states to experiment with alternative forms of universal health insurance, if a state wanted to experiment with such an approach the citizens in other states, and therefore the nation as a whole, would have much to gain and little to lose from the experiment.

4. SHORT- AND LONG-RUN SOLUTIONS

The twin goals of achieving equal access and restraining the growth of health-care costs create a very strong case for a publicly financed National Health Insurance system. Two other arguments strengthen that case. First, researchers have found that increases in health-care spending are crowding out other public spending. Most recently, a study by Thomas Kane and Peter Orszag (2003) indicates that increased spending on Medicaid has displaced spending on higher education and other benefits, such as early childhood education, at both the federal and state level. Restraining health-care spending is a prerequisite for shifting from ever increasing spending on the elderly to more productive spending on children. Second, a publicly financed system of National Health Insurance can help reverse the seemingly inexorable trend to increased inequality. Employer-provided health insurance, for the most part, assures that each employee pays for his or her own health insurance. If health insurance costs $5,000 per person, under employer-provided insurance, then each employee pays $5,000, in the form of reduced wages. By way of contrast, if health insurance were publicly financed by a proportional tax, the richest fifth of the population which earns about 60 percent of total income would pay for 60 percent of the cost or about $15,000 per person, while the poorest fifth which earns only about 5 percent of total income would pay only about $1,500 per person.

A publicly financed universal National Health Insurance program, even with private insurers as agents, would promote opportunity by equalizing access to health care, reduce inequality by increasing the progressivity of financing, and increase economic efficiency by restraining the growth in health-care costs.

Although the case for a single-payer National Health Insurance system is strong, achieving such a national system is likely to be politically difficult for the foreseeable future. A single-payer system has very powerful opponents, including the private health insurance industry, the medical technology and hospital industries, and the American Medical Association. Feder (2008) and most other analysts argue that health-care reform cannot immediately include the abandonment of the employer-based system and use of private insurers which undergird access for the middle class. They advocate building on the employer-based private health insurance system and subsidizing the costs of those not covered by employers so as to achieve complete (or nearly so) national coverage. Further, they argue that government testing for cost effectiveness of new treatments and technologies can help steer coverage to the most cost-effective levels and reduce variance across communities and states (Wennberg et al., 2008). Those who wanted more coverage, or other types of coverage, would have to pay more from their own pockets for these features. The cost, as noted above, would be about $105 to $125 billion. President Barak Obama favors this approach. But, as argued above, it is highly unlikely that building on employer-provided insurance will restrain costs.

The United States cannot avoid tackling the issue of financing health insurance for very long. Medicare is due to run out of money in 10 short years (SSA, 2008), so something must be done to restrain the growth of costs and make them correspond more closely to overall economic growth.

It is ironic that to stem the tide in the social costs of health insurance the US most likely needs to increase taxes to finance a single-payer system. This irony illustrates one elementary lesson of cost-benefit analysis—government costs are not in general a good measure of total social costs. Still, it is difficult to say when the American system will place an acceptable floor under health care for all Americans, while at the same time restraining the growth of health-care costs.

State innovations, as health-care experts Henry Aaron on the left and Stuart Butler on the right have advocated, may help break the logjam. Several states have already taken large steps in the direction of achieving universal coverage. But so far attempts to achieve universal coverage seem to be failing in both California and Massachusetts where the costs are increasingly higher than estimates (Gruber, 2008). Thus, the issue has returned to the federal level and has become a key focus of Congress and of the Obama administration.

As the country explores and debates the merits of retaining the employer-based system versus adopting a tax-based, single-payer system, we recommend three positive steps which do not resolve this fundamental issue, but represent compromise steps forward that are compatible with either a single-payer system or retention of the employer-based system. The first two are to adopt both a tax-financed National Health Insurance program for children up to age 22 or 25, and to adopt proposals for achieving universal coverage by building upon the employer-based system. A National Health Insurance system for children would be a good first federal step both in terms of equalizing opportunity for children and as a practical matter. The extra tax costs of insuring children are relatively small. Symbolically, achieving universal coverage for children would convey an orientation to the future. Building on the employer-provided, private health insurance industry is the least disruptive method of achieving universality of coverage for the working-age population. Both reforms will also inject more revenue into the health-care system, which should make the third step more palatable and more likely to succeed. The third step would be to enact federal legislation that would allow states to use all federal funding for health care in their states to reconfigure their state health-care systems in alternative ways subject to a set of constraints, such as universal coverage and no increases in costs in excess of the growth in national income and the aging of the population. Combining a budget limit with decentralization is another huge compromise philosophically that would achieve both a slowing of the growth rate of health-care expenditures and enable greater experimentation that comes from decentralized government.

III. Restoring American pre-eminence in education

Welfare state programs in all rich nations transfer substantial resources from the working-age population to the elderly population. As populations have grown older in all rich nations, old-age pensions and medical care have become the biggest welfare state programs. As the populations of rich countries continue to age, the costs of these programs will grow larger. The economic demographer Sam Preston, in his famous presidential address to the Population Association of America (1984), called attention to the danger that the increasing burden of cash and in-kind transfers to the aged would crowd out investments in children.

Investing in children now will increase their future productivity, thereby increasing future earnings and the tax base and allowing the same level of support at lower tax rates. Conversely, investing inadequately now in children will lower future productivity, reduce incomes and the tax base, and require higher tax rates. Thus, ironically, perhaps, nations with aging populations must invest all the more in children in order to make the future burden of supporting the aged more tolerable (Esping-Anderson, 2005). In this section, we discuss investments that would restore American pre-eminence in education. In the following section, we discuss other complementary investments in children.

Universal pre-school for three and four year olds

Extending the age of compulsory schooling downward to age three by enacting universal pre-school programs would increase productivity and reduce poverty and inequality. A 2003 National Academy of Sciences study estimated the cost of such a program at $25–35 billion above and beyond the $25–30 billion in public funds which we now spend on various public and non-profit pre-school programs (Smolensky and Gootman, eds, 2005: 7–8).

Children who begin school at age three are more likely to enjoy learning and do better not only in school but also in adult life. Of children age three to five whose mothers are college-educated, 70 percent already attend pre-school. Only 38 percent of children whose mothers did not complete high school attend pre-school. Children whose mothers are high school drop-outs have the most to gain from pre-school, and the broader society will benefit the most from educating these children in high-quality public schools beginning at age three. But, more generally, because of the public benefits of education, everyone will benefit from universal pre-school.

Researchers have gathered very strong evidence that the benefits of high-quality early childhood education exceed the costs, especially for disad-vantaged children. The strongest evidence comes from the Perry pre-school experiment initiated more than 30 years ago in Ypsilanti, Michigan, where children from disadvantaged families were randomly selected to be in either the experimental group or a control group. Children in the experimental group were eligible to participate in a very high-quality pre-school program. As the children grew older, those in the experimental group outperformed those in the control group in many ways. They did better in school, needed less remedial assistance, completed more years of schooling, committed fewer crimes, were less likely to be dependent upon welfare, earned more money, and paid more taxes. Even though high-quality pre-school is quite expensive—more than $16,000 for a two-year half-day program in 2004 dollars—and though most of the benefits come much later than costs are incurred and therefore get discounted, James Heckman reports in *Science* (2006) that the present discounted value of the benefits was nearly nine times the costs—or about $144,000! Evaluations of other good pre-school programs, including Head Start, also find positive effects.[11]

Universal high-quality pre-school would produce much smaller benefits for more advantaged children for two reasons. Many are already enrolled in such programs, and more advantaged children are less at risk for special education, grade retention, dropping out of school, crime, and welfare dependence. That does not mean, however, that the benefits would be zero. A Rand Corporation study by Lynn Karoly and James Bigelow, of a universal pre-school program in California, finds that half of all students who use special education, get held back a grade, or drop out of school are from families in the middle three quintiles of the income distribution. Moreover, there is some direct evidence of positive effects of pre-school on more advantaged children. But even if only the most at-risk children— the bottom 11 percent—derived any benefits and if the benefits were only one-fourth as large as those of the Perry pre-school, the Rand study estimates that benefits to California residents would exceed cost by nearly 2 to 1. Assuming more realistically that the benefits decline gradually from highest for those most at risk to zero for those least at risk, the study finds that for Californians the benefits of universal pre-school exceed costs by 2.6 to 1.

The Rand study, as the authors note, underestimates the benefits to the state of universal pre-school education because it does not measure several benefits, including most importantly the long-term effects on economic growth. As we discussed in Chapter 2, economists agree, in general, that increased education accounts for a large part of economic growth. And, in a recent study, William Dickens, Isabel Sawhill, and Jeffrey Tebbs (2006) estimate specifically that the effects of universal pre-school education on economic growth are likely to be quite large—leading to a higher GDP in 2080 of between 1 and 4 percent. The increase in state taxes resulting from their preferred estimate of increased GDP would more than pay for the costs of the program in 2080![12]

Pre-schools, in addition to being an investment in children, provide childcare for parents. In view of the large share of mothers of three and four year olds who work, childcare is a very important service. Half-day pre-schools provide half as much childcare as full-day pre-schools. For this reason, most proposals for pre-school programs combine half-day schooling with at least half-day childcare. Even full-day pre-schools, however, do not provide adequate childcare for parents who work full time. Therefore, pre-schools will also need to be funded to provide extended childcare services to parents who request the service.

Though universal high quality pre-school education would be a good investment for any state and for the nation as a whole, low-quality pre-school education may not be a good investment and might even do more harm than good.[13] Some analysts favor a high-cost high-quality pre-school program that is targeted at low-income families, rather than being universal, because they fear that a high-quality universal program would be so costly that taxpayers would be unwilling to fund it and that, as a result, quality would be reduced to lower costs. That is certainly possible and is a danger to be avoided. But it is at least as likely that political support for high-quality pre-school programs will be stronger if the program is universal rather than income-tested. In any case, low-quality pre-school education should be avoided, but probably won't be in many states.

UNIVERSALITY OR A FLOOR VERSUS A SAFETY NET

The federal government in the United States has been supporting pre-school-age education for poor children since 1965 via the Head Start program. Why should the nation shift towards universal provision? All of the general arguments in Chapter 3 about the long-term superiority of floors to safety nets apply here, and with special force to education. The external, or spillover, benefits of education are uniquely large, which means that all of us benefit a great deal from the education of all children. Universal pre-school will also lead to reductions in income, racial and ethnic, and gender inequality. It will lead to greater assimilation across cultural, racial and ethnic lines. Universal programs lead to direct reductions in income inequality, as we saw in Chapter 3, because they provide equal benefits to all income classes, and the tax bite on the upper classes is much higher for universal programs than for income-tested programs. Universal provision will reduce future inequality by providing investments in poor, lower-middle income, and middle-income children that the upper-middle and upper-income families already provide to their children. Because black and Hispanic children are disproportionately disadvantaged in terms of income, the education of their mothers, and single parenthood, they will benefit disproportionately from universal pre-school.[14] Finally, universal pre-school will also promote gender equality by freeing mothers to pursue other activities, including market employment, while their children are in pre-school. Promoting gender equality only at the bottom of the income distribution by limiting benefits to the poorest children is a dangerous recipe. Other institutions, most especially higher education, promote gender equality at the top of the income distribution. The lower-middle class and middle class, as usual in the non-universal world, disproportionately fall between the cracks. This mixture is dangerous for a country where the bottom fifth is much more black and brown than the second and third fifths. The lower-middle and middle-income mothers come to resent both their upper-class and their lower-class sisters for their greater gender equality and at the same time despise their behavior.

STATE INITIATIVES AND VOUCHERS

States are taking the lead in enacting universal pre-school programs because public education is traditionally and remains today predominantly a state and local responsibility. A few including Georgia, Oklahoma, and New York, have already adopted, but have not yet fully funded, universal pre-school education programs. Complementary federal funding is needed to make these programs financially viable for all states, not just the few who have begun to formulate such programs.

Some states may elect to experiment with vouchers in providing early childhood education, particularly because vouchers are already common in childcare. Choice and competition could lead to better education. But vouchers raise two major concerns. First, if the voucher covers only part of the tuition that schools charge, in the long run they will undermine public support for education. All of those with above-average incomes will have an incentive to vote for reductions in the voucher because their reduction in taxes will exceed the increase in the tuition they will have to pay. If vouchers can be used only at schools where tuition does not exceed the voucher, this danger can be avoided. Second, in the United States, public education is responsible for inculcating a common American set of values in a very diverse set of children. That concern, however, applies with less force to three and four year olds than to older children.

Although elementary and secondary education has traditionally been a state and local function, the federal government already provides funding for Head Start and for childcare. Thus, the federal government will continue to play a much bigger role in early childhood education and care than it plays in elementary and secondary education. Though states have taken the leadership to date, federal leadership can speed up the process and underwrite state investment. Just as President Bush became the "education president" by leading Congress to enact his "no child left behind" policy for education output measurement in elementary and secondary schools, President Obama could become the "fair and equal start" president by persuading the Congress to provide federal matching funds for states that establish high-quality, universal pre-schools for all three to five year olds. The president's proposed budget includes a huge increase in federal funding for early childhood education.

K-12

As we have seen, the US public education system is producing, at best, mediocre results compared with that of other rich nations. Compared with all nations globally, of course, the results are outstanding. Nearly one in five adults in the world are still illiterate and, in most countries, a majority still do not complete high school. But the world is catching up. As of 2005, over 60 percent of adults in India were literate and in China the figure is 90 percent (UNDP, 2007/2008). And Japan, South Korea, Taiwan, and Singapore are now on par with or have surpassed the United States. In the United States, 75 percent of the cohort that was age 20 in 1980 graduated from high school, but in 2005, 70 percent graduated (Fiske, 2008). Though adoption of universal pre-school programs is the most important change that states and the nation as a whole must make, K-12 education also requires change.

There is some debate in the economics profession about how important school spending is in producing better school outcomes (Akin and Garfinkel, 1980; Burtless, 1996; Hanushek, 1996; Card and Krueger, 1996). But all parties to the debate seem to agree that high-quality teachers improve school outcomes. Raising teacher salaries will attract higher-quality teachers and also raise costs. Moreover, wealthy suburban localities appear willing to tax themselves sufficiently to attract the best teachers and build the best school facilities. We expect that the better-off localities will continue to adequately fund the schools their children attend.

A large part of the problem lies within large cities with disproportionate concentrations of poor families, which are, in turn, disproportionately ethnic, black, and made up of the children of recent immigrants. The children of these families need better-than-average teachers and other resources to succeed, but their parents have much less-than-average capacity to pay for schooling. The tax base lives in and pays taxes to the suburbs. Many states have been grappling with these financing issues for quite some time, and the trend has been for a greater share of total financing of education to come from the state rather than the locality, and for spending per pupil to become more equal (Evans, Murray, and Schwab, 2003; Wilson, Lambright, and Smeeding, 2006). With luck, this trend will not only continue but intensify as Americans once more put greater emphasis on promoting opportunity, equality, and economic security.

Though most improvements in K-12 education will take place on the state level, the federal role should grow. Richard Murnane (2006), an economist at Harvard's School of Education, recommends a modest reform agenda that builds on the No Child Left Behind Act and that Congress is likely to adopt. The recommendations involve several elements: improving accountability by modifying the annual yearly progress requirements of the No Child Left Behind; creating incentives for schools to align curricula with post-secondary education and work needs; monitoring progress by requiring all schools to administer revised 12th grade national (NAEP) tests instead of less difficult state tests; and building state capacity by offering competitive matching grants for state and local programs that offer incentives for teachers to work and to stay in schools that serve high-poverty populations. In this way, federal funds can help hard-pressed central cities fulfill their missions. Together with universal pre-schools, such changes will lead to a relative improvement in graduation rates and college attendance.

Higher education

Higher education graduation rates for children from low-income families are very low (Haveman and Smeeding, 2006). Only 8 percent of all children born into the lowest-income quartile in 1966–70 graduated from college (within six years of finishing high school), as against 50 percent of top-quartile children. A study of elite colleges finds that, among all enrollees, 44 percent of lower-quartile children and 78 percent of higher-quartile enrollees now graduate. In fact, most disadvantaged kids, and especially minority kids, first enroll in two-year community colleges, from which only about a third go on to four-year colleges and universities (Goldhaber and Kiefer, 2007). Because Americans are committed to greater social mobility, we hope that once these facts are widely known and understood, we will see a number of modest but important changes in United States higher education policy, at both federal and state levels, to address these inequities.

Achieving greater success in higher education for low-income children will require several changes. Students must be better prepared in high school, by taking the right courses, by developing better study habits, by taking standardized examinations, and by applying for admission to colleges. Secondary schools must take the lead here, especially with better career counseling, mentoring, and better information on the true costs of college (not the daunting "sticker prices" at very selective schools). State and federal governments need to expand needs-based financial aid. Researchers have now amassed good evidence that higher tuition subsidies and direct grants increase both college attendance and completion (Dynarksi, 2005).

Moreover, though zero-cost tuition reduces dropout rates in higher education by nearly 50 percent, it does not eliminate them (Stinebrickner and Stinebrickner, 2003). Recent evidence from Turner (2006) and Pallais and Turner (2007) suggests that college-going is an ever-lengthening process that is stretching itself out beyond five to six years after secondary school graduation. To reduce the time it takes them to earn a degree, students must not only become better prepared when they first enter college, but polices to retain students who are at risk of dropping out for non-academic reasons must be expanded (Tinto, 1998; Dickert-Conlin and Rubenstein, 2007). Thus, in addition to zero-cost tuition for students from low-income families, higher education policy should increasingly turn to the important issue of enrollment management and persistence to degree by instituting strategies that produce higher rates of graduation for those who enter post-secondary education.

Finally, a major policy focus for low-income youth will be community and two-year colleges, where the majority of both black and Latino children first enter higher education. These schools will need to provide remedial education for four-year college-bound students who are not well enough prepared, and to provide direct skill-based technical education for those who do not want to pursue a four-year degree.

None of these steps by themselves are very costly, but none is costless. The costs of all of the steps add up and mustering political support for them will not be easy. Once again, however, the Obama administration is taking steps in the right direction, instituting polices to lower costs for student loans, to increase Pell grants, and to influence high school and college graduation rates.

IV. Making other productive investments in children

Restoring American pre-eminence in education will also require other complementary investments in children. In this section, we briefly discuss four other investments in children—paid parental leave, a post-birth home-visiting service, child allowances in the form of refundable tax credits, and an assured child support benefit—that would further promote both equity and efficiency. They are complementary in the sense that they are likely to increase the returns to the education and health investments outlined above. The four complementary investments discussed are not meant to be exhaustive, but rather illustrative. There are many other productive investments, but those discussed seem especially promising. All add to the American floor of social investment and protection. Our exclusive focus on floors does not indicate that we think improvements in safety nets are not important. Elsewhere, we have written about the short-comings of and sensible improvements to the American safety net for families with children (Garfinkel and McLanahan, 1986; Garfinkel, 1992,

1996, and 2001). Our focus on floors rather than safety nets reflects our belief that raising the floor for all children will maximize both reductions in poverty and inequality and increases in efficiency and productivity.

Paid parental leave

Universal paid parental leave polices have been adopted in all rich countries save Australia and the US (Gornick and Meyers, 2007). A number of employers and states within the US have also made pioneering efforts. Based on the scientific evidence of its productivity and equity effects, these countries, employers, and states have made wise decisions, which the US as a whole would do well to imitate.

In the United States, more than half of all mothers now work during the first year of their child's life. Yet an increasing body of scientific evidence shows that children from all income groups who are cared for by one of their parents during their first year do better than children who are cared for by others (Waldfogel, 2006). Paid family leave encourages mothers and fathers to take time off from work and care for their newborn infants. Research based on differences in parental leave policies across rich nations and within nations over time finds that longer periods of leave are associated with better child health, especially post neo-natal mortality—death between 28 days and one year of life (Ruhm, 2000; Tanaka, 2005).

Children are the primary beneficiaries of paid parental leave. But parents also benefit. Longer periods of paid family leave (across and within rich nations) are also associated with lower maternal mortality (Tanaka, 2005) and higher maternal mental health (Chatterji and Brooks-Gunn, 2004). Paid family leave is an essential ingredient to balancing work and family. Caring for and raising a child is difficult work. When both parents work, as is quite common now, it is difficult financially for one parent to stop working. Because paid family leave replaces a large share (normally 50 to 75 percent of pay up to some maximum) of the earnings of the leave-taker, it allows one parent to stop working temporarily at little financial sacrifice.

Because eligibility for paid parental leave is contingent on having work and earnings, it reinforces work even as it releases parents from work for a time-limited period to care for their newborns. Paid parental leave also creates an incentive for women to delay childbirth until they have established a work record that enables them to qualify for the benefit.

Paid parental leave insurance, like old-age insurance, is a way of redistributing income over the life course to a period when income-generating potential is low. To the extent that the earnings replacement rate is higher for low earners than high earners, it is also a non-stigmatizing way to transfer income to low-income families. Additionally, as opposed to welfare transfers, paid family leave is not only by nature time-limited, but it also by nature, as discussed above, reinforces work.

Some feminists object to paid family leave because it reinforces the traditional gender division of labor in which men work in the market and women work at home. They point out that even in Sweden, where fathers as well as mothers are eligible for leave and the full length of leave is available only if both parents take some of the leave, mothers are much more likely than fathers to take leave. Gender differences in leave-taking are driven initially by biology. Mothers carry the child and give birth, both of which are physically taxing. Similarly, mothers are capable of nursing the newborn. But gender differences in leave-taking persist well beyond the first six months of the child's life when biological differences are strongest. Thus, there is truth to the argument that paid family leave reinforces the traditional gender division of labor. But the overall effect is not likely to be large. Assuming that the maximum length of leave is one year, that only mothers take leave, and that the average mother has two children, on average, mothers would miss two years of work. That amounts to only 5 percent of a normal work life of 40 years. Moreover, even in the absence of paid family leave, many mothers will stay home to take care of their newborns for some period. Finally, only women who work become eligible for leave. In theory, this pro-work feature of paid family leave could actually outweigh the negative effects of leave-taking. For all these reasons, despite the opposition of some feminists, most women support paid family leave and have been the leading advocates at the state and national level for its adoption.

The United States and Australia are now the only rich nations without national paid family leave. The length of paid leave, earnings replacement rates, and the degree to which fathers as well as mothers are encouraged to take leave varies in other countries (Gornick and Meyers, 2003). A few states—California, Washington, and New Jersey—have adopted paid family leave programs as extensions of state unemployment or disability insurance programs, or both. Other states are likely to follow the lead of these pioneers and adopt paid parental leave programs. Ultimately, federal legislation to nationalize the program is desirable. The legislation could create a federal/state program along the lines of Unemployment Insurance, which allows for great variations across states, or a pure federal program like Old Age Insurance, or something in between.

Post-birth nurse home-visiting service

In the United Kingdom, all parents are visited by a nurse in their home soon after the birth of their child. The visit is viewed as a follow-up to the care and instruction received during the short period the mother stays in the hospital after giving birth. In the United States, following the positive results from an experiment conducted by David Olds, a number of states and localities have implemented visiting nurse services for at-risk children (Olds, 2002; Olds et al., 2002). More states should adopt visiting nurse services and, over time as the health-care system becomes more universal and other costs are restrained, this service should become universal. The logic is the same as with pre-school education.

Child allowances or a fully refundable child tax credit

With the partial exception of the United States, all rich nations have children's allowances—a universal cash benefit paid to parents of all income classes. Though the benefit is substantial in France and Sweden, in most countries it is small. Similarly, in most countries, it is paid out during the course of the year. In some countries, the benefit increases with the number of children. The United States is only a partial exception because the federal income tax contains a partially refundable tax credit for children equal to $1,000 per child. A tax credit of $1,000 offsets tax liability up to $1,000 and is therefore worth $1,000 to everyone who owes taxes of $1,000 or more. At the upper end of the earnings spectrum, the child tax credit is reduced at a rate of $50 for every $1,000 of earnings above $110,000. At the bottom of the spectrum, families with no income tax liability receive a credit worth 15 percent of earnings above the eligibility threshold, currently $12,050, and indexed for inflation. If the credit were fully refundable, like the earned income tax credit, the government would refund or pay families, who had less tax liability than the credit, the difference between the two. As of 2005, 20 million children were getting nothing or less than the full credit because it was not fully refundable (CBPP, 2005) and over 6 million get nothing or less than the full credit because of the phase out.

A *fully* refundable tax credit of $1,000 per child, which is not phased out for high-income families, would be worth $1,000 for every child and therefore would be perfectly equivalent in economic terms to a $1,000 per child allowance. Making the credit fully refundable would extend the benefit to the poorest children who do not now receive it. Like the EITC, the refundable credit would raise the incomes of low- and moderate-income families. Unlike the EITC, however, because a fully refundable child tax credit is worth $1,000 for every child, no matter what the income of its parents, it would be easy and administratively efficient to electronically deposit the funds to all families with children on a monthly basis.

As with any floor, child allowances redistribute income from richer to poorer. Child allowances also transfer income from those without children to those with children. Because most adults eventually have children, however, child allowances primarily transfer income over the life cycle—from before and after the childrearing years to during childrearing years. Child allowances also transfer incomes to larger families. Child allowance programs reflect a social recognition of the extra costs of childrearing and the value to society of parental willingness to undertake childrearing. These considerations justify the US child tax credit and more generally child allowances in rich nations.

Making the federal child tax credit fully refundable is not terribly costly—about $12 billion—and would improve both equity and efficiency. (Eliminating the phase out for high-income families would cost another $6 billion.)[15] Providing a child allowance to everyone but the poor and near-poor is on its face inequitable. Extending the benefit to the poorest children will increase their standard of living outside TANF, food stamps, and other safety nets, thereby reducing reliance on TANF and other safety nets.

In this area, too, the Obama administration has already made progress. The American Recovery and Relief Act (ARRA), popularly referred to as the stimulus Bill, temporarily expands the child tax credit provisions in the income tax code for two years, aiding 3 million additional children and increasing benefits by as much as $825 per child for another 10 million already-participating children. The Obama administration budget, if adopted by the Congress, would make these tax cuts permanent.

An assured child support benefit

More than half of American children will live apart from one of their natural parents before reaching adulthood (Bumpass and Lu, 2000). The overwhelming majority will live in a single-mother family. Though the United States leads the rich world in the share of its children who grow up with a single mother, single motherhood is experienced by approximately one third of children in the Northern European rich countries, and even in Italy, by one in eleven children (McLanahan, 2004). What should be done to aid children in single-parent families is therefore of great concern to all rich nations.

Children in single-parent families are disadvantaged compared with those in two-parent families precisely because there is only one parent. Just as Survivors' Insurance is a social invention to ensure that parents who die can support their children, a child support assurance system that both enforces the obligation of living parents to share income with their children and undergirds the system, with a public guarantee of a minimum level of support, would ensure that parents who live apart from their children nonetheless support them. In the United States, as we have seen, states and the federal government have already substantially strengthened enforcement of private child support. Other rich nations, learning from the US experience, are also strengthening their enforcement systems. But enforcing private support is inherently limited. Child support from fathers with low and irregular earnings, at best, will be low and irregular. The Scandinavian countries and a few of the continental European nations have advanced maintenance benefits that guarantee minimum child support payments and thereby create a floor in the child support system (Kahn and Kamerman, 1988; Kunz, Villeneuve, and Garfinkel, 2001).

Creating a child support floor—a publicly financed minimum child support benefit—that is conditional on being legally entitled to receive private child support reduces the poverty and insecurity of single mothers and their children, and increases mothers' incentives to cooperate in identifying the fathers of their children, establishing paternity, and securing a child support award (Garfinkel, 1992).[16] Assured child support, like other universal benefits, will further reduce the dependence of single mothers on TANF and other safety-net programs.

Minimum benefits are common in social insurance programs. The enforcement features of the American system of assuring child support increasingly resemble social insurance. Non-resident fathers are required to pay a share of their income for child support, and the obligations are deducted from their paychecks. Adding a minimum benefit to the system is consistent with this evolution.

An assured child support benefit is a relatively cheap floor that would substantially reduce the poverty and economic insecurity of single mothers and their children and simultaneously strengthen child support enforcement.[17]

Summary and conclusion: laggard or leader?

Is the American welfare state a laggard or leader? The sub-title of our book is deliberatively provocative. We suspect that, before reading the book, most would have dismissed the question as being obvious. Like the majority of welfare state scholars, the reader would have failed to include education as part of the welfare state. Yet elementary and secondary education, like public assistance and health and social insurance, is a publicly financed transfer. We hope that we have persuaded most of our readers, including the scholars who have omitted education, that, of course, education is a part of the welfare state.

Including education profoundly changes the image of the welfare state. All rich nations have large welfare states because capitalism combined with critical doses of socialism—in education, health, and social insurance—enriches nations. To omit education is to omit the most productivity-enhancing part of the welfare state. Public health is also clearly productivity enhancing. Health and social insurance enhance security and economic well-being and may indirectly enhance productivity by promoting solidarity and social peace.

In the most productivity-enhancing segment of the welfare state—mass education—for most of the nineteenth and twentieth centuries, the United States was a leader, not a laggard. As a nation, it was amply rewarded as public education contributed mightily to its economic growth and to equality of opportunity.

But the United States no longer leads in mass education, even at the college level, and in early childhood education and care it now lags. Although the United States used to offer more opportunity for upward mobility—except to its black minority—than other rich nations, it now offers less. The United States spends much more than other rich nations on health insurance, yet 15 percent of the population is uninsured and the financial burden of paying for health insurance is the least fairly shared. The American population is now less healthy and less well educated than populations in other rich nations. Finally, during the last quarter-century, inequality has increased in all the rich nations, but it has increased most markedly in the United States, returning by 2007 to the Roaring 1920s peak.

Will the United States be a leader or laggard in the future? The American welfare state faces three major challenges: (1) making the old-age insurance program fiscally sound; (2) achieving universal health insurance and restraining the growth in health-care costs; and (3) restoring American pre-eminence in education and making other productive and complementary investments in children. The overarching challenge is to increase opportunity and security and reduce poverty and inequality in ways that enhance productivity. Minor tinkering with the existing system—a mix of small benefit cuts and small increases in taxes—will restore fiscal balance in the old-age insurance system. The second challenge is far more difficult. Achieving universality in health care will increase costs. Aging of the population and, more important, costly improvements in medical care also drive up health-care costs. Restraining health-care costs is probably the more daunting of the twin health-care challenges. The third challenge may be the most difficult of all because, in the face of an aging population, the first two must be resolved to free up the resources to adequately invest in American children. Restoring American pre-eminence in education and other public investments in children is the most important challenge not just in terms of the US being true to its historical self, but also in terms of future American wealth and productivity.

The United States, like every other nation, has responded both poorly and well to past challenges, but, on balance, the record is pretty good. Despite serious, fundamental flaws in its social, economic, and political framework, throughout most of its history, the United States of America has been a beacon of hope, inspiration, and leadership in the struggle for democracy and equality. The victory of the Democratic Party candidate Barack Obama in the 2008 presidential election indicates that the long swing right in American politics has come to an end. Americans and citizens of other nations, rich and poor, are excited by the prospect that the United States of America has elected a black man as president. As a foreign friend said to one of us with much admiration, as the saying goes, "Only in America." No one knows for sure what the future portends. We are hopeful.

Notes

1. Rates available at <http://www.ssa.gov/pubs/10003.html>. Though employers pay half of the tax and workers the other half, economists generally assume that the full tax is borne by labor.
2. However, these changes would not maintain solvency in the 76th year and beyond. See Diamond and Orszag (2005) and Feldstein (2005) for plans that achieve permanent or perpetual fiscal balance.

3. The large size of the so-called Baby Boom cohort born after World War II temporarily exacerbates the problem caused by the more fundamental long-term trends of increases in life expectancy and decreases in fertility.

4. For example, the precipitous decline in the stock market in 2008 appears to have induced an increasing number of older workers to delay retirement (Norris, 2008). To the extent that this effect continues, the expected future deficit will decrease due to higher taxes paid by older workers.

5. In 2000, 62 percent of Americans strongly agreed and another 22 percent agreed somewhat with the following statement "Health care should be provided equally to everyone, just as public education is." Similarly, 48 percent strongly agreed and another 28 percent agreed somewhat to the question "Do you agree or disagree with people who say access to health care should be a right?" (Kaiser/News hour, 2000).

6. Indeed, the United States veterans' health-care system has been cost constrained, but has become much more cost effective in its use of care as a result (Jha, Perlin, Kizer, and Dudley, 2003).

7. Cutler is reluctant to advocate a universal government-run health insurance system because, as an economist, he prefers competition to monopoly and, more fundamentally, because the benefits of health care are so much larger than costs.

8. Finkelstein (2007) estimates that half of the increase in per capita health spending between 1950 and 1990 was due to the spread of health insurance. Her estimate relies upon pre-existing differences across states in private insurance and medical care spending, and differences across states in changes in medical care spending induced by the introduction of Medicare in 1965. Her work overturns the previous consensus in the economics literature, which flew in the face of common sense that insurance played a small role in the increase in health expenditures. As she notes, however, the previous consensus was based on applying the micro-experimental results from the Rand Health Insurance Experiment. Medicare, by providing health insurance to 100 percent of the aged as compared to the 25 percent of the aged who were insured privately before Medicare, made it economically worthwhile for hospitals and pharmaceutical companies to invest in developing services and medicines to help the newly profitable aged group.

9. Sheils and Haught (2005) have a slightly lower estimate (11 percent) for the state of California.

10. See note 8.

11. The only other experiment with high-quality early child education and care directed at very disadvantaged children that was initiated long enough ago to allow for follow-up of the children through adulthood also finds equally impressive long-term benefits. But the Abecedarian program provided high-quality care beginning a few months after birth until the children entered

kindergarten. For an outstanding review of the literature on the short- and long-term effects of early childhood education, see Karoly and Bigelow (2005).

12. Dickens, Sawhill, and Tebbs (2006) estimate that 20 percent of the increase in GDP goes to increases in federal taxes. We assumed that state taxes increase by one sixth as much as federal taxes.

13. There is evidence that boys who spend substantial time in average childcare are more likely to have behavioral problems. On the other hand, boys who are randomly assigned to high-quality childcare do no worse or better in terms of behavioral problems (Waldfogel, 2006: 56–62).

14. Poor Black and Hispanic children already benefit disproportionately from Head Start and other subsidies for children in poor families. But such children also disproportionately fill the ranks of the near-poor and lower-middle class and, as discussed above in Chapter 3, the near-poor and lower-middle class are the biggest gainers from universal provision.

15. In 2008, we spent approximately $56 billion on the CTC, both refundable and non-refundable. According to the Brookings-Urban Tax Policy Center, it would cost $12.2 billion in 2009 to make the credit fully refundable at the bottom. In 2007, there were 74 million children under age 18, implying that the gross cost of a fully refundable credit with no phase outs would be $74 billion (Table 2: Annual Estimates of the Population by Sex and Selected Age Groups for the United States: April 1, 2000 to July 1, 2007 (NC-EST2007–02), Population Division, US Census Bureau, May 1, 2008).

16. Reducing welfare benefits by one dollar for each dollar of child support paid reduces mothers' incentive to cooperate and fathers' incentive to pay child support. Counting only a portion of support in determining eligibility and benefits would increase cooperation and payments. It would also increase costs, at least in the short run. In the long run, however, if the proportion of fathers paying support increases sufficiently, it might not even increase costs. Rather than restoring the old AFDC $50 set aside for child support payments, Congress should consider requiring or encouraging states to ignore a substantial portion—say 50 percent—of child support payments in determining TANF eligibility and payments.

17. So long as the guaranteed minimum benefit is conditional on legal entitlement to support, the costs of even a very generous minimum benefit is modest—in 1985, under $5 billion (Meyer, Garfinkel, Oellerich, and Robins, 1994). If the benefit is not conditional on entitlement to private child support, the incentive to obtain legal entitlement is eliminated and costs increase substantially.

References

Aaron, Henry. 1982. *Economic Effects of Social Security*. Washington, DC: The Brookings Institution.

Aaron, Henry J., and Stuart M. Butler. 2004. "How Federalism Could Spur Bipartisan Action On The Uninsured." *Health Affairs*, 23: 168–78 (published online 31 March 2004): <http://www.10.1377/hlthaff.w4.168>.

Aaron, Henry J., and William B. Schwartz. 1984. *The Painful Prescription: Rationing Hospital Care*. Washington, DC: Brookings Institution.

Aaron, Henry, and Robert Reischauer. 2001. *Countdown to Reform: The Great Social Security Debate*. Washington, DC: Brookings Institution.

Aaron, Henry J., William B. Schwartz, and Melissa Cox. 2005. *Can We Say No?: The Challenge of Rationing Health Care*. Washington, DC: Brookings Institution Press.

Adema, William, and Maxime Ladaique. 2005. "Net Social Expenditure, 2005 Edition: More Comprehensive Measures of Social Support." *OECD Social, Employment and Migration Working Papers* 29. Paris: Organisation for Economic Co-operation and Development.

Agell, Jonas. 1996. "Why Sweden's Welfare State Needed Reform." *Economic Journal*, 106: 000–000.

Akerlof, George. 1970. "The Market for Lemons: Quality Uncertainty and the Market Mechanism." *Quarterly Journal of Economics* 84(3): 488–500.

Akin, John S. and Irwin Garfinkel. 1980. "The Quality of Education and Cohort Variation in Black–White Earnings Differentials: Comment." *American Economic Review* 70(Mar.): 186–91.

Alderson, Arthur S., and Francois Nielsen. 2002. "Globalization and the Great U-Turn: Income Inequality Trends in Sixteen OECD Countries." *American Journal of Sociology* 107(5): 1244–99.

Alesina, Alberto, and Edward L. Glaeser. 2004. *Fighting Poverty in the US and Europe: A World of Difference*. Oxford: Oxford University Press.

Alesina, Alberto, Reza Baqir, and William Easterly. 1999. "Public Goods and Ethnic Divisions." *Quarterly Journal of Economics* V. 114(4): 1243–84.

Alesina, Alberto, Sule Ozler, Nouriel Roubini, and Phillip Swagel. 1996. "Political Instability and Economic Growth." *Journal of Economic Growth* 1(2): 189–211.

References

American Academy of Orthopedic Surgeons. 2003. *AAOS Bulletin 2003*. Rosemont: AAOS.

American Council on Education. 2007. *Fact Sheet on Higher Education*. Washington, DC: American Council on Education, Center for Policy Analysis.

Anderson, Gerald, and B. Frogner. 2008. "Health Spending in OECD Countries: Obtaining Value Per Dollar." *Health Affairs* 27(6): 1718–29.

Anderson, Gerald F., Uwe E. Reinhardt, Peter S. Hussey, and Varduhi Petrosyan. 2003. "It's the Prices, Stupid: Why the United States is So Different from Other Countries." *Health Affairs* 22(3): 89–105.

Arrow, Kenneth J. 1963. "Uncertainty and the Welfare Economics of Medical Care." *American Economic Review* 53(5): 941–73.

Arts, Wil, and John Gelissen. 2002. "Three Worlds of Welfare Capitalism or More? A State-of-the-Art Report." *Journal of European Social Policy* 12: 137–58.

Ashenfelter, Orley, and Cecilia Rouse. 1998. "Income, Schooling, and Ability: Evidence from a New Sample of Identical Twins." *Quarterly Journal of Economics* 113: 253–84.

Atkinson, Anthony B. 1983. *The Economics of Equality*, 2nd edn. Oxford: Clarendon Press.

Atkinson, A. B. 1995. *Public Economics in Action: The Basic Income/Flat Tax Proposal.* New York: Oxford University Press.

Atkinson, Anthony B. 1997. "Bringing Income Distribution in from the Cold." *Economic Journal* 107(441) (March): 297–321.

Atkinson, Anthony B., and Francois Bourguignon. 2000. "Introduction: Income Distribution and Economics." In *Handbook of Income Distribution.* New York: Elsevier-North Holland, pp. 1–58.

Atkinson, Anthony B., Lee Rainwater, and Timothy M. Smeeding. 1995. "Income Distribution in OECD Countries: Evidence from the Luxembourg Income Study (LIS)." *Social Policy Studies* 18 (October). Paris: Organisation for Economic Co-operation and Development.

Atkinson, A. B., and Universität München. Center for Economic Studies. 1999. *The Economic Consequences of Rolling Back the Welfare State, Munich Lectures in Economics.* Cambridge, MA: MIT Press.

Autor, David, and Mark Duggan, 2006. "The Growth in the Social Security Disability Rolls: A Fiscal Crisis Unfolding." *Journal of Economic Perspectives,* 20 (3) (summer): 71–96. American Economic Association.

Baker, Dean, and David Rosnick. 2005. *The Burden of Social Security Taxes and the Burden of Excessive Health Care Costs.* Washington, DC: Center for Economic and Policy Research.

Ball, Robert. 1998. *Straight Talk about Social Security.* New York: Century Foundation Press.

Ball, Robert M. 2006. *Meeting Social Security's Long-Range Shortfall: How We Can Cope—Calmly—with a Readily Manageable Challenge.* New York: The Century Foundation.

Banthin, Jessica S., and Didem M. Bernard. 2006. "Changes in Financial Burdens for Health Care—National Estimates for the Population Younger than 65 Years, 1996 to 2003." *Jama-Journal of the American Medical Association* 296(22): 2712–19.

Barr, Nicholas. 1992. "Economic Theory and the Welfare State: A Survey and Interpretation." *Journal of Economic Literature* 30(2): 741–803.

Barr, Nicholas, ed. 2001. *Economic Theory and the Welfare State*. The International Library of Critical Writings in Economics #132. Cheltenham, UK: Edward Elgar Publishing Limited.

Barro, Robert J. 2001. "Human Capital and Growth." *The American Economic Review* 91(2): 12.

Bartels, Larry M. 2007. *Unequal Democracy: The Political Economy of the New Gilded Age*. New York, Russell Sage Foundation.

Baum, Sandy, and Patricia Steele. 2007. *Trends in Student Aid 2007*. The College Board, 2007, available at: <http://www.collegeboard.com/prod_downloads/ about/news_info/trends/ trends_aid_07.pdf>.

Becker, Gary S. 1986. "Human Capital and the Rise and Fall of Families." *Journal of Labor Economics* 4(3): S1–S39.

Becker, Gary S. 1991. *A Treatise on the Family*. Chicago, IL: University of Chicago Press.

Becker, Gary S. 1993. *Human Capital: A Theoretical and Empirical Analysis, with Special Reference to Education*. Chicago, IL: The University of Chicago Press.

Becker, Gary S., and Kevin M. Murphy. 1988. "The Family and the State." *Journal of Law & Economics* 31(April): 1–18.

Behrman, Jere R., Robert A. Pollak, and Paul Taubman. 1982. "Parental Preferences and Provision for Progency." *Journal of Political Economy*, 90(1): 52–73.

Behrman, Jere R., Mark R. Rosenzweig, and Paul Taubman. 1994. "Endowments and the Allocation of Schooling in the Family and in the Marriage Market: The Twin Experiment." *Journal of Political Economy* 102(6): 1131–74.

Beller, Emily, and Michael Hout. 2006. "Intergenerational Social Mobility: The United States in Comparative Perspective." *The Future of Children* 16(2) (fall): 19–36.

Bergh, Andreas. 2006. "Is the Swedish Welfare State a Free Lunch?" *Econ Journal Watch* 3(2): 210–35.

Bergmann, Barbara R. 1986. *The Economic Emergence of Women*. New York: Basic Books.

Bergmann, Barbara R. 1997. *Saving Our Children from Poverty: What the United States Can Learn from France*. New York: Russell Sage Foundation.

Berlin, Gordon L. 2007. "Rewarding the Work of Individuals: A Counterintuitive Approach to Reducing Poverty and Strengthening Families." In *The Next Generation of Anti-Poverty Policies*, 17(2): 17–42. Princeton, NJ: Future of Children.

Bernstein, Eduard. 1899. *Evolutionary Socialism*, reprinted in 1961. New York: Schocken Books.

References

Blackman, Amy, Kenndard T. Wing, and Thomas Pollack. 2008. *The Non-Profit Sector in Brief*. Washington, DC: National Center for Charitable Statistics, Urban Institute.

Blank, Rebecca M. 2002. "Evaluating Welfare Reform in the U.S." *Journal of Economic Literature 40*(4): 1105–66.

Blank, Rebecca M. 2007. "Improving the Safety Net for Single Mothers Who Face Serious Barriers to Work." In *The Next Generation of Anti-Poverty Policies*, 17(2): 183–97. Princeton, NJ: Future of Children.

Blinder, A. 1988. "Why is the Government in the Pension Business?" In Susan Wachter, ed., Social *Security and Private Pensions: Providing for Retirement in the Twenty-first Century*. Lexington, MA: D.C. Heath & Co., pp. 17–34.

Borger, Christine, Sheila Smith, Christopher Truffer, Sean Keehan, Andrea Sisko, John Poisal, and M. Kent Clemens. 2006. "Health Spending Projections through 2015: Changes on the Horizon." *Health Affairs* 25(2): 61–73.

Borjas, George. 2006. "Making it in America: Social Mobility in the Immigrant Population." *The Future of Children* 16(2): 19–36.

Bowles, Samuel, and Herbert Gintis. 1976. *Schooling in Capitalist America: Educational Reform and the Contradictions of Economic Life*. New York: Basic Books.

Bowles, Samuel, Herbert Gintis, and Melissa Osborne Groves, eds. 2005a. *Unequal Chances: Family Background and Economic Success*. New York: Russell Sage Foundation.

Bowles, Samuel, Frank Roosevelt, and Richard Edwards. 2005b. *Understanding Capitalism: Competition, Command, and Change*. Oxford: Oxford University Press.

Bradley, David, Evelyn Huber, Stephanie Moller, François Nielsen, and John Stephens. 2003. "Distribution and Redistribution in Postindustrial Democracies." *World Politics* 55(2): 193.

Branch, Taylor. 1988. *America in the King Years 1954–1963*. New York: Simon & Schuster.

Brandolini, Andrea, and Timothy S. Smeeding. 2009. "Income Inequality in Richer and OECD Countries." In W. Salverda, B. Nolan, and T. M. Smeeding, eds, *Oxford Handbook of Economic Inequality*. Oxford: Oxford University Press, ch.4.

Brands, H. W. 2000. *The First American: The Life and Times of Benjamin Franklin*. New York: Doubleday.

Breen, Richard, and Jan O. Jonsson. 2005. "Inequality of Opportunity in Comparative Research: Recent Research on Educational Attainment and Social Mobility." *Annual Review of Sociology* 31: 223–43.

Brinkley, Alan. 1995. *The End of Reform: New Deal Liberalism in Recession and War*. (A Borzoi Book.) New York: Alfred A. Knopf.

Brittain, John A. 1971. "The Incidence of Social Security Payroll Taxes." *American Economic Review* 61(1): 110–25.

Brooks, David. (2007, November 9). "History and Calumny." *New York Times*.

Brooks-Gunn, J., Jane Waldfogel, and Wen Han. 2002. "Maternal Employment and Child Outcomes in the First Three Years of Life: The NICHD Study of Early Childcare." *Child Development* 73: 1052–72.

Brown, J. R., and A. Finkelstein. 2007. "Why is the Market for Long-term Care Insurance so Small?" *Journal of Public Economics*, 91(10): 1967–91.

Buchanan, James M. 1968. "Social Insurance in a Growing Economy: A Proposal for Radical Reform." *National Tax Journal* 21(4): 386–95.

Bumpass, L., and Lu, H.-H. 2000. "Trends in Cohabitation and Implications for Children's Family Contexts in the United States." *Population Studies* 54: 29–41.

Bureau of Labor Statistics. 1982. *Current Population Survey: A Databook* (BLS Bulletin 2096). Washington, DC: US Government Printing Office.

Burtless, Gary. 1996. *Does Money Matter? The Effect of School Resources on Student Achievement and Adult Success*. Washington, DC: Brookings Institution.

Bush, G. W. 2005. Speeches. Pensacola, FL (3/18/05); Tuscon, AZ (3/21/05); and Albuquerque, NM (3/22/05).

Cannon, Lou. (2007, November 18). "Reagan's Southern Stumble." *New York Times*.

Card, David, and Alan B. Krueger. 1996. "Labor Market Effects of School Quality: Theory and Evidence." In Gary Burtless, ed., *Does Money Matter? The Effect of School Resources on Student Achievement and Adult Success*. Washington, DC: Brookings Institution, pp. 97–140.

Card, David, and A. Abigail Payne. 2002. "School Finance Reform, the Distribution of School Spending, and the Distribution of Student Test Scores." *Journal of Public Economics*, 83(1) (January): 49–82.

Case, Charles E., Greeley, Andrew M., and Stephan Fuchs. 1989. "Social Determinants of Racial Prejudice." *Sociological Perspectives* (32) 4: 469–83.

Cassetty, Judith. 1978. *Child Support and Public Policy: Securing Support From Absent Husbands*. Lexington, MA: Lexington Books.

Castles, Francis Geoffrey (ed.). 1989. *The Comparative History of Public Policy*. Cambridge, UK: Polity.

Castles, Francis Geoffrey. 2004. *The Future of the Welfare State: Crisis Myths and Crisis Realities*. Oxford: Oxford University Press.

Catlin, Aaron, Cathy Cowan, Stephen Heffler, and Benjamin Washington (the National Health Expenditure Accounts Team). 2007. "National Health Spending in 2005: The Slowdown Continues." *Health Affairs,* 26(1): 142–53.

CBO. 2008. *Technological Change and the Growth of Heath Care Spending*. Washington, DC: CBO. January 31. Available at: <http://www.cbo.gov/ftpdocs/89xx/doc8947/01–31-TechHealth.pdf>.

Census Bureau. 2004. *Ancestry 2000*. Washington, DC.

Centers for Medicare & Medicaid. 2007. *National Health Expenditures by Type of Service and Source of Funds: Calendar Years 2006–1960*. Retrieved February 15, 2008, from <http://www.cms.hhs.gov/NationalHealthExpendData/02_NationalHealthAccountsHistorical.asp>.

Chatterji, Pinka, and Jeanne Brooks-Gunn. 2004. "WIC Participation, Breastfeeding Practices and Well-Baby Care Among Unmarried, Low-Income Mothers." *American Journal of Public Health* 94: 1324–7.

References

Chernick, Howard. 1998. "Fiscal Effects of Block Grants for the Needy: An Interpretation of the Evidence." *International Tax and Public Finance* 5(2): 205–33.

Cipolla, C. M. 1969. *Literacy & Development in the West*. Great Britain: Cox & Wyman Ltd.

Clearinghouse on International Developments in Child, Youth, and Family Policy at Columbia University. Website: <http://www.childpolicyintl.org/>.

Cobbett, Thomas. 1812. *Cobbett's Parliamentary Debates*. Cambridge MA: Harvard University.

Cogan, John F., R. Glenn Hubbard, and Daniel P. Kessler. 2005. *Healthy, Wealthy, and Wise: Five Steps to a Better Health Care System*. Washington, DC/Stanford, CA: AEI Press/Hoover Institution.

Committee for Economic Development. 2002. *Preschool for All: Investing in a Productive and Just Society*. New York: Committee for Economic Development, Research and Policy Committee.

Cook, Bryan J., and Jacqueline E. King. 2007. *Status Report on the Pell Grant Program*. American Council on Education Center for Policy Analysis. June 2007. Available at: <http://www.acenet.edu/AM/Template.cfm?Section=Publications&Template=/CM/ContentDisplay.cfm&ContentFileID=3434>.

Corak, Miles (ed.). 2004. *Generational Income in North America and Europe*. Cambridge, UK: Cambridge University Press.

Corak, Miles. 2006. "Do Poor Children Become Poor Adults? Lessons from a Cross Country Comparison of Generational Earnings Mobility." IZA DP No. 1993. Bonn, Germany: Institute for the Study of Labor (IZA). March. <http://ftp.iza.org/dp1993.pdf>.

Currie, Janet. 2006. *The Invisible Safety Net: Protecting the Nation's Poor Children and Families*. Princeton, NJ: Princeton University Press.

Cusack, Thomas R. (1997). "Partisan Politics and Public Finance: Changes in Public Spending in the Industrialized Democracies, 1955–1989." *Public Choice* 91(3): 375–95.

Cutler, David. 2004. *Your Money or Your Life: Strong Medicine for America's Health Care System*. Oxford: Oxford University Press.

Cutler, David M., and Mark McClellan. 2001. "Is Technological Change in Medicine Worth It?" *Health Affairs*, 20(5) (September/October): 11–29.

Cutler, David, Angus Deaton, and Adriana Lleras-Muney. 2006. "The Determinants of Mortality." *NBER Working Paper* No. W11963. Cambridge, MA: National Bureau of Economic Research.

Cutler, David, Allison B. Rosen, and Vijan Sandeep. 2006. "The Value of Medical Spending in the United States, 1960–2000." *New England Journal of Medicine* 355 (9) (August, 31): 920–7.

Danziger, Sheldon H., and Robert Haveman. 2002. *Understanding Poverty*. Cambridge, MA: Harvard University Press.

Danziger, Sheldon H., Robert Haveman, and Eugene Smolensky. 1977. "The Measurement and Trend in Inequality: Comment." *The American Economic Review*, 67(3): 505–12.

Danziger, Sheldon H., Robert Haveman, and Robert Plotnick. 1981. "How Income Transfer Programs Affect Work, Savings, and the Income Distribution: A Critical Review." *Journal of Economic Literature* 19(3): 975–1028.

De Beaumont, M. Gustave. 1835. *Marie, or Slavery in America*. Paris: Gosselin.

de Condorcet, Antoine-Nicolas. [1795] 1955. *A Sketch for the Historical Picture of the Progress of the Human Mind*, trans. J. Barraclaugh, and ed. S. Hampshire. London.

Denison, Edward F. 1962. "Education, Economic Growth, and Gaps in Information." *The Journal of Political Economy* 70(5): 124–8.

Diamond, P., and Orszag, M. 2005. "Saving Social Security." *Journal of Economic Perspectives* 19(2): 11–32.

Dickens, Charles. 2004. *David Copperfield*. New York: Penguin Classics.

Dickens, William T., Isabel V. Sawhill, and Jeffrey Tebbs. 2006. *The Effects of Investing in Early Education on Economic Growth*. Washington, DC: Brookings Institution.

Dickert-Conlin, S., and Rubenstein, R. 2007. *Economic Inequality and Higher Education: Access, Persistence and Success*. Eds: Stacy Dickert-Conlin and Ross Rubenstein. New York. NY: Russell Sage Foundation.

Downs, Anthony. 1982. "Comment," and discussion portion of Chapter 4 "Income Testing and Politics: A Theoretical Model by Gordon Tullock." In Irwin Garfinkel, ed., *Income-Tested Transfer Programs: The Case For and Against*. New York: Academic Press, pp. 117–28.

Duncombe, William, and John Yinger. 1997. "Why is it So Hard to Help Central City Schools?" *Journal of Policy Analysis and Management* 16(1) (winter): 85–113.

Dunn, Thomas A., and John W. Phillips. 1997. "The Timing and Division of Parental Tranfers to Children." *Economic Letters*, 54: 135–7.

Dynarski, Susan. 2005. "Building the Stock of College-Educated Labor." *NBER Working Paper* No. 11604 (September). Cambridge, MA: National Bureau of Economic Research.

Edelman, Peter. (1997, March). "The Worst Thing Bill Clinton Has Done." *The Atlantic* 279(3): 43–58.

Ellwood, David T. 1988. *Poor Support: Poverty in the American Family*. New York: Basic Books.

Ellwood, David T., and Christopher Jencks. 2004. "The Spread of Single-Parent Families in the United States Since 1960." In Daniel Patrick Moynihan, Timothy M. Smeeding, and Lee Rainwater, eds, *The Future of the Family*. New York: Russell Sage Foundation, pp. 25–65.

Employee Benefit Research Institute. 2004. "Employer Spending on Benefits: 2002." FACTS from EBRI. Washington, DC: EBRI. May. <http://www.ebri.org/facts/0504fact.pdf>.

References

Erikson, Robert, and John H. Goldthorpe. 2002. "Intergenerational Inequality: A Sociological Perspective." *Journal of Economic Perspectives* 16(3) (summer): 31–44.

Ermish, John, and Marco Francesconi. 2000. "Educational Choice, Families and Young People's Earnings." *Journal of Human Resources* 35(1): 146–76.

Esping-Andersen, Gøsta. 1990. *The Three Worlds of Welfare Capitalism*. Princeton, NJ: Princeton University Press.

Esping-Andersen, Gøsta. "Government and the Distribution of Skills." *DemoSoc Working Paper* #17, Universitat Pampeu Fabra, July 2006. Available at: <http://sociodemo.upf.edu/papers/DEMOSOC17.pdf>.

Estes, C. L., L. Glasse, and T. M. Smeeding. 1999. "Social Security in the 21st Century More than Deficits: Strengthening Security For Women." In *The Gerontological Society of America,* pp. 1–8.

European Union. "Eurydice." website: <http://www.eurydice.org>.

Evans, W. M., Murray, S. E., and Schwab, R. M. 2003. "The Changing Distribution of Education Finance: 1972–1997." In K. Neckerman, ed., *Social Inequality*. New York, NY: Russell Sage Foundation, pp. 433–65.

Fagan, Jeffrey, and Garth Davies. 2003. "Street Stops and Broken Windows: *Terry,* Race, and Disorder in New York City." *Fordham Urban Law Journal* 28: 457–504.

Falkingham, Jane, and John Hills. 1995. "Redistribution Between People or Across the Life Cycle." In J. Falkingham and J. Hills, eds, *The Dynamics of Welfare: The Welfare State and the Life Cycle*. Hempstead: Princeton Hall, pp. 137–49.

Feder, Judith. 2008. *Our Troubled Health Care System: Why is it so Hard to Fix?* Center for Policy Research, Policy Brief No. 37/2008. CPR, Maxwell School of Syracuse University.

Feldman, R., Parente, S. T., Abraham, J., Christianson, J. B., and Taylor, R. (2005). Health Savings Accounts: Early Estimates of National Take-up. *Health Affairs* 24(6): 1582–91.

Feldstein, Martin S. 1973. "The Welfare Loss of Excess Health Insurance." *The Journal of Political Economy* 81(2): 251–80.

Feldstein, Martin S. 1974. "Social Security, Induced Retirement, and Aggregate Capital Accumulation." *The Journal of Political Economy* 82(5): 905–26.

Feldstein, Martin S. 1976. "Temporary Layoffs in the Theory of Unemployment." *The Journal of Political Economy* 84(5): 937–58.

Feldstein, Martin S. 1980. "International Differences in Social Security and Saving." *Journal of Public Economics* 14(2): 225–44.

Feldstein, Martin S. 1982. "Social Security and Private Savings: Reply." *Journal of Political Economy* 90(3): 630–42.

Feldstein, Martin S. 1987. "Should Social Security Benefits Be Means Tested?" *Journal of Political Economy* 95: 468–84.

Feldstein, Martin S. 1996. "Social Security and Saving: New Time Series Evidence." *National Tax Journal* 49: 151–64.

Feldstein, Martin S. 2005. "Structural Reform of Social Security." *Journal of Economic Perspectives* 19(2): 33–55.

Ferrie, Joseph. 2005. "History Lessons: The End of American Exceptionalism? Mobility in the United States since 1850." *Journal of Economic Perspectives* 19(3): 199–215.

Finkelstein, Amy. 2007. "The Aggregate Effect of Health Insurance: Evidence from the Introduction of Medicare." *Quarterly Journal of Economics* 122(1): 1–37.

Finkelstein, Amy, and Robin McKnight. 2005. "What Did Medicare Do (and was it worth it)?" *NBER Working Paper* No. 11609. Cambridge, MA: National Bureau of Economic Research.

Fischer, Claude S., and Michael Hout. 2006. *Century of Difference: How America Changed in the Last One Hundred Years*. New York: Russell Sage Foundation.

Fiske, Edward B. 2008. "A Nation at Loss." *New York Times*, April 25th. Available at: <http://www.nytimes.com/2008/04/25/opinion/25fiske.html?_r=1&scp=1&sq =Fiske,%20edward%202008%20"A%20Nation%20at%20a%20Loss,"%20by% 20Edward%20B.%20 Fiske%20(Op-Ed,%20April%2025),%20&st=cse>.

Fitzpatrick, Maria, and Sarah E. Turner. 2007. "Blurring the Boundary: Changes in the Transition from College Participation to Adulthood." In Sheldon Danziger and Cecilia Elena Rouse, eds, *The Price of Independence: The Economics of Early Adulthood*. Russell Sage Press, pp. 107–38.

Flora, Peter, and Arnold J. Heidenheimer, eds. 1995. *The Development of Welfare States in Europe and America*. New Brunswick, NJ: Transaction Publishers.

Fogel, Robert William. 2004. "The Escape from Hunger and Premature Death, 1700–2100: Europe, America, and the Third World." Vol.8, Cambridge Studies in Population, Economy, and Society in Past Time. Cambridge, UK; New York: Cambridge University Press.

Follain with David C. Ling. 1991. "The Federal Tax Subsidy to Housing and the Reduced Value of the Mortgage Interest Deduction." *National Tax Journal*, XLIV (2) (June): 147–68.

Freeman, Richard B., Robert H. Topel, and Birgitta Swedenborg. 1997. *The Welfare State in Transition: Reforming the Swedish Model*. Chicago, IL: University of Chicago Press.

Fremantle, Anne. 1960. *This Little Band of Prophets: The British Fabians*. New York: Mentor Books.

Freund, D., and T. M. Smeeding. Forthcoming. "The Future Costs of Health Care in Aging Societies: Is the Glass Half Full or Half Empty?" In S. Tuljapurkar, N. Ogawa, and A. Gauthier (eds), *Riding the Age Waves: Responses to Aging in Advanced Industrial States*. New York, NY: Springer Kluwer Press. Friedman, Milton. 1962. *Capitalism and Freedom*. Chicago, IL: University of Chicago Press.

Friedan, Betty. 1963. *The Feminine Mystique*. New York: W. W. Norton.

Fullerton, Don, and Diane Lim Rogers. 1993. *Who Bears the Lifetime Tax Burden?* Washington, DC: Brookings Institution.

Garber, Alan, and John Skinner. 2008. "Is American Health Care Uniquely Inefficient?" August 5, 2008, mimeo, Hanover, NH: Dartmouth College, and Stanford, CA: Stanford University. Available online at: <http://www.dartmouth.edu/~jskinner/ documents/garberskinnerAug2008_000.pdf>. April 8, 2008, mimeo.

References

Garfinkel, Irwin. 1972. "Equal Access, Minimum Provision, and Efficiency in Financing Medical Care." *Journal of Human Resources* 7(2): 242–9.

Garfinkel, Irwin. 1982. *Income Tested Transfer Programs: The Case for and Against.* New York: Academic Press.

Garfinkel, Irwin. 1992. *Assuring Child Support: An Extension of Social Security.* New York: Russell Sage Foundation Publications.

Garfinkel, Irwin. 1994. "The Child-Support Revolution." *The American Economic Review* 84(2): 81–5.

Garfinkel, Irwin. 1996. "Economic Security for Children: From Means Testing and Bifurcation to Universality." In I. Garfinkel, J. Hochschild, and S. McLanahan, eds, *Social Policies for Children.* Washington, DC: Brookings Institute, pp. 33–82.

Garfinkel, Irwin. 2001. "Child Support in the New World of Welfare." In R. Blank and R. Haskins, eds, *The New World of Welfare.* Washington, DC: Brookings Institution Press, pp. 442–60.

Garfinkel, Irwin, and Annemette Sorensen. 1982. "Sweden's Child Support System: Lessons for the United States." *Social Work* 27(6): 509–15.

Garfinkel, Irwin, and Sara McLanahan. 1986. *Single Mothers and Their Children: A New American Dilemma.* The Changing Domestic Priorities Series. Washington, DC: Urban Institute Press.

Garfinkel, Irwin, Rainwater, Lee, and Smeeding, Timothy. 2006. "A Re-examination of Welfare States and Inequality in Rich Nations: How In Kind Transfers and Indirect Taxes Change the Story." *Journal of Policy Analysis and Management* 25(4): 897–918.

Gibson-Davis, C. M., and J. Brooks-Gunn. 2006. "Couples' Immigration Status and Ethnicity as Determinants of Breastfeeding." *American Journal of Public Health* 96: 641–6.

Glennister, Howard. 1992. *Paying for Welfare: The 1990's.* London: Harvester/Wheatsheaf.

Goldhaber, Dan, and Gretchen Kiefer. 2007. "Higher Education and Inequality: The Increasingly Important Role Community Colleges Play in Higher Education." In Stacy Dickert-Conlin and Ross Rubenstein, eds, *Economic Inequality and Higher Education: Access, Persistence and Success.* New York: Russell Sage Foundation, pp. 101–1127.

Goldin, Claudia. 1998. "Americans Graduation from High School: The Evolution and Spread of Secondary Schooling in the Twentieth Century." *The Journal of Economic History* V. 58(2) (June), 345–74.

Goldin, Claudia, and Lawrence F. Katz. 2008. *The Race Between Education and Technology.* Cambridge, MA: Harvard University Press.

Goodwin, Doris Kearns. 1976. *Lyndon Johnson and the American Dream.* New York: Harper & Row.

Gompers, Samuel. 1925. *Seventy Years of Life and Labor.* New York: E.P. Dutton.

Gordon, Margaret, S. 1988. *Social Security Policies in Industrial Countries: A Comparative Analysis.* Cambridge: Cambridge University Press.

Gornick, Janet C., and Marcia K. Meyers. 2003. *Families that Work: Policies for Reconciling Parenthood and Employment.* New York: Russell Sage Foundation.

Gough, Ian. 1979. *The Political Economy of the Welfare State.* London: Macmillan.

Grawe, Nathan. 2004. "Intergenerational Mobility for Whom? The Experience of High and Low Earning Sons in International Perspective." In Miles Corak, ed., *Generational Income Mobility in North America and Europe*, ch. 4.

Greeley, Andrew. 1976. *Ethnicity, Denomination and Inequality.* Beverly Hills, CA: Sage Publications.

Greeley, Andrew. 1988. *The Irish Americans: The Rise to Money and Power.* New York: Warner Books.

Gruber, Jonathan. 2008. "Covering the Uninsured in the United States" *NBER Working Paper* No. 13758. Cambridge, MA: NBER.

Gruber, Jonathan, and David A. Wise (eds). 1999. *Social Security and Retirement around the World.* Chicago, IL: University of Chicago Press.

Gustafsson, Bjorn, and Mats Johansson. 1999. "In Search of Smoking Guns: What Makes Income Inequality Vary over Time in Different Countries?" *American Sociological Review* 64 (4): 585–605.

Hacker, Jacob S. 2002. *The Divided Welfare State: The Battle over Public and Private Social Benefits in the United States.* Cambridge/New York: Cambridge University Press.

Hacker, Jacob S. 2006. *The Great Risk Shift: The Assault on American Jobs, Families, Health Care, and Retirement and How You Can Fight Back.* Oxford/New York: Oxford University Press.

Hacker, Jacob, Suzanne Mettler, and Diane Pinderhughes. 2005. "Inequality and Public Policy." In Lawrence Jacobs and Theda Skocpol, eds, *Inequality and American Democracy.* New York: Russell Sage Foundation, pp. 156–213.

Haggard, Stephen, and Robert R. Kaufman. 2008. *Development, Democracy, and Welfare States: Latin America, East Asia and Eastern Europe.* Princeton, NJ: Princeton University Press.

Hamilton, Alexander, John Jay, and James Madison. [1787] 1941. *The Federalist: A Commentary on the Constitution of the United States*, with an introduction by Edward Mead Earle. New York: Modern Library Edition.

Hans-Jurgen, Engelbrecht. 2003. "Human Capital and Economic Growth: Cross-Section Evidence for OECD Countries." *Economic Record* 79: S40.

Hanushek, Eric A. 1996. "School Resources and Student Performance." In Gary Burtless, ed., *Does Money Matter? The Effect of School Resources on Student Achievement and Adult Success.* Washington, DC: Brookings Institution, pp. 43–73.

Harris, Tim. 1999. "The Effects of Taxes and Benefits on Household Income." *Economic Trends* 545: <http://www.statistics.gov.uk/cci/nscl.asp?id=7727>.

Harrison, Paige M., and Allen J. Beck. 2006. "Prisoners in 2005." NCJ 215092. Washington, DC: Bureau of Justice Statistics.

Hartney, C. 2006. *U.S. Rates of Incarceration: A Global Perspective.* Oakland, CA: National Council on Crime and Delinquency: <http://www.nccdcrc.org/nccd/n_pubs_main.html>.

References

Haskins, Ron. 2006. *Work Over Welfare*. Washington, DC: Brookings Institution Press.

Haveman, R., and T. M. Smeeding. 2006. "The Role of Higher Education in Social Mobility." *Future of Children* 16(2): 125–50.

Heckman, James J. 2006. "Skill Formation and the Economics of Investing in Disadvantaged Children." *Science* 312(5782): 1900–2.

Heclo, H. 1995. "The Social Question." In K. Mc Fate, R. Lawson, and W. J. Wilson (eds), *Poverty, Inequality, and the Future of Social Policy*. New York: Russell Sage Foundation, pp. 665–92.

Heidenheimer, Arnold J., and John Layson. 1982. "Social Policy Development in Europe and America: A Longer View on Selectivity and Income Testing." In Irwin Garfinkel, ed., *Income Tested Transfer Programs: The Case For and Against*. New York: Academic Press, pp. 141–66.

Herbert, Bob. (2007, November 13). "Righting Reagan's Wrongs?" *New York Times*.

Hibbs, Douglas. 1977. "Political Parties and Macroeconomic Policy." *American Political Science Review* 71 (December): 1467–87.

Hill, Herbert. 1996. "The Problem of Race in American Labor History." *Reviews in American History* 24(2) (June): 189–208.

Hills, John. 2004. *Inequality and the State*. Oxford: Oxford University Press.

Hills, J., and Stewart, K. (eds) 2005. *A More Equal Society?: New Labour, Poverty, Inequality and Exclusion*. Bristol: Policy Press.

Hills, Jennifer L., Jeanne Brooks-Gunn, Jane Waldfogel, and W. Han. 2005. "Maternal Employment and Child Development: A Fresh Look Using Newer Methods." *Developmental Psychology* 41(6): 833–50.

Hochguertel, Stefan, and Henry Ohlsson. 2000. "Compensatory Inter Vivos Gifts," *Working Papers in Economics* 31. Göteborg: Göteborg University.

Howard, Christopher. 2007. *The Welfare State Nobody Knows: Debunking Myths About U.S. Social Policy*. Princeton, NJ: Princeton University Press.

Hoyt, E. H., V. Schiraldi, B. V. Smith, and J. Ziedenberg. 2001. *Pathways to Juvenile Detention Reform: Reducing Racial Disparities in Juvenile Detention*. Available from: <http://www.aecf.org>.

House Committee on Ways and Means. 1994. *Green Book*. Washington, DC: US Governement Printing Office.

Huber, Evelyne, Charles Ragin, and John Stephens. 1993. "Social Democracy, Christian Democracy, Constitutional Structure and the Welfare State." *American Journal of Sociology* 99(3): 711–49.

Huber, Evelyne, and John D. Stephens. 2001. *Development and Crisis of the Welfare State: Parties and Policies in Global Markets*. Chicago, IL: University of Chicago Press.

Huber, John D., and Ronald Inglehart. 1995. "Expert Interpretations of Party Space and Party Locations in 42 Societies." *Party Politics* 1: 73–111.

Hussey, Peter S., Gerard F. Anderson, Robin Osborn, Colin Feek, Vivienne McLaughlin, John Millar, and Arnold Epstein. 2004. "How Does the Quality of Care Compare in Five Countries?" *Health Affairs* 23(3): 89–99.

Institute of Medicine (US). Committee on the Consequences of Uninsurance. 2003. *Hidden Costs, Value Lost: Uninsurance in America, Insuring Health.* Washington, DC: National Academies Press.

International Monetary Fund. 1998–2006. *Government Finance Statistics Yearbook.* Washington, DC: International Monetary Fund.

Isaacson, Walter. 2003. *Benjamin Franklin: An American Life.* New York: Simon & Schuster.

Iverson, Torben, and David Soskice. 2002. "Insurance and Representation: Why Do Some Democracies Redistribute More Than Others?" Presented at the 2002 Annual Meetings of the American Political Science Association, Boston.

Iverson, Torben, and David Soskice. 2005. "Electoral Institutions, Parties, and the Politics of Class: Why Some Democracies Redistribute More Than Others." Presented at the workshop on the economic consequences of democratic institutions, Department of Political Science, Duke University, April 1–2, 2005.

Jäntti, Markus, Bernt Bratsberg, Knut Röed, Oddbjørn Raaum, Robin Naylor, Eva Österbacka, Anders Björklund, and Tor Eriksson. 2006. "American Exceptionalism in a New Light: A Comparison of Intergenerational Earnings Mobility in the Nordic Countries, the United Kingdom and the United States." IZA DP No. 1938. Bonn, Germany: Institute for the Study of Labor (IZA). January. <http://ftp.iza.org/dp1938.pdf>.

Jencks, Christopher, and Laura Tasch. 2005. "Would Equal Opportunity Mean More Mobility?" RWP05–037. Cambridge, MA: Kennedy School of Government, Harvard University.

Jenkins, Roy. 2001. *Churchill: A Biography.* New York: Farrar, Straus, and Giroux.

Jensen, R.T. 2003. "Do Private Transfers 'Displace' the Benefits of Public Transfers? Evidence from South Africa." *Journal of Public Economics* 88: 89–112.

Jha, Ashish K., Jonathan B. Perlin, Kenneth W. Kizer, and R. Adams Dudley. 2003. "Effect of the Transformation of the Veterans Affairs Health Care System on the Quality of Care." *The New England Journal of Medicine*, 348(22) (May 29): 2218–27.

Johnson, Richard, Gordon Mermin, and C. Eugene Steuerle. 2006. *Work Impediments at Older Ages.* Washington, DC: Urban Institute.

Johnston, David Cay. December 15, 2007. "Report Says Rich are Getting Rich Faster, Much Faster." *New York Times.*

Jones, Gareth Stedman. 2004. *An End to Poverty?* London: Profile.

Kaestle, Carl F. 1983. *Pillars of the Republic: Common Schools and American Society, 1780–1860.* Edited by Eric Foner. New York: Hill and Wang.

Kahn, Alfred J., and Sheila Kamerman. 1988. *Child Support: From Debt Collection to Social Policy.* Newbury Park, CA: Sage Publications.

Kaiser/News hour Uninsured Survey. 2000. *National Survey on the Uninsured.* (April). Available at: <http://www.pbs.org/newshour/health/uninsured/highlights.pdf>.

References

Kamerman, Sheila B. 1976. *Child-Care Programs in Nine Countries*. Washington, DC: US Department of Health, Education, and Welfare.

Kamerman, Sheila B., and Alfed J. Kahn. 1978. *Family Policy: Government and Families in Fourteen Countries*. New York: Columbia University Press.

Kamerman, Sheila B., and Alfred Kahn, eds. 1991. *Child Care, Parental Leave, and the Under 3s: Policy Innovation in Europe*. New York: Auburn House.

Kane, Thomas, and Peter Orszag. 2003. "Higher Education Spending: The Role of Medicaid and the Business Cycle." *Brookings Policy Brief* 124. Washington, DC: Brookings Institution.

Karoly, Lynn, and James H. Bigelow. 2005. *The Economics of Investing in Universal Preschool Education in California*. Santa Monica: Rand Corporation.

Katz, Michael B. 1971. *Class, Bureaucracy, and Schools: The Illusion of Education Reform in America*. New York: Praeger.

Katz, Michael B. 1987. *Reconstructing American Education*. Cambridge, MA: Harvard University Press.

Katz, Michael B. 1996. *In the Shadow of the Poorhouse: A Social History of Welfare in America*. New York: Basic Books.

Katznelson, Ira. 2005. *When Affirmative Action Was White: An Untold History of Racial Inequality in Twentieth Century America*. New York: W.W. Norton.

Katznelson, Ira, and Margaret Weir. 1985. *Schooling for All: Class, Race, and the Decline of the Democratic Ideal*. New York: Basic Books.

Kenworthy, Lane. 2004. *Egalitarian Capitalism: Jobs, Incomes, and Growth in Affluent Countries*. New York: Russell Sage Foundation.

Kenworthy, Lane, and Jonas Pontussan. 2005. "Rising Inequality and the Politics of Redistribution in Affluent Countries." *Perspectives on Politics* Sept. V. 3(3): 449–71.

Koebel, C. T. (1999). "Sustaining Sustainability: Innovation in Housing and the Built Environment." *Journal of Urban Technology* 6(3): 75–94.

Korpi, Walter. 1985. "Economic Growth and the Welfare State: Leaky Bucket or Irrigation System?" *European Sociological Review* 1(2): 97–118.

Korpi, Walter. 1996. "Eurosclerosis and the Sclerosis of Objectivity: On the Role of Values among Economic Policy Experts." *Economic Journal*, 106: 1727–46.

Krugman, Paul. "Always Low Wages. Always (5/13/05)," "Americans Want Security (5/23/05)," and "Played for a Sucker (11/16/07)." *New York Times*.

Krugman, Paul. (2007, November 19). "Republicans and Race." *New York Times*.

Kumlin, Staffan, and Bo Rothstein. 2005. "Making and Breaking Social Capital: The Impact of Welfare State Institutions." *Comparative Political Studies* 38 (4) (May 2005): 339–65.

Kunz, James, Villeneuve, Patrick, and Garfinkel, Irwin. 2001. "Child Support Among Selected OECD Countries: A Comparative Analysis." In K. Vleminckx, Tim Smeeding, eds, *Child Well-Being in Modern Nations: What Do We Know?* Bristol: Policy Press, pp. 485–500.

Lampman, Robert. 1971. *Ends and Means of Reducing Income Poverty*. Chicago, IL: Markham-Rand McNally.

Lampman, Robert J. 1984. *Social Welfare Spending: Accounting for Changes from 1950 to 1978*. Orlando: Academic Press.

Lampman, R. J., and Smeeding, T. M. (1983). "Interfamily Transfers as Alternatives to Government Transfers to Persons." *Review of Income and Wealth* 29(1): 45–66.

Lebergott, Stanley. 1976. *The American Economy: Income, Wealth, and Want*. Princeton, NJ: Princeton University Press.

Lee, Chul-In, and Gary Solon. 2006. "Trends in Intergenerational Income Mobility." *NBER Working Paper* No. 12007 (February). Cambridge, MA: National Bureau of Economic Research.

Le Grand, Julian. 1978. "The Distribution of Public Expenditure: The Case of Health Care." *Economica* 45(178) (May): 125–42.

Leigh, Andrew. 2006. "How Closely Do Top Income Shares Track Other Measures of Inequality?" *Economic Journal*, 117(524) (2007): F619–F633.

Leigh, Andrew, and Christopher Jencks. 2007. "Inequality and Mortality: Long-run Evidence from a Panel of Countries." *Journal of Health Economics* 26 (2007): 1–24.

Levy, F., and P. Temin. 2007. "Inequality and Institutions in 20th Century America." *MIT Department of Economics Working Paper No. 07–17*. Cambridge, MA: MIT Press.

Lewis, Charles E., Irwin Garfinkel, and Qin Gao. 2007. "Incarceration and Unwed Fathers in Fragile Families." *Journal of Sociology and Social Welfare* 34: 77–94.

Lieberman, Robert. 1998. *Shifting the Color Line: Race and the American Welfare State*. Cambridge, MA: Harvard University Press.

Lieberson, Stanley, and Mary C. Waters. 1988. *From Many Strands: Ethnic and Racial Groups in Contemporary America*. New York: Russell Sage Foundation.

Lindbeck, Assar. 1994. "The Welfare State and the Employment Problem." *American Economic Review*, 84(2) (May): 71–5. American Economic Association.

Lindbeck, Assar. 1996. "Incentives in the Welfare-State; Lessons for Would-Be Welfare-States." Papers 604, *International Economic Studies*. Stockholm.

Lindbeck, Assar. 1997. "The Swedish Experiment." *Journal of Economic Literature* 35 (September): 1273–1319.

Lindert, Peter H. 2000. "Three Centuries of Inequality in Britain and America." In A. B. Atkinson and F. Bourguignon, eds, *Handbook of Income Distribution*, 1st edn, vol. 1. Elsevier, ch. 3, pp. 167–216.

Lindert, Peter H. 2004. *Growing Public: Social Spending and Economic Growth since the Eighteenth Century*. New York: Cambridge University Press.

Lindert, Peter H. 2006. "The Welfare State is the Wrong Target: A Reply to Bergh," *Econ Journal Watch* 3(2): 236–50.

Lipset, Seymour Martin. 1977. "Why No Socialism in the U.S." In S. Bialer and S. Sluzer, eds, *Sources of Contemporary Radicalism*, I. Boulder, CO: Westview Press, pp. 31–149.

Lipset, Seymour Martin. 1996. *American Exceptionalism*. New York: W.W. Norton & Co.

References

Lowell, Josephine Shaw. 1890. "The Economic and Moral Effects of Public Outdoor Relief." Reprinted from the *Seventeenth Annual Report of the National Conference of Charities and Corrections* (Baltimore, May 14–21). In William Rhinelander Stewart, ed., *The Philanthropic Work of Josephine Shaw Lowell*. Montclair, NJ: Patterson Smith, [1911] 1974.

Lucas, Robert E. 1988. "On the Mechanics of Economic Development." *Journal of Monetary Economics* 22(1): 3–42.

McClellan, Mark, and Skinner, Jonathan. 2006. "The Incidence of Medicare." *Journal of Public Economics*, Elsevier, 90(1–2) (January): 257–76.

McGarry, Kathleen. 1999. "Inter Vivos Transfers and Intended Bequests." *Journal of Public Economics*, 73: 321–51.

McGarry, Kathleen. 2000. "Testing Parental Altruism: Implications of a Dynamic Model." *NBER Working Paper* No. 7593.

McGarry, Kathleen, and Robert F. Schoeni. 1995. "Transfer Behavior in the Health and Retirement Study: Measurement and the Redistribution for Resources Within the Family." *Journal of Human Resources* 30: S184–S226.

McGarry, Kathleen, and Robert F. Schoeni. 1997. "Transfer Behavior Within the Family: Results from the Asset and Health Dynamics Study." *The Journals of Gerontology* 52B: 82–92.

McLanahan, Sara. 2004. "Diverging Destinies: How Children Are Faring Under the Second Demographic Transition" *Demography* 41(4) (November): 607–27.

McLanahan, Sara, and Lynne Casper. 1995. "Growing Diversity and Inequality in the American Family." In R. Farley, ed., *State of the Union: America in the 1990s*. New York: Russell Sage Foundation, pp. 1–45.

McLennan, W. 1996. "The Effects of Government Benefits and Taxes on Household Income, 1993–94 Household Expenditure Survey Australia." No. 6537.0. Australian Bureau of Statistics: <http://www.abs.gov.au/Ausstats/abs@.nsf/e8ae5488b598839cca25682000131612/b9b3916f5652bf79ca256aa80081f81f!OpenDocument>.

Mankiw, Gregory N., David Romer, and David N. Weil. 1992. "A Contribution to the Empirics of Economic Growth." *Quarterly Journal of Economics* 107: 407–37.

Manski, Charles, and Irwin Garfinkel, eds. 1992. *Evaluating Welfare and Training Programs*. Cambridge, MA: Harvard University Press.

Mares, Isabela. 2003. *The Politics of Social Risk: Business and Welfare State Development, Cambridge Studies in Comparative Politics*. Cambridge, UK/New York: Cambridge University Press.

Marical, François, Marco Mira d'Ercole, Maria Vaalavuo, and Gerlinde Verbist. 2006. 2006. "Publicly-provided Services and the Distribution of Resources." *OECD Social Employment and Migration Working Papers No. 45*. Paris: Organisation for Economic Co-operation and Development. Available at: <http://oberon.sourceoecd.org/vl=3184858/cl=11/nw=1/rpsv/cgibin/wppdf?file=5l4w2bzk6f5b.pdf>.

Mauer, M. 1999. *Race to Incarcerate*. New York: The New Press.

Mazumder, Bhashkar. 2005. "Fortunate Sons: New Estimates of Intergenerational Mobility in the United States Using Social Security Earnings Data." *Review of Economics and Statistics* 87(2) (May): 235–55.

Meade, J. E. 1978. *The Structure and Reform of Direct Taxation: Report.* London: Allen and Unwin for the Institute of Fiscal Studies.

Mencher, Samuel. 1967. *Poor Law to Poverty Program: Economic Security Policy in Britain and the United States.* Pittsburg, PA: University of Pittsburg Press.

Mermin, Gordon B. T., and C. Eugene Steuerle. 2006. "Would Raising the Social Security Retirement Age Harm Low-Income Groups? Retirement Policy Project." Issue Brief, #19, Urban Institute, December; available at: <http://www.urban.org/UploadedPDF/311413_Raising_Retirement_Age.pdf>.

Merx, H., K. Dreinhofer, P. Schrader, T. Sturmer, W. Puhl, K-P Gunther, and H. Brenner. 2002. "International Variation in Hip Replacement Rates." *Ann Rheum Dis* 62: 222–6.

Mettler, Suzanne. 2005. *Soldiers to Citizens: The G.I. Bill and the Making of the Greatest Generation.* Oxford/New York: Oxford University Press.

Meyer, Daniel R., Irwin Garfinkel, Donald Oellerich, and Philip K. Robins. 1994. "Who Should Be Eligible for an Assured Child Support Benefit?" In Irwin Garfinkel, Sara S. McLanahan, and Philip K. Robins, eds, *Child Support Assurance.* Washington, DC: The Urban Institute Press, pp. 159–88.

Meyers, Marcia K. 2003. "Early Childhood Education Estimates for 12 Nations." e-mail communication. October 1.

Micklewright, John, and Sylke Schnepf. 2004. "Educational Achievement in English-Speaking Countries: Do Different Surveys Tell the Same Story?" IZA DP No. 1186. Institute for the Study of Labor. June.

Miles-Ferretti, Gian Maria, Roberto Perotti, and Massimo Rostagno. 2002. "Electoral Rules and Public Spending." *Quarterly Journal of Economics* 117: 609–58.

Miller, Paul W., Charles Mulvey, and Nick Martin. 1995. "What Do Twins Studies Reveal About the Economic Returns to Education? A Comparison of Australian and U.S. Findings." *American Economic Review* 85(3): 586–99.

Mincer, Jacob. 1993. "Studies in Human Capital." *The Collected Essays of Jacob Mincer.* Brookfield, VT: Elgar.

Moffitt, Robert. 1992. "Incentive Effects of the U.S. Welfare System: A Review." *Journal of Economic Literature* 30(1): 1–61.

Moffitt, Robert. 1998. "The Effect of Welfare on Marriage and Fertility." In Robert A. Moffitt, ed., *Welfare, the Family, and Reproductive Behavior.* Washington, DC: National Academy Press, pp. 50–97.

Moffitt, Robert. 2003. "The Negative Income Tax and the Evolution of U.S. Welfare Policy." *Journal of Economic Perspectives*, 17(3)(summer): 119–40.

Moffitt, Robert. 2008. "Welfare Reform: The U.S. Experience." *Institute for Research on Poverty*, Discussion paper no. 1334–08.

References

Moller, Stephanie, David Bradley, Evelyne Huber, Francois Nielsen, and John D. Stephens. 2003. "Determinants of Relative Poverty in Advanced Capitalist Democracies." *American Sociological Review* 68(1): 22–51.

Moon, Marilyn. 2006. *Medicare: A Policy Primer.* Washington, DC: Urban Institute Press.

Morison, Samuel Eliot. 1965. *The Oxford History of the American People.* New York: Oxford University Press.

Munnell, Alicia. 1974. "The Impact of Social Security on Personal Savings." *National Tax Journal,* 27(4) (December): 553–67.

Murnane, Richard. 2007. "Children Living in Poverty." In *The Next Generation of Anti-Poverty Policies,* 17(2): 161–82. Princeton, NJ: Future of Children.

Musgrave, Richard. 1959. *The Theory of Public Finance.* New York: McGraw Hill.

Musgrave, Richard Abel, and Peggy B. Musgrave. 1984. *Public Finance in Theory and Practice,* 4th edn. New York: McGraw-Hill.

Myrdal, Gunnar. 1944. *An American Dilemma: The Negro Problem and Modern Democracy* New York: Harper & Brothers.

National Commission on Children. 1991. *Beyond Rhetoric: A New American Agenda for Children and Families.* Washington, DC: US Government Printing Office.

National Immigration Law Center. 2005. *Immigrant Eligibility for Public Benefits.* Washington, DC: NILC.

National Center for Education Statistics (NCeS). 1985–95. *International Education Indicators: A Time Series Perspective, 1985–1995.* Available at: <http://nces.ed.gov/pubsearch/pubsinfo.asp?pubid=2000021>.

Neal, D. 2006. "Why Has Black/White Skill Convergence Stopped?" In E. Hanushek and F. Welch, eds, *The Handbook of Economics of Education,* vol. 1. Amsterdam: North-Holland, pp. 511–76.

Newhouse, Joseph P. 2002. *Pricing the Priceless: A Health Care Conundrum.* Cambridge, MA: MIT Press.

Newhouse, Joseph P. et al., 1993. *Free for All? Lessons from the RAND Health Insurance Experiment.* Cambridge, MA: Harvard University Press.

Noble, Holcomb B. (2006, November 17). "Milton Friedman, 94, Free-Market Theorist, Dies." *New York Times.*

Norris, Floyd. (2008, December 13). "Younger Job-Seekers Have It Worse." *New York Times.*

OASDI Trustees. 2006. *The 2006 Annual Report of the Board of Trustees of the Federal Old-Age and Survivors Insurance and Disability Insurance Trust Funds* (May 1).

O'Connor, James (1973). *The Fiscal Crisis of the Welfare State,* New York: St Martin's Press.

Offe, Claus. 1972. "Advanced Capitalism and the Welfare State." *Politics Society* 2: 479.

O'Higgins, Michael. 1988. "The Allocation of Public Resources to Children and the Elderly in OECD Countries." In John Palmer, Timothy Smeeding, and Barbara Boyle Torrey, eds, *The Vulnerable.* Washington, DC: Urban Institute Press, pp. 201–28.

Okun, Arthur M. 1975. *Equality and Efficiency, the Big Tradeoff.* Washington, DC: The Brookings Institution.

Organisation for Economic Co-operation and Development. 2004a. *Learning for Tomorrow's World: First Results from PISA 2003*. Paris: Organisation for Economic Co-operation and Development.

Organisation for Economic Co-operation and Development. 2004b. *Social Expenditure Database (SOCX) 1980–2001*. Paris: Organisation for Economic Co-operation and Development.

Organisation for Economic Co-operation and Development. 2004c. *Towards High-Performing Health Systems*. Paris: Organisation for Economic Co-operation and Development. Available at: <http://www.oecd.org/document/58/0,3343,en_2649_33929_31786874_1_1_1_1,00.html>.

Organisation for Economic Co-operation and Development. 2004d. *OECD 1980–2001: 20 Years of Social Expenditure*—the OECD Database. Paris: Organisation for Economic Co-operation and Development. Available at: <http://www.oecd.org/dataoecd/3/63/2084281.pdf>.

Organisation for Economic Co-operation and Development. 2006a. "Science Competencies for Tomorrow's World Executive Summary." PISA. Available at: <http://www.oecd.org/dataoecd/15/13/39725224.pdf>.

Organisation for Economic Co-operation and Development. 2006b. *Education at a Glance*. Paris: Organisation for Economic Co-operation and Development.

Organisation for Economic Co-operation and Development. 2007a. *Health Care Costs at a Glance*. Paris: Organisation for Economic Co-operation and Development.

Organisation for Economic Co-operation and Development. 2007b. *SourceOECD* (<http://www.sourceoecd.org>). Paris: Organisation for Economic Co-operation and Development.

Organisation for Economic Co-operation and Development. 2007c. *OECD Factbook 2007: Economic, Environmental and Social Statistics*. Paris: Organisation for Economic Co-operation and Development.

Orloff, Ann. 1993a. "Gender and the Social Rights of Citizenship: The Comparitive Analysis of Gender Relations and Welfare States." *American Sociological Review* 58: 303–28.

Orloff, Ann. 1993b. *The Politics of Pensions: A Comparative Analysis of Britain, Canada and the United States, 1880–1940*. Madison, WI: University of Wisconsin Press.

Orr, Larry. 1976. "Income Transfers as a Public Good: An Application to AFDC." *American Economic Review* 66(3) (June): 359–71.

Osberg, Lars, Timothy M. Smeeding, and Jonathan Schwabish. 2004. "Income Distribution and Public Social Expenditure: Theories, Effects, and Evidence." In K. Neckerman, ed., *Social Inequality*. New York, NY: Russell Sage Foundation, pp. 821–59.

Owcharenko, Nina. 2004. "Health Savings Accounts: How to Broaden Health Coverage for Working Families." Web Memo #481, Heritage Foundation, Washington, DC, at: <http://www.heritage.org/Research/HealthCare/wm481.cfm>.

Pager, Devah. 2003. "The Mark of a Criminal Record." *American Journal of Sociology*, 108(5) (March): 937–75.

Pager, Devah. 2005. "Walking the Talk: What Employers Say Versus What They Do." *American Sociological Review* 70(3): 355–80.

Paglin, Morton. 1975. "The Measurement and Trend of Inequality: A Basic Revision." *The American Economic Review* 65(4): 598–609.

Paine, Thomas. 1776. *Common Sense*. Philadelphia: R. Bell.

Pallais, Amanda, and Sarah Turner. 2007. "Access to Elites: The Growth of Programs to Increase Opportunities for Low-Income Students at Selective Universities." In Stacy Dickert–Conlin and Ross Rubenstein, eds, *Economic Inequality and Higher Education: Access, Persistence, and Success*. New York: Russell Sage Foundation, pp. 128–56.

Palmer, John L. 2006. "Entitlement Programs for the Aged: The Long-Term Fiscal Context." *Research on Aging* 28(3): 289–302.

Parsons, Talcott. 1969. *Politics and Social Structure*. New York: Free Press.

Peacock, Alan T., and Jack Wiseman. 1961. *The Growth of Public Expenditure in the United Kingdom*. Princeton, NJ: Princeton University Press.

Persson, Torsten, and Guido Tabellini. 2003. *The Economic Effects of Constitutions, Munich Lectures in Economics*. Cambridge, MA: MIT Press.

Phillips, K. 1969. *The Emerging Republican Majority*. New York: Arlington House.

Pierson, Paul. 1994. *Dismantling the Welfare State?: Reagan, Thatcher, and the Politics of Retrenchment, Cambridge Studies in Comparative Politics*. Cambridge, UK/New York: Cambridge University Press.

Pierson, Paul. 2000. "Three Worlds of Welfare State Research." *Comparative Political Studies* 33(6/7): 791–821.

Piriano, Patrizio, and Robert Haveman. 2006. "Generational Income Mobility: Review Article." *Review of Income and Wealth* 52(3) (September): 477–86.

Piven, Frances Fox, and Richard A. Cloward. 1972. *Regulating the Poor: The Functions of Public Welfare*. New York: Vintage Books.

Pontusson, Jonas. 2005. *Inequality and Prosperity: Social Europe vs Liberal America*. Ithaca, NY: Cornell University Press.

Popenoe, D. 1988. *Disturbing the Nest*. Hawthorne, NY: Aldine de Gruyter.

Preston, Samuel H. 1975. "The Changing Relation between Mortality and Level of Economic Development." *Population Studies* 29(2): 231–48.

Preston, Samuel H. 1980. "Causes and Consequences of Mortality Declines in Less Developed Countries During the 20th Century." In Richard A. Easterlin, ed., *Population and Economic Change in Developing Countries*. Chicago, IL: University of Chicago Press, pp. 289–360.

Preston, Samuel H. 1984. "Children and the Elderly: Divergent Paths for America's Dependents." *Demography* 21(4) (November): 435–57.

Preston, Samuel H. 1996. "American Longevity: Past, Present, and Future." New York: Syracuse University Policy Brief No 7.

Project on the Federal Social Role. 1985. *The Report of the Committee on Economic Security of 1935*, 50th anniversary edn. Washington, DC: National Conference on Social Welfare.

References

Putnam, Robert D. 2001. *Bowling Alone: The Collapse and Revival of American Community.* New York: Simon & Schuster.

Qin, Duo, Marie Anne Cagas, Geoffrey Ducanes, Xinhua He, Rui Liu, and Shiguo Liu. 2006. "Income Disparity and Economic Growth: Evidence from People's Republic of China." *ERD Working Paper Series, No. 84, Asian Development Bank.*

Quadagno, Jill. 1994. *The Color of Welfare: How Racism Undermined the War on Poverty.* Oxford: Oxford University Press.

Rainwater, Lee. 1982. "Stigma in Income-Tested Programs." In Irwin Garfinkel, ed., *Income-Tested Transfer Programs: The Case For and Against.* New York: Academic Press, pp. 19–46.

Rainwater, Lee, Richard P. Coleman, and Gerald Handel. 1959. *Workingman's Wife.* New York.

Rainwater, Lee, and Timothy M. Smeeding. 2003. *Poor Kids in a Rich Country: America's Children in Comparative Perspective.* New York: Russell Sage Foundation; paperback edn, 2004.

Ravitch, Diane. 2000. *The Great School Wars: A History of the New York City Public Schools.* Baltimore, MD: Johns Hopkins University Press.

Rawls, J. 1972. *A Theory of Justice.* Cambridge, MA: Harvard University Press.

Reichman, Nancy, Teitler, Julien, Garfinkel, Irwin, and Garcia, Sandra. 2004. "Variations in Maternal and Child Wellbeing Among Financially Eligible Mothers By TANF Participation Status." *Eastern Economics Journal* 30(1): 101–18.

Reichman, N., Teitler, J., and Curtis, M. 2005. "TANF Sanctioning and Hardship." *Social Service Review* 79(2): 215–36.

Reichman, Nancy, Teitler, Julien, Garfinkel, Irwin, and Garcia, Sandra. 2004. "Variations in Maternal and Child Wellbeing Among Financially Eligible Mothers By TANF Participation Status." *Eastern Economics Journal* 30(1): 101–18.

Reinhardt, U. E., P. S. Hussey and G. F. Anderson. 2004. "U.S. Health Care Spending in an International Context." *Health Affairs* 23: 10–25.

Reno, Virginia P., and Joni Lavery. 2005a. "Options to Balance Social Security Funds Over the Next 75 Years." *Social Security Brief* 18. Washington, DC: National Academy of Social Insurance.

Reno, Virginia P., and Joni Lavery. 2005b. "Social Security: What Role for Life Annuities in Individual Accounts? Issues, Options, and Tradeoffs." *Social Security Brief* 19. Washington, DC: National Academy of Social Insurance.

Reno, Virginia P., Michael J. Graetz, Kenneth S. Apfel, Joni Lavery, and Catherine Hill, eds. 2005. *Uncharted Waters: Paying Benefits from Individual Accounts in Federal Retirement Policy,* Study Panel Final Report. Washington, DC: National Academy of Social Insurance.

Robert, J. Barro. 2001. "Human Capital and Growth." *The American Economic Review* 91(2): 12.

Roemer, John E. 2004. "Equal Opportunity and Intergenerational Mobility: Going Beyond Intergenerational Income Transition Matrices." In Miles Corak, ed.,

Generational Income Mobility in North America and Europe. New York: Cambridge University Press, pp. 101–18.

Ruhm, Christopher. 2000. "Parental Leave and Child Health." *Journal of Health Economics* 19(6) 931–60.

Sack, Kevin. 2008. "In Massachusetts, Universal Coverage Strains Care." *New York Times*, April 5, p. 1.

Sala-I-Martin, Xavier. 1996. "Transfers, Social Safety Nets, and Economic Growth." *IMF Working Papers* 96/40. International Monetary Fund.

Schrantz, Dennis, and Jerry McElroy. 2000. *Reducing Racial Disparity in the Criminal Justice System*. Washington, DC: United States Department of Justice.

Schuck, Peter H., and Richard J. Zeckhauser. 2006. *Targeting in Social Programs: Avoiding Bad Bets, Removing Bad Apples*. Washington, DC: Brookings Institution Press.

Schultz, Theodore W. 1971. *Investment in Human Capita: The Role of Education and of Research*. New York: Free Press.

Schultz, Theodore W. "The Value of Children: An Economic Perspective." *Journal of Political Economy*, Part II: New Economic Approaches to Fertility (March–April 1973), 81(2): S2–13. University of Chicago Press. Available at: <http://www.jstor.org/stable/pdfplus/1840410.pdf>.

Schultz, Theodore W. 1993. "The Economic Importance of Human Capital in Modernization." *Education Economics* 1(1): 13–19.

Schumpeter, Joseph Alois. 1942. *Capitalism, Socialism, and Democracy*, 2nd edn. New York, London: Harper & Brothers.

Scott, Janny. 2005. "Life at the Top in America Isn't Just Better, It's Longer." *The New York Times*, May 16.

Sefton, Tom. 2002. "Recent Changes in the Distribution of the Social Wage." *Centre for Analysis of Social Exclusion (CASE) Paper No. 62* (December). London: London School of Economics and Political Science. Available at: <http://sticerd.lse.ac.uk/dps/case/cp/CASEpaper62.pdf>.

Sen, Amartya. 1982. *Poverty and Famines: An Essay on Entitlement and Deprivation*. Oxford: Oxford University Press.

Sen, Amartya. 1992. *Inequality Re-examined*. Cambridge, MA: Harvard University Press.

Shaw and Shapiro. 2002. "The Polls-Trends: Poverty and Public Assistance." *Public Opinion Quarterly*, 66(1): 105–28.

Sheils, John F., and Randall A. Haught. 2005. *The Health Care For All Californians Act: Cost and Economic Impacts Analysis*. Falls Church, VA: The Lewin Group.

Sierminska, Eva, and Thesia I. Garner. 2002. "A Comparison of Income, Expenditures, and Home Market Value Distributions Using Luxembourg Income Study Data from the 1990s." *LIS Working Paper No. 338* (December). Syracuse, NY: Center for Policy Research, Syracuse University. Available at: <http://www.lisproject.org/publications/liswps/338.pdf>.

References

Skocpol, Theda. 1992. *Protecting Soldiers and Mothers: The Political Origins of Social Policy in the United States*. Cambridge, MA: Harvard University Press.

Skocpol, Theda, and Edwin Amenta. 1986. "States and Social Policies." *Annual Review of Sociology* 12: 131–57.

Smeeding, Timothy M. 1982. "Alternative Methods for Valuing Selected In-Kind Transfers and Measuring Their Effect on Poverty." *US Bureau of the Census Technical Report No. 50* (April). Washington, DC: US Government Printing Office.

Smeeding, T. M. 1999. "Social Security Reform: Improving Benefit Adequacy and Economic Security for Women." *Center for Policy Research Policy Brief Series No. 16*, The Maxwell School. Syracuse, NY: Syracuse University, pp. 1–25.

Smeeding, Timothy M. 2004. "Twenty Years of Research on Income Inequality, Poverty, and Redistribution in the Developed World." *Socio-Economic Review* 2(2): 149–63.

Smeeding, Timothy M. 2005. "Public Policy, Economic Inequality, and Poverty: The United States in Comparative Perspective." *Social Science Quarterly* 86(5): 955–83.

Smeeding, Timothy M. 2006a. "Government Programs and Social Outcomes: Comparison of the United States with Other Rich Nations." In Alan J. Auerbach, David Card, and John M. Quigley, eds, *Poverty, the Distribution of Income, and Public Policy*. New York: Russell Sage Foundation, ch.4, pp. 149–218.

Smeeding, Timothy M. 2006b. "Poor People in a Rich Nation: The United States in Comparative Perspective." *Journal of Economic Perspectives* 20(1): 69–90.

Smeeding, Timothy M., Michael O'Higgins, and Lee Rainwater. 1990. *Poverty, Inequality, and Income Distribution in Comparative Perspective: The Luxembourg Income Study (Lis)*. Washington, DC: Urban Institute Press.

Smeeding, Timothy M., and J. Thompson. 2008. "Income from Wealth and Income from Labor: Stocks, Flows and More Complete Measures of Well Being." Unpublished manuscript (June). University of Wisconsin-Madison.

Smeeding, Timothy M., Peter Saunders, John Coder, Stephen P. Jenkins, Johan Fritzell, Aldi J. M. Hagenaars, Richard Hauser, and Michael Wolfson. 1993. "Poverty, Inequality and Family Living Standard Impacts across Seven Nations: The Effect of Noncash Subsidies for Health, Education, and Housing." *Review of Income and Wealth* 39(3): 229–56.

Smith, Adam. 1991. *The Wealth of Nations, Everyman's Library*. New York: Knopf; distributed by Random House.

Smith, James P., and Finis R. Welch. 1989. "Black Economic Progress after Myrdal." *Journal of Economic Literature* 27(2): 519–64.

Smolensky, Eugene, and Jennifer Appleton Gootman, eds. 2005. *Working Families and Growing Kids: Caring for Children and Adolescents*. Washington, DC: National Research Council, Institute of Medicine, The National Academies Press.

Social Security Administration. 2002. *Annual Statistical Supplement*. Washington, DC: Office of Research and Statistics.

Social Security Administration. 2003. *Social Security Programs Throughout the World: The Americas*. Washington, DC: Office of Research and Statistics.

Social Security Administration. 2004a. *Social Security Programs Throughout the World: Asia and the Pacific*. Washington, DC: Office of Research and Statistics.

Social Security Administration. 2004b. *Social Security Programs Throughout the World: Europe*. Washington, DC: Office of Research and Statistics.

Social Security Administration. 2005. *Social Security Programs Throughout the World: The Americas*. Washington, DC: Office of Research and Statistics.

Social Security Administration. 2006a. *2006 Annual Report of the Board of Trustees of the Federal Old-Age and Survivors Insurance and Disability Insurance Trust Funds*. Washington, DC: Social Security Administration.

Social Security Administration. 2006b. *Social Security Programs Throughout the World: Europe*. Washington, DC: Office of Research and Statistics.

Social Security Administration. 2008. "Status of the Social Security and Medicare Trust Funds, Summary Report." April 3, 2008. Accessed at: <http://www.ssa.gov/OACT/TRSUM/index.html>.

Solon, Gary. 2004. "A Model of Intergenerational Mobility Variation over Time and Place." In Miles Corak, ed., *Generational Income Mobility in North America and Europe*. New York: Cambridge University Press, pp. 38–47.

Sowell, Thomas, ed. 1978. *American Ethnic Groups*. Washington, DC: Urban Institute.

Sowell, Thomas. 1983. *The Economics and Politics of Race: An International Perspective*. New York: William Morrow.

Sowell, Thomas. 1998. *Race, Culture, and Equality*. Stanford, CA: Hoover Institution on War, Revolution and Peace.

Sperling, Gene. 2005. "A Progressive Framework for Social Security Reform." Washington, DC: Center for American Progress. January 10.

Steuerle, C. E., and J. M. Bakija. 1994. *Retooling Social Security for the 21st Century: Right and Wrong Approaches to Reform*. Washington, DC: Urban Institute.

Steuerle, Eugene, and Adam Carasso. 2005. *The True Tax Rates Confronting Families With Children*. Washington, DC: Urban Institute.

Steuerle, E., and P. Van de Water. 2007. *Administering Health Insurance Mandates*. Washington, DC: NASI, March 3, 2008.

Stiglitz, Joseph, with Michael Rothschild. 1976. "Equilibrium in Competitive Insurance Markets: An Essay on the Economics of Imperfect Information." *Quarterly Journal of Economics*, 90: 629–49.

Stinebrickner, Todd R., and Ralph Stinebrickner. "Understanding Educational Outcomes of Students from Low Income Families: Evidence from a Liberal Arts College with a Full Tuition Subsidy Program." *Journal of Human Resources*, 38(3) (summer 2003): 591–617.

Sweezy, Paul M. 1942. *The Theory of Capitalist Development; Principles of Marxian Political Economy*. New York: Oxford University Press.

235

References

Tanaka, Sakiko. 2005. "Parental Leave and Child Health Across OECD Countries," *Economic Journal* 115: F7–LF28.

Tanzi, V., and Schuknecht, L. 2000. *Public Spending in the 20th Century: A Global Perspective*. Cambridge: Cambridge University Press.

Tawney, R.H. 1931. *Equality*. London: Unwin Books.

Thompson, Jeffrey, and Timothy Smeeding. 2007. "Income from Wealth and Income from Labor: Stocks, Flows and More Complete Measures of Well Being," mimeo, June 21. Syracuse, NY: Center for Policy Research, Syracuse University. Available at: <http://www.irp.wisc.edu/aboutirp/people/affiliates/Smeeding/14-INCOME-FROM-WEALTH_6_21_07.pdf>.

Tinto, Vincent. 1993. *Leaving College: Rethinking the Causes and Cures of Student Attrition*, 2nd edn. Chicago, IL: University of Chicago Press.

Tinto, Vincent. 1998. "Colleges as Communities: Taking Research on Student Persistence Seriously." *Review of Higher Education* 21(2) (winter): 167–78.

Titmus, Richard M. 1958. *Essays on the Welfare State*. London: George Allen & Unwin.

Tobin, James, Joseph A. Pechman, and Peter M. Mieszkowski. 1967. "Is a Negative Income Tax Practical?" *Yale Law Journal* 77(1): 1–27.

Tocqueville, Alexis de. 1835. *Democracy in America*, 3d edn. London: Saunders and Otley.

Tullock, Gordon. 1982. "Income Testing and Politics: A Theoretical Model and Comment by Anthony Downs and Larry Orr." In Irwin Garfinkel, ed., *Income Tested Transfer Programs: The Case For and Against*. New York, NY: Academic Press, pp. 97–116.

Turner, Frederick Jackson. 1893. "Significance of the Frontier in American History." *Proceedings of the State Historical Society of Wisconsin, 1893*. Madison, Wisconsin.

Turner, Frederick Jackson. 1921. *The Frontier in American History*. New York: Henry Holt and Company.

Turner, Sarah. 2006. "Higher Tuition, Higher Aid and the Quest to Improve Opportunities for Low Income Students in Selective, Public Higher Education." In Ronald Ehrenberg, ed., *What's Happening to Public Higher Education?* Westport, CT: Greenwood Press for the American Council on Education, pp. 251–74.

UC Berkeley Center for Labor Research and Education. 2007. "Individual Mandates: Lessons from Abroad." Policy Brief. Berkeley, CA: UC Berkeley.

United Nations Development Program (UNDP) 2007/2008. Human Development Report 2007/2008: *Fighting Climate Change: Human Solidarity in a Divided World*. New York: UNDP. Available at: <http://hdr.undp.org/en/reports/global/hdr2007-2008/>.

US Bureau of the Census. 2004. *U.S. Interim Projections by Age, Sex, Race, and Hispanic Origin*. Available at: <http://www.census.gov/ipc/www/usinterimproj/>.

US Bureau of the Census. 2008. Table 2: Annual Estimates of the Population by Sex and Selected Age Groups for the United States: April 1, 2000 to July 1, 2007 (NC-EST2007–02), Population Division, US Census Bureau, May 1, 2008. Available at: <http://www.census.gov/popest/national/asrh/NC-EST2007/NC-EST2007–02.xls>.

Van de Water, Paul. 2008. "Achieving Universal Participation in Social Insurance Systems." NASI Policy Brief #11. Washington, DC: NASI.

Van Parijs, Philippe, ed. 1992. *Arguing for Basic Income: Ethical Foundations for a Radical Reform*. London: Verso.

Van Parijs, Philippe et al. 2001. *What's Wrong with a Free Lunch?* Boston: Beacon Press.

Voltaire, Francois-Marie Arouet. [1759] 1950. *Candide*. Harmondsworth: Penguin Classics.

Waldfogel, Jane. 2006. *What Children Need*. Cambridge, MA: Harvard University Press.

Waldfogel, Jane, Wen-Jui Han, and Jeanne Brooks-Gunn. 2002. "The Effects of Early Maternal Employment on Child Cognitive Development." *Demography* 39 (2): 369–92.

Weich, Ronald, and Carlos Angulo. 2000. *Justice on Trial: Racial Disparities in the American Criminal Justice System*. Washington, DC: Leadership Conference on Civil Rights.

Weisbrod, Burton Allen. 1969. *Collective Action and the Distribution of Income: A Conceptual Approach*. Madison, WI: University of Wisconsin, Institute for Research on Poverty.

Welch, Finis. 1973. "Black–White Differences in Returns to Schooling." *American Economic Review* 63: 893–907.

Wennberg, J.E., E.S. Fisher, D.C. Goodman, and J S. Skinner. 2008. "Tracking the Care of Patients with Severe Chronic Illness." *Dartmouth Atlas of Health Care 2008*. Available at: <http://www.dartmouthatlas.org>; accessed on April 8, 2008.

White, Chapin. 2007. "Health Care Spending Growth: How Different is the United States from the Rest of the OECD?" *Health Affairs* 26(1): 154–61.

Widerquist, Karl. 2001a. "Perspectives on the Guaranteed Income, Part II." *Journal of Economic Issues* 35(4): 1019–30.

Widerquist, Karl. 2001b. "Perspectives on the Guaranteed Income, Part I." *Journal of Economic Issues* 35(3): 749–57.

Wilensky, Harold L. 2002. *Rich Democracies: Political Economy, Public Policy, and Performance*. Berkeley and Los Angeles, CA: University of California Press.

Wilensky, Harold L., and Charles N. Lebeaux. 1965. *Industrial Society and Social Welfare*, 1st edn. New York: Free Press.

Wilson, Kathryn S. 2000. "Using the PSID to Examine the Effects of School Spending." *Public Finance Review* 28(5): 428–51.

Wilson, K., K. Lambright, and T. M. Smeeding. 2006. "School Finance, Equivalent Educational Expenditure and Income Distribution: Equal Dollars or Equal Chances for Success?" *Education Finance and Policy* 1(4): 396–424.

Wilson, Kathryn, Robert Haveman, and Timothy Smeeding. 2007. "Higher Education and Social Mobility in the United States: What Difference Does the Index of Mobility Make?" Paper presented to the Barcelona EQUAL SOC Conference. (September 2006).

References

Wilson, Kathryn S., Kristina T. Lambright, and Timothy M. Smeeding. 2006. "School Finance and Equality of Opportunity: Equal Dollars or Equal Chances for Success?" *Education Finance and Policy* 1(4)(fall): 396–424.

Witte, Edwin E. 1963. *The Development of the Social Security Act. A Memorandum on the History of the Committee on Economic Security and Drafting and Legislative History of the Social Security Act.* Madison, WI: University of Wisconsin Press.

Wolfe, Barbara. 2002. "Unpublished Estimates of Health Care Subsidies for the Uninsured using the Medical Care Expenditure Survey." Mimeo. November 16. Madison, WI: University of Wisconsin-Madison.

Wolfe, Barbara, and Robert Haveman. 2003. "Social and Non Market Benefits from Education in an Advanced Economy." In Yolanda Kodrzycki, ed., *Education in the 21st Century: Meeting the Challenges of a Changing World.* Boston, MA: Federal Reserve Bank of Boston, pp. 97–131.

Woodward, Bob, and Carl Bernstein. 1974. *All the President's Men.* New York: Simon & Schuster.

Woolhandler, Steffie, Terry Campbell, and David Himmelstein. 2003. "Cost of Health Care Administration in the United States and Canada." *The New England Journal of Medicine* 349(8): 768–75.

World Bank. 2007. *World Development Indicators.* Washington, DC: World Bank Group.

World Health Organisation. 2004. *Meeting the MDG Drinking Water and Sanitation Target: The Urban and Rural Challenge of the Decade.* Geneva: World Health Organisation.

Wright, Erik Olin, ed. 1996–2006. *The Real Utopias Project* (vols II, III, and IV). New York: Verso.

Zuvekas, Samuel H., and Joel W. Cohen. 2007. "Prescription Drugs and the Changing Concentration of Health Care Expenditures." *Health Affairs* 26(1): 249–57.

Index

Note: page numbers in *italics* refer to Figures and Tables.

Index